INCLUSION AND EXCLUSION: UNEMPLOYMENT AND NON-STANDARD EMPLOYMENT IN EUROPE

Inclusion and Exclusion: Unemployment and Non-standard Employment in Europe

Edited by
JENS LIND
IVER HORNEMANN MØLLER

Routledge
Taylor & Francis Group
LONDON AND NEW YORK

First published 1999 by Ashgate Publishing

Reissued 2018 by Routledge
2 Park Square, Milton Park, Abingdon, Oxon, OX14 4RN
711 Third Avenue, New York, NY I 0017, USA

Routledge is an imprint of the Taylor & Francis Group, an informa business

A Library of Congress record exists under LC control number: 98073855

ISBN 13: 978-1-138-32054-3 (hbk)
ISBN 13: 978-0-429-45322-9 (ebk)

Contents

Acknowledgements

This book is the result of an ongoing research process involving rather many people over a number of years. A grant from the Danish Social Science Research Council in 1993 enabled the start of a joint research project on 'New structures and everyday life' in the Centre for Social Integration and Differentiation (CID) at Copenhagen Business School. During the work with this project we came into contact with the then newly established European Network called 'Social Exclusion and the Development of European Citizenship' (SEDEC) which later gave birth to a thematic network on 'Social Inclusion Policy' and a research project on 'Inclusion and Exclusion in Social Policies and Everyday Experiences in Central and Peripheral Areas' (INPART). Both the network and the research project are until the end of 1999 parts of the European Commission's work programme: Targeted Socio-Economic Research (TSER).

Our participation in these European fora has been both fruitful and stimulating, and also opened the opportunity to widen and strengthen co-operation among European researchers in the field of inclusion within work. One example was a European-wide conference in Lund, Sweden, in May 1996 where we arranged a workshop on 'Work and social integration'. The papers given at this workshop are, after several revisions, the main part of this book.

We are grateful to both Danish and European sources of research funding for making these projects, meetings and seminars possible, and we are grateful to all our colleagues who in one way or the other have contributed to the process. We thank especially the participants in the Lund conference for valuable comments on the first drafts of the articles, and we thank the contributors to this anthology for their commitment and patience in the process of finalising the book.

Emeritus professor John Westergaard has been a great help in making linguistic improvements to parts of the text. Dr Kjell Eriksson, University of Lund, has shown great skill and experience in setting out the text for publication.

Jens Lind and Iver Hornemann Møller
July 1998

Preface

The main content of this book is about unemployment and non-standard employment and about policies aiming to reduce the social exclusion caused, among other things, by labour market marginalisation. Four European countries are in focus: Denmark, the UK, the Netherlands and Portugal. These countries to some extent represent the different types of welfare state regime in Europe: a Scandinavian, social-democratic model; a liberal, Anglo-Saxon model; a corporate, 'Bismarckian' model; and a southern 'variant'. The analyses intend to give a thorough insight into the variety of issues in recent labour market developments and a related overview of the major schemes and programmes to combat social exclusion.

On the one hand the variety of issues and policies underline the notion that there is no single and common pattern for exclusion and inclusion in Western Europe. National and regional specificities are still very much the case. On the other hand, however, we are able to identify some common traits in labour market developments and in the associated modes of social regulation. There is a clear trend to identify labour market marginalisation as a major social issue and to emphasise measures which 'activate' the unemployed instead of just paying them benefits. The social implications of the latter are, however, not without ambiguities. One way of seeing it is that the unemployed and marginalised are provided with assistance from the welfare state in order to be re-included within an important social institution: namely working life. Another viewpoint is that this 'workfare policy' is a disciplinary and punitive measure to maintain commitment to the work ethic, and that the South European unemployed should be happy not to be targets of this policy. The most radical alternative to the 'workfare policy' is some sort of 'freedom from work' in terms of citizen's income or basic income scheme. Another strategy is to improve the quality of working life, through 'freedom at work'.

The last two aspects are discussed in the first chapter of the anthology and should be seen as an underlying theme for the other articles, which present a range of national descriptions and analyses. In the last chapter of the book we offer a discussion of convergences versus national specificities and try to identify the contours of a West European labour market policy.

Jens Lind and Iver Hornemann Møller

1. Introduction

JENS LIND AND IVER HORNEMANN MØLLER

The restructuring of working life, unemployment and labour market marginalisation are among the most important social issues on the agenda in Western Europe. It is a common observation that changes in the world economy are taking place at a very high speed under influence of increasing globalisation of markets and the implementation of significant and revolutionary new technology. This process is furthered by the assumption and recommendation that national and regional economies have to avoid protectionism and instead keep up with these changes to secure competitiveness through more flexible production and a more flexible labour market.

There are many facets of this development and interpretations of the risks and opportunities are not at all unambiguous. From one point of view it seems that the industrialised societies are in a situation where 'human labour is being systematically eliminated from the production process' (Rifkin 1995:3). This is in accordance with Habermas when he sees an end to the work-society and a shift of paradigm from that to the society of communication (Habermas 1984) and it echoes of course a main thesis of Gorz's in his Farewell to the Working Class (1982) with its identification of the 'non-class of non-workers'.

These ideas on the decline of the role of work in society should not be completely abandoned just because it is difficult to envisage exactly how and when they would materialise. Yet for the time being it seems that, despite a lack of work, work is becoming increasingly important to most people's lives because it is becoming increasingly important for the social structure in general and for social stratification in particular as a still salient and even more widespread public norm: any decent citizen within normal working age should have paid employment or some other legal income- creating activity.

This continuing importance of work-norms and the status of paid employment is contrary to the thesis of Beck (1986) and Bauman (1992) who both argue that work is no longer a key source of social identity at the end of the twentieth century, and that the organization of work – most notably, the occupational order – no longer provides a useful framework with which social institutions and behaviour may be analyzed. These arguments have been paralleled by a growing emphasis upon the causal significance of consumption rather than production-related activities in contemporary societies.

The arguments developed by Beck and Bauman seem to have been implicitly constructed in relation to the Fordist model of work and employment relations. As the Fordist model of employment changed, so employment and work themselves were effectively downgraded as a framework for analyses and causal explanations. Although we agree that the Fordist model is less dominant today we find, however, this rejection a bit premature and suggest that employment still remains among the most important determinants of life chances for the majority of the population.

From another point of view the thesis is that we are just in a period of capitalist restructuring which is causing some transitional and temporary social problems which will soon be eliminated once the adjustments to the new technology and the global market have taken place. The main challenge is to chose the right strategy out of it, preferably a strategy which involve people as full participiants in social life and decision making (Standing 1997).

This is also the overall concern linking the contributions to this anthology, namely that the goal of social citizenship includes, apart from civil, political and social rights, not only a right to but also a real opportunity for participation in the reproduction of society. Participation in legal income-giving activities might be considered as the most important participative activity for members of any European society. This importance of work is also emphasised by Dahrendorf when he claims that work is a 'central social institution and an essential part of peoples lives' (Dahrendorf 1988), and by Prixley who takes the stand that 'employment is very much a part of being a citizen and that the issue of employment must be cast in terms of rights and obligations that make it possible to participate in the life of the society' (Pixley 1993).

This emphasis on a real opportunity for participation in working life does not deny that wage-work and other income creating activities, as pointed out among others by Offe (1985), have undergone significant changes in the last decades. It is evident, as mentioned above, that much 'traditional' industrial work has been displaced by machines and automatic technology and that rationalisations and electronic steering increasingly are penetrating work processes. Furthermore, the type and content of work have changed significantly with the increasing importance of private and public service industries as vast growing employment areas. It is also generally agreed that official working hours, at least for the majority of employees, have been declining since the beginning of the century and that the time spent in 'working-life' today is shorter than ever before. Still, however, employment in general is steadily rising or has remained stable and the members of the nuclear family (in Scandinavia) today are working many more hours in paid employment outside the family (Bojo and Nielsen 1993) than in the heyday of 'the male breadwinner' family model.

The end of the industrial society (Bell 1973) and the coming of a post-Fordist era (Aglietta 1979), with new production concepts (Kern & Schumann 1984) and managerial paradigms, may herald improvements in the quality of working life for some. More flexible employment patterns may indeed be an advantage for a lot of people who can create a more coherent everyday life by a pleasant combination of family and working life. These are the opportunities and they are available for some. The risks are that other groups of people cannot find sufficient work at sufficient pay to secure decent standards of living. They may be unemployed for long periods or employed in temporary or low paid jobs and in this way risk social marginalisation.

The ongoing transition of the welfare states has already to some extent reflected these social issues. Today it seems that Jessop was right when he argued (1991) that the Keynesian welfare state would be succeeded by an emerging post-Fordist state, which he described as a 'Schumpeterian workfare state' whose objectives would be 'to promote product, process, organizational and market innovation in open economies in order to strengthen structural competitiveness of the national economy on the supply-side'. This emerging workfare state, directed to sustaining free market forces, of course, first and foremost, marks a clear break with the Keynesian welfare state. Full employment is de-prioritized in favour of competitiveness, and redistributive welfare rights take second place to a productivist re-ordering of social policy and other welfare policies. So, a major re-orientation of welfare policies is indeed taking place: away from redistributive concerns towards cost-saving and productivist concerns. The welfare state has added a new and stronger emphasis on its role as a disciplinary force in society to maintain the work ethic. Workers looking for jobs or other access to the means of subsistence do not just face the employers as obstacles to a decent life, but are also confronted with the demands of the 'workfare' state.

This can clearly be seen from the experience of the employment or unemployment policies in countries throughout Western Europe. For some policy makers non-standard employment and unemployment are seen as a remedy or the cure for the present problems of restructuring economic life. These neo-liberal ideas have for many years now been very influential in Western Europe. They present themselves as the salvation from old fashioned socialist strategies based upon rigid regulation of societies by means of state intervention or collective bargaining, which in turn are seen as the main reason for the present problems of unemployment etc. The neo-liberals have traditionally been the strongest proponents of more flexibility in the labour market, to be achieved by market regulation; but during the past ten years or so, socialists, too, have gradually adopted a lot of neo-liberal ideas. Perhaps the main difference between liberals and socialists (at least the social democratic labour parties) nowadays is that socialists are a bit more concerned about the quality of social policies than are the liberals.

It is a strong belief among liberals that a deregulated and flexible labour market will provide people with the best employment opportunities and living conditions in the longer term perspective. A low paid, temporary job is often seen as a stepping stone into a better job. As a recent report from the OECD (1997) shows, this is often the case; but it is also noteworthy that the report emphasises 'that "escaping" from a low-paid job can be a temporary phenomenon' and that the escapes take a longer period of time in the liberal, market-regulated economies, such as the USA and the UK, than in the relatively more public-regulated labour markets like Denmark, France, Germany and Italy (OECD 1997:VIII). This may indicate that the liberal mode of regulating the labour market tends to maintain social inequalities to a greater extent than is the case in societies with a higher degree of state regulation of the labour market.

Anyway, there is no coherent and convincing alternative strategy to liberalism among the policy makers in Western Europe, but most of them are on the other hand not attracted to the way things are done in the UK, USA and New Zealand. 'Working poor' are not a European ideal, and in this sense perhaps a distinct 'European Model' is emerging; but defining and shaping such a model to deal with unemployment and underemployment is a task still to be done. In the EU Commission's Green Paper on 'Partnership for a new Organisation of Work' the challenge to policy makers is described as 'how to develop or adapt policies which support, rather than hinder, fundamental organisational renewal and how to strike a productive balance between the interests of business and the interests of workers, thereby facilitating the modernisation of working life. An essential objective is to achieve such a balance between flexibility and security throughout Europe.' (COM(97)128).

To achieve such a balance at times where the interests of workers obviously are on the retreat is not an easy task. It is not sufficient to rely on individual workers' expressions of interest as presumed in the neo-liberal universe. Therefore policies must ensure 'that participants in the labour market must have a secure capacity to bargain and influence the character of employment, to have an adequately strong 'voice' to ensure that distributive justice is pursued' (Standing 1997:29).

Whatever the future may be, it seems very likely that Europe will have to adapt to the changes in one way or the other and that a lot of ordinary people's lives will be profoundly changed. A step in the direction of identifying a 'European Model' could be to look into what is actually going on in the various countries. By doing this here, however, we do not intend to end up with a well defined 'European Model' of labour market regulation. We hope that we can contribute to a better understanding of the issues of unemployment and non-standard employment in the various countries, and the different modes of social regulation to deal with these issues; and from these experiences then draw some useful conclusions.

Focusing on work, new types of differentiation and integration, as we are in this anthology, analysis of the specific forms and configurations of labour market regulation becomes crucial. The single elements of labour market regulation derive from the key institutions on the labour market: the market, the organisations and the state, with their specific forms of regulation, rationality, sets of relations, values and consequent strategies. Labour market regulation in a specific society has its own particular configuration of these dimensions regulating the production of labour (qualifications etc.), the exchange of labour and the deployment of labour; and these tools for analysing labour market regulation can be useful for identifying different strategies and how these strategies are being developed over time.

Table 1.1 Regulation of labour market relations

Institution	***Market***	***Interest organisations***	***State***
Form of regulation	*Market forces*	*Collective agreement*	*Legislation*
Rationality	*Economic*	*Economic/social*	*Social/political*
Relations	*Competition*	*Cooperation*	*Cooperation*
Values	*Individualism*	*Collectivism*	*Collectivism*
Strategy	*Liberal*	*Liberal/socialist*	*Socialist*

In a slightly expanded perspective these elements can be seen as key features in identifying welfare state models or regimes, and the four countries analysed in this anthology, Portugal, UK, Netherlands and Denmark, do in some sense represent examples of typical forms of national labour markets and regulation regimes. We suggest that the identification of such regimes should not be taken too seriously, as it is always problematic to categorise because the dimensions applied and the judgements made can always be criticised (Castles and Mitchell 1992; Hill 1996). But inspired by Esping-Andersen (1990) and following Liebfried and Pierson (1995) in their addition of a south European model, we can distinguish among four models: a Scandinavian, social-democratic model; a liberal, Anglo-Saxon model; a corporate, 'Bismarckian' model; and a southern 'variant'. The latter might have some conservative features in common with the corporate model, as Rhodes emphasises, but similar observations can be made of common traits between the other models, especially if specific countries within the categories are compared with countries representing another model. For instance labour market regulation in Denmark has many similarities with both the liberal and corporate model, and regulation in Holland with the liberal and Scandinavian model.

Taking these considerations into account, we suggest that Portugal might be seen as representing the south European, catholic and family oriented reproduction structure; the UK the Anglo-Saxon liberal society; the Netherlands the corporate welfare state regime; and Denmark as representing the Scandinavian welfare state society. As indicated, this does not mean we assume that the study of these countries provides us with a full understanding of developments across all Europe. It may, however, give us an opportunity to see both the range of diversities among the countries and, having in mind the representativity of the countries within the various categories of welfare regimes, an insight into patterns of labour market issues and modes of regulation.

We have not imposed a completely unitary theoretical and conceptual apparatus onto the various contributors. At first glance such an approach might seem to be an advantage for the internal coherence of the anthology. Having in mind, however, that the configuration of the social institutions differs widely between the various countries, a completely unitary interpretation of the relationship between non-standard employment, unemployment and social marginalisation on the one side and modes of labour market regulation, approaches to citizenship and concern with inclusion/exclusion on the other could easily violate the analysis of these specific relationships in the various countries.

That a completely unitary approach would look nice at first sight but might be followed by irrelevant and misleading interpretations and analyses is clearly illustrated when one deals with the concept of integration. As shown in the anthology's individual country analyses, the restructuring of working life and the growth of unemployment and labour market marginalisation are everywhere followed by new types of labour market integration and differentiation. One need not go through much of the literature on integration before it is clear that the concept has many different meanings and has been used in a lot of different contexts. From further reading and attempts to classify conceptions and definitions of integration (Mortensen 1995; Møller 1998) it is evident that integration is an umbrella concept, and that a single unitary conception of integration in society should not be the aim because the different conceptions reflect a real complexity. They show that a number of different observations of 'integration in society' exist at one and the same time, without any of them standing out as convincingly more important than the others.

Lockwood's article from 1964 in many ways set the scene for the debate on integration that followed over the next decades. When he, Habermas, Rex, Mouzelis and others talk about integration they operate with structures and actors at the macro level. System integration, according to Lockwood, is then conceived as a set of more or less compatible relationships between different parts or sub-systems in the society at large, while social integration is seen as a question of more or less orderly or conflicting relations between the collective actors of a social system.

This dual type of understanding concerning systems' and social actors' integration, is applied throughout the anthology. It does, however, not deal with the attachment or involvement of individuals and certain groups of individuals within society or within function systems hereof. For that purpose at least one more conception of integration is needed, namely the 'inclusion/exclusion understanding'. This is inspired by Niklas Luhmann, according to whom the question is whether or not individuals have a role from where they communicate and act in the sub-systems into which the society is conceived to be differentiated (work, economic, political, cultural, family, networks, etc.): inclusion within a specific sub-system means to have such a role; exclusion means not to have such a role. However, not only do the roles the individuals possess differ according to power and other resources but also the type and combination of societal differentiation into sub-systems differs from country to country. Consequently, the inclusion/exclusion approach to individuals' integration will not be entirely identical in Portugal, the Netherlands, UK and Denmark.

The contributions also differ according to the sort of non-standard employment which is emphasised and how it is related to unemployment and social marginalisation. In some countries changes in the legal forms of employment, like self-employment, sub-contracting and temporary work, have been most important in the reshaping of working life, while the flexibilisation of labour and other forms of non-standard employment, like part-time and temporary employment, seems to have been more typical and important in the case of other countries. These differences are clearly related to differences in social, economic and political structures and have to be interpreted within the framework of these before we can extract further and general, European, analyses.

References

Aglietta, M. (1979), *A Theory of Capitalist Regulation,* London: New Left Books.

Bauman, Z. (1982), *Intimations of Postmodernity,* London: Routledge.

Beck, U. (1992. *Risikogesellschaft. Auf dem Weg in eine andere Moderne,* Frankfurt/M: Suhrkamp.

Bell, D. (1973), *The Coming of Post-Industrial Society,* New York: Basic Books.

Boje, T.P. and Nielsen, L.D. (1993), 'Flexible Production, Employment and Gender', in T.P. Boje, S.E. Olsson Hort (eds), *Scandinavia in the New Europe,* Oslo: Scandinavian University Press, pp. 137-170.

Castles, F.G. and Mitchell, D. (1992), 'Identifying Welfare State Regimes: The Links Between Politics, Instruments and Outcomes', *Governance: An International Journal of Policy and Administration,* Vol. 5, No. 1, January, pp. 1-26.

Dahrendorf, R. (1988), *The Modern Social Conflict,* Berkeley/Los Angeles: University of California Press.

Esping-Andersen, G. (1990), *The Three Worlds of Welfare Capitalism,* Oxford: Polity Press

European Commission COM (97) 128, *Partnership for a New Organisation of Work,* Brussels.

Gorz, A. (1982), *Farewell to the Working Class,* London: Pluto.

Hill, M. (1996), *Social Policy – A Comparative Analysis,* London: Prentice Hall.

Jessop, B. (1991), 'The Welfare State in Transition from Fordism to Post-Fordism', in B. Jessop et al., *The Politics of Flexibility: Restructuring the State and Industry in Britain, Germany and Scandinavia,* London: Edward Elgar.

Kern, H. and Schumann, M. (1984), *Das Ende der Arbeitsteilung?,* München.

Leibfried, S. and Pierson, P. (eds) (1995), *European Social Policy,* Washington D.C.:The Brookings Institute.

Møller, I.H. (1998), *On the Spoor of Conceptual Clarification,* Working paper for the INPART: Inclusion through Participation.

OECD 1997, *Employment Outlook,* July.

Offe, C. (1985), *Disorganised Capitalism,* Cambridge: Polity Press.

Pixley, I. (1993), *Citizenship and Employment: Investigating Post-Industrial Options,* Cambridge/Melbourne: Cambridge University Press.
Rifkin, J. (1995), *The End of Work,* New York: G.P. Putnam's Sons.
Standing, G. (1997), 'Globalization, Labour Flexibility and Insecurity: The Era of Market Regulation', *Journal of Industrial Relations,* Vol. 3, No. 1, pp. 7-37.

Part I

Freedom from work or freedom through work?

2. Citizen's income as a heretical, political discourse: The Danish debate about citizen's income

ERIK CHRISTENSEN

Introduction

The idea that everyone should be guaranteed a minimum income goes a long way back. Members of the European association for research on citizen's income, BIEN (Basic Income European Network) refer to Juan Luis Vives, Mayor of Bruges in 1526, as the first to have formulated notions of providing a guaranteed income for all citizens.

In the period after World War II the idea of a citizen's income has come to be associated especially with the English liberal economist and politician, Lady Juliet Rhys-Williams (Rhys-Williams 1943), who in 1942 proposed a 'social dividend' as a counterpart to the Beveridge plan. Whereas Beveridge's prime concerns were with employment and people retired from it, Rhys-Williams set out a scheme to provide everybody with a social dividend.

There seems, internationally, to be much conceptual confusion around the notion of a citizen's income. A multiplicity of different terms are used in English: 'negative income tax', 'basic income', 'state bonus', 'social credit', 'social wage', 'social dividend', 'guaranteed income', 'universal benefit', 'citizen's wage' or 'citizen's income'. The latter, rather than 'basic income', was agreed in 1992, when the cross-national European association for research on the subject decided to adopt a single term in common.

In Danish, too, the labels vary: citizen's wage, social wage, guaranteed minimum income, social income; and ideas of this sort spread quite widely in Denmark following publication of a book, *Oprør fra midten* (Revolt from the centre, Meyer et al. 1978), which used the term 'citizen's wage'. In its alternative form of 'citizen's income', this is the term I shall use in what follows because it is the one that most clearly expresses the ideas involved.

What I want to do here is to present the results of an analysis of the debate in Denmark about a citizen's income, seen in international perspective, with a view to both re-defining and developing further the ideas at issue.

The concept of a citizen's income: as an idea, as part of a scientific paradigm and as a political discourse

A citizen's income may be defined as a general right of all citizens to receive from the state sufficient support to maintain a modest material level of living, without any general obligation to make themselves available in the labour market.

This is usually regarded only as a specific policy for labour market arrangements. However, I discern four layers within the notion of a citizen's income: these concern respectively values, theory, politics and more practical or technical matters. The notion is then to be seen variously as an idea within a framework of conceptual understanding; as a paradigm within a framework of scientific understanding; as political discourse within a framework of political understanding; and, finally, as a set of concrete, technical measures for political and economic affairs.

Conceptually the idea of a citizen's income reflects a particular interpretation of the relationships between the fundamental social values of sustainability, justice, freedom, equality and material security. In addition it can be seen as an element within various social scientific paradigms concerning the allocation of resources and rights. Finally it figures as a political discourse in the competitive contests of politics.

There are to ideas, paradigms and discourses alike features of values, theory and strategy; but these differ with respect to purpose, function and logic. Within the ideological framework, the value element is to the fore; within the paradigmatic framework, the element of theory; in political discourse, the element of strategy. There are links between the various layers of the concept and distinct social arenas. The conceptual layer of values is aligned to the arena of ideological politics, that of theory to the scientific arena, that of politics to the political arena.

It is analytically important to distinguish between the conceptual layers, because the social arenas to which they correspond are different by way of function and logic. The function of ideas is to provide ideological meaning and motivation for action; that of paradigms, to create new knowledge and understanding; that of political discourses, to bring about political understanding and support from political actors for certain political solutions, to the exclusion of other and undesired solutions. There are to a degree, nonetheless, value-related determining influences from one layer to another. Specific interpretations of the relationship between freedom, equality and justice will, for example, set the shape of the various scientific theories and paradigms that bear on resource distribution. Social scientific paradigms in turn play a part in determining the problem-specifications of political discourse. Finally, considerations of political strategy may set the course for or against concrete policy proposals.

The Danish debate of the 1990s around the subject showed that the political discourses both for and against a citizen's income drew on scientific paradigms. The hegemonic growth-discourse thus sought support from the interpretations dominant in economic science, in order to exclude opposing citizen's-income discourse from the agenda. Adherents of the latter discourse, by contrast, drew on the work of critical social scientists influenced by new citizen's-income paradigms emerging in international social science.

The distinction between different analytical layers within the concept of a citizen's income makes sense and helps towards clarity, because the past twenty years' debate in Denmark around the idea has moved unevenly, and has been conducted on different stages and with different actors, in three periods as follows.

1. The late 1970s and early 1980s saw the launch of notions of a citizen's income by 'outsiders' in various ideological milieux. This meant that the debate then stayed mainly at the layer of values and theory.
2. In the course of the 1980s a new social movement, Midteroprøret (the Centre Revolt), arose which, inspired by the book *Oprør fra midten* (Meyer et al. 1978 and 1982), turned the issue of a citizen's income into a new political discourse through its attempts to place the question onto the political agenda. In the same period the idea cropped up in the scientific arena, both internationally and in Denmark, to become a feature of a number of new social scientific paradigms.
3. New formulations of citizen's income as political discourse were brought to bear in the early 1990s. Debate about the notion now spread among the public at large, as an item on the general political agenda concerning renewal of the welfare state. That debate was set going both 'from the bottom up' by initiatives from new political networks, and 'from the top down' by initiatives from various reporting commissions, research workers and politicians.

The emergence of a new idea of citizen's income in the 1970s

The interesting feature of the climate of ideological debate in the 1970s is that, in relative independence of one another, 'outsiders' in four different ideological settings – social-democratic, socio-liberal, Marxist and liberal – advanced parallel notions of introducing new social provision for maintenance of livelihood without traditional wage labour in return.

1. The Swedish economist, Gunnar Adler-Karlsson, then a professor at Roskilde University Centre in Denmark, published a couple of books in the mid-1970s (Adler Karlsson, 1976 and 1977) which put a social-democratic case for a 'guaranteed minimum income'.
2. The idea of a citizen's income aroused widespread public attention in Denmark especially through publication of the book *Oprør fra midten,* by the philosopher Villy Sørensen, the natural scientist Niels I. Meyer and the politician Kristen Helveg Petersen, in February 1978. This linked the idea to socio-liberal circles and to new 'green' aspirations for 'a humanely balanced society'.
3. At around the same time the ideas of the French socialist André Gorz about introduction of a 'social income' came to be known, in socialist circles especially, through translation of several of his books (Gorz 1979, 1981 and 1983).
4. Finally, a former co-operative society director, Niels Hoff, launched the notion of a 'citizen's stipend' for debate in liberal circles (Hoff 1983).

These very diverse authors were at one and the same time each linked to a particular ideological milieu while yet having an outsider status in relation to it. They figured as typical heretics, conceptual innovators and provocateurs, who 'stood things on their head', broke away from established ideological frameworks and challenged industrial society's conventional growth discourse.

Common to the four strands of thought was an assured awareness that the familiar measures to solve societal problems were inadequate, and that prevailing conceptions of nature and humankind in industrial society were wide open to question. With these authors' shifts of conceptual framework went also shifts in the language and the metaphors they used. New views of problems and solutions will usually find reflection in language. For in the designation of one thing as a problem and another as a solution, problems are often described negatively, solutions positively. If you then switch things around, you will commonly need new words to reflect your new insights.

So there was turbulence in four separate ideological settings; and, if hesitantly and tentatively, a movement emerged towards formulation of a new common ideology, towards a sustainable development that was to include within it the notion of a citizen's income in some form or other. To borrow a term from the philosopher of science Thomas Kuhn (Kuhn 1962), the situation was pre-paradigmatic. But though there were many similarities of approach between the four currents of thinking, there were nonetheless also significant differences; and no dialogue between them came about.

A new grassroots movement and its formation of a political discourse about citizen's income in the 1980s

The thoughts of Adler-Karlsson, Gorz and Hoff came to be known only within small circles and were quickly forgotten. It was *Oprør fra midten* and its conception of a citizen's income that stirred public debate.

Publication of this book led to the establishment of a new periodical, the formation of a new grassroots movement and publication of a series of further books. A network was set up, which served as a political agent to disseminate the new ideas. It came as a surprise for the initiators that the notion of a citizen's income proved to be among those ideas that attracted greatest immediate support. It was this notion, therefore, which the new grassroots movement took up first with a view to translation into concrete policy.

So an attempt was made in the 1980s to turn the idea into a 'political issue', to set a political discourse going about citizen's incomes. It followed that the idea had to be linked to solution of a series of specific political problems, and that efforts must be made to form a coalition or political alliance around the issue. The means adopted to this end were a number of conferences, publication of discussion books and pamphlets, interviews with leading politicians. The prime objective was to build a political alliance around the issue between the trade union movement, the Social Democratic Party, the Radical Liberals and the Socialist People's Party.

The new grassroots movement had to engage actively in the game of practical politics, and show that it was not just preoccupied with utopian ideas, in order to get into debate and dialogue with the political parties and the union movement. It therefore put forward an alternative national budget, and made specific proposals to provide a citizen's income for young people and for others to have access to 'sabbatical leave'. The movement for 'revolt from the centre' failed in its endeavours to recruit the old political parties that were its target for its policies of citizen's incomes, or to persuade them to incorporate similar proposals in their programmes. Yet although its hopes of thus putting the issue directly onto the everyday political agenda failed in the first instance, its ideas about general provision for state-supported sabbatical leave were to prove significant for the subsequent acceptance of schemes of this sort in the late 1980s and early 1990s.

It must be said, then, that the political counter-discourse initiated in the 1980s took only a weak form.

Its weakness of strategy was that its proponents failed to link the idea, with sufficient clarity and certainty, to a wider range of concrete social problems. It was not made clear that citizen's incomes imply a strategy towards a multiplicity of goals. There was a failure to specify the relevance of the idea to resolution of the problems confronting the unemployed, social assistance recipients, people on early retirement schemes, disability pensioners and so on, in respect of their circumstances of dependency as against their claims to personal autonomy. There was also in the 1980s, moreover, an unfortunate tendency for division of the debate around citizen's incomes into two parts, one ideological and the other more practical, with the result that the new and weak political discourse came quickly to figure in a form bereft of conceptual elaboration and coherence.

The idea of a citizen's income had now taken material root in a social movement which sought to place the issue on the political agenda. But this also meant that the movement for 'revolt from the centre' had acquired a 'monopoly' on the issue, which in turn prevented the formation of a cross-political forum between social democrats, 'greens', liberals and Marxists to take the matter further.

Citizen's income as a political discourse in the arena of politics in the 1990s

In the early 1990s – especially in the years 1992-94 – the citizen's-income debate re-appeared in different guise. A new discourse on the theme was created in the form of a counter-discourse to the dominant discourse around the labour market and social policy concerning renewal of the welfare state.

The idea of a citizen's income took on new shape as a political discourse, because the movement-oriented, the scientific and the political strands of debate about the issue came now, for a short time, to be twined together. A number of parties took up the question. New cross-political fora were created, and the idea became a subject of social scientific analysis. For a brief period the new citizen's-income discourse thus managed to give voice to sentiments widespread among the population, and to sow the seeds of a new pattern of alliance between groups across a series of political divides.

The interesting feature of the 1990s' debate about the issue was that the idea of a citizen's income was brought onto the political agenda both 'from the bottom upwards' and 'from the top downwards'. It came 'from the bottom upwards' in the sense that it was promoted by marginalised people themselves, by 'outsiders' on the fringes of the worlds of business and trade unions, by spinners of ideas and by a few practitioners and controversialists of social science; and a new journal, SALT, strove to join the debates in the party-political arena with the debates in the arenas of social science and social movements. 'From the top downwards', in turn, the new discourse was met by attempts to delimit, diminish or exclude it: attempts to those ends were made by the leadership of the established political parties, by a number of ministers, and by public commissions of enquiry and civil servants.

The fact that the issue of citizens' incomes got onto the official agenda of politics in the years 1992-94 can be ascribed to the development of a particular political context and its coincidence with a set of economic, institutional and political circumstances.

The problems of unemployment and transfer payments were attracting growing attention, since joblessness continued to rise until the turn of the year 1994-95. At the beginning of the 1990s the government had set up a series of commissions of enquiry, whose tasks were to devise a more rational system of labour market arrangements and public benefit provision: the targets were simplification and savings. In 1993, moreover, the new social-democratic government had enacted a set of measures for reform of the labour market. On the one hand, these widened employees' opportunities to take periods of paid leave away from work; on the other hand, they gave significantly more scope for 'activation', that is to say enforcement on the jobless of obligations to enter training schemes or find work.

By 1992-93 the hegemonic growth-discourse was in crisis over its legitimacy in popular eyes. The majority of the population had lost faith in the ideology of full employment. Public opinion polls showed widespread attitudes in favour of rethinking labour market policies and experimenting with alternative models for distribution: 'dustmen's deal' models, for instance, along the lines for job-sharing proposed by the dustmen in Aarhus; or measures for reduced working-time, or for a citizen's income. In that situation, the latter notion indeed came to figure as a serious alternative. Politicians and their parties were forced into taking some stance on the idea of citizens' incomes, and to spell out arguments against such new and more radical modes of problem solution.

The fact that the discourse for a citizen's income vanished again from the official political arena around the turn of the year 1994/95 must be attributed to a change then in the conjuctures of economics and politics, and to associated success for the hegemonic growth discourse in its endeavours to exclude the rival discourse. That exclusion of the citizen's-income discourse took place, at a rhetorical level, in public political debate and within the political parties; and this was matched, at an institutional level, by exclusion of discourse about job sharing, sabbatical leave provision and citizens' incomes from the work of the Social Commission, the Welfare Commission and the government's Economic Secretariat. It is the task of a hegemonic discourse to set the official definitions of what are to be recognised as problems, and of how those problems fit in with existing institutions. The aim is to maintain a viable common identity and a political coalition. This is often done by way of public commissions of enquiry and civil service reports; and the concrete means to the end are the terms of reference set for commission enquiry, the appointments made to commissions, and the formulation of their professional and technical discourse.

The fact that it proved hard for the idea of a citizen's income to make headway within the political parties is connected with the point that, to a greater or lesser extent, most of the parties were coloured by and linked into the ideologies and organisational forms of established industrial society, whose hegemonic discourse was challenged by the discourse for a citizen's income. Those parties most clearly committed to the goal of economic growth were also the parties most strongly opposed to the idea of a citizen's income; while parties semi-critical of growth – such as the Socialist People's Party and the Radical Liberals – held views on the idea that were ambivalent and unclear. The Social Democrats and the right-of-centre Agrarian Liberals now found themselves with a new enemy in common, under the name of citizen's income, against whom they were in agreement to keep the societal goal of economic growth intact and to step up compulsory 'activation' for work and job-training. Both these parties then amended their programmes to distance themselves from the idea of a citizen's income.

The failure of the citizen's-income discourse to gain a foothold was tied up also with the fact that it achieved little support from circles central in social critique of the time. For these the notion either seemed too controversial and so was ignored, or it was ridiculed as unrealistic. The leading spirits of the women's movement thus dismissed the idea without explicitly addressing it. And the left-wing think-tank CASA (Centre for Alternative Social Analysis), which served as an expert body for the left in trade union and political affairs, opposed the hegemonic discourse for economic growth yet held back from taking any stance on the idea of a citizen's income. CASA instead looked to an enlargement of wage earning work as the way forward, to be achieved through job-sharing and the creation of new 'green' jobs in the public sector. An independent cross-political debating group similarly held apart from the citizen's-income discourse, and proposed that wage-employment be expanded by means of new jobs in the private service sector. Taken together, these responses demonstrated the continuing hold of the ideology of wage labour over even the critical flank of public commentary.

Citizen's income as a metaphor in various framework-narratives

For the purpose of my analysis I see conceptions of a citizen's income as an interesting new societal metaphor.

A metaphor is a descriptive image of an object or a relationship that sets out to view the world in a different manner. Metaphors can be used as epistemological tools for conceptual and scientific analysis towards the creation of new ideas and approaches. Concepts and scientific models derive from some basic metaphors, and scientific innovations often take the form of a shift of metaphors. Metaphors are organised into hierarchical structures of meaning or frameworks of understanding. All theories of society may therefore be seen as metaphorical systems based upon some foundational metaphors or 'metaphors in depth'.

For all citizen's-income theorists, development of the concept involves endeavours to establish a new language, including new metaphors distinct from those of the dominant scientific paradigms and political discourses. To talk about a citizen's income or wage is an attempt to give a name to a new situation by creating a new concept through a combination of old concepts. A 'wage' is an economic concept that has something to do with markets, whereas the concept of 'citizen' has something to do with state, society and democracy. The new concept of a 'citizen's wage' implies a proposal to add to the market wage another wage that is politically determined. This in turn means giving democracy a more prominent part in distribution, and so implies a new priority for the role of fellow-citizenship vis à vis the role of markets.

Public welfare payments are usually seen as providing a 'safety net'. Some critics of the welfare state argue, however, that many such benefits have become rather a 'hammock' that encourages idleness. Many therefore talk about how to turn welfare provision into a 'springboard' for work enterprise instead. All these phrases are examples of the widespread use of metaphors.

So too with the notion of a citizen's income which is to be, not a benefit payment contingent on restrictively defined need or past contribution but a universal personal entitlement. It thus shatters the familiar one-sided view of transfer incomes. The aims of a citizen's income are multiple; and just which aims are to prevail will be a matter for individual recipients to decide. So citizens' incomes can be seen as both a 'safety net' and a 'springboard'; and yet they can be used as a 'hammock' too. For people have a need also to rest, and to decide just how and when for themselves.

A number of current transfer payments and arrangements in support of enterprise can be replaced by, and re-conceived as, a universal citizen's income. When such re-conceptions are followed through, an entirely different understanding emerges, a new vision. The new metaphor of a citizen's income thus helps to change society's economic-cum-political conception of normality. Everyone will be normal and equal by way of common entitlement to an assured citizen's income. The old concepts are left behind – transfer payments, welfare benefits, social assistance, leave of absence, compensation and so on, all of which in some way or other incorporate the notion of wage labour as the norm. A citizen's income will not abolish wage labour; but it will relativise it, by depriving it of its monopoly on normality and so of its hegemonic role.

Citizen's income figures as a new metaphor within frameworks of understanding which conceive society as primarily a commonalty, a democracy or a civil society, and for which the market metaphor has only secondary significance. So, as a new metaphor, that of citizen's income points to a new scale of priorities among the various societal metaphors applied to current welfare society. A society of citizens' incomes is one that is understood to be, first and foremost, not a labour market but rather a democracy, so set as to ensure autonomy and security of living vis à vis the labour market and the state within a civil society. Provision for citizens' incomes will not have the power to dissolve the market character of society or its features of political compulsion. But it will set some clearer limits to that character and those features; and arrayed against this vision are most of those sceptics or opponents of the idea of citizens' incomes who, consciously or unconsciously, see society primarily as a market and the market metaphor as basic.

Frameworks of understanding are systems of metaphors. Coherence within a framework of understanding is created out of narratives, and it is through narratives that metaphors and the pattern they form become visible. The metaphor of citizen's income can be located within four different frame-setting narratives.

At the most general level the idea of citizens' incomes may be understood by reference to a narrative about the crises of ideologies and industrialism, and about the limits to growth, in which citizen's income figures as part of a new narrative concerning sustainable development. The seeds of this new narrative were planted by the citizen's-income theorists of the 1970s and acquired scientific form in the work especially of the ecologically oriented economist Herman E. Daly (Daly 1977).

Next, the idea of citizens' incomes may be set within the story of the historical development of democracy and the welfare state, where it appears as a further stage of welfare provision and a full realisation of social citizenship: the formation of some sort of 'third way society', where the aspiration is to unite old and new political forces in a new manner.

Within those parameters in turn, citizens' incomes can be viewed more narrowly by reference to a smaller narrative about the problems of the welfare state and about endeavours towards greater autonomy for the citizen vis à vis state, market and civil society alike.

Finally, the idea of a citizen's income may be seen as a feature of some more technical narratives about simplification and rationalisation of a series of welfare-societal mechanisms.

Citizen's income as metonymy and a target of negative political stereotyping

In the early 1990s the citizen's-income debate took the form of an ideological contest over the norms implied by linguistic usage. Supporters of the idea fought for acknowledgement of the concept of citizens' income as a new term with a core meaning that was neutral, and a complementary meaning that was positive. Opponents sought instead to accord to the term both core and complementary meanings of negative character.

While supporters used the concept as metaphor, opponents used it as metonymy to the effect of negative political stereotyping. Whereas metaphors are aimed to create new meanings through conjoining two different contexts, metonomy involves the making of links only between features that conventionally belong to one and the same context. Thus opponents of the citizen's-income idea strove to associate it with a range of adverse features of the established system. They described provision for it as provision for 'enforced passivity', as something that would 'set no challenges', as 'morally demeaning'. They argued that some particular negative features of current welfare provision would be writ large in any institution of citizen's incomes. And from this they drew general inferences about the nature of a new entity, the citizen's-income society, which they then stamped as undesirable.

Metaphorical use of the concept of citizen's incomes aims to open people's eyes to an alternative social order involving a new enhancement of the rights of fellow-citizenship and a sustainable development of civil society. Metonymic use of the concept, by contrast, has been deployed to strengthen the foundations of the established order.

Citizen's income as a pointer to a shift of ideas, paradigms and problem resolutions

Another theoretical perspective on the idea of a citizen's income is to see it as a sign of a shift of values at the normative level and a shift of paradigms at the scientific level.

At the normative level, the shift involved is from values that emphasise economic growth and equality (distributive justice) to values that emphasise freedom (autonomy), justice and sustainability. At the scientific level, the concept of a citizen's income can be seen as an element to a set of new social-scientific paradigms which stand in opposition to the paradigms prevailing in that field of knowledge.

Political ideologies and scientific theories alike may be described as larger coherent systems for problem resolution, within which there are internal connections of common logic among the descriptions and explanations offered of the various problems and problem-solutions in focus. What is characteristic of a paradigm shift is that problems and solutions get turned around through a change of viewpoints, values and language. Previous conceptions of what constitutes a problem are radically reformulated. The problem itself takes on new character and shape. Problems change places with solutions, in the sense that they come to be seen as parts of the solution, while what previously figured as solutions come now to be seen as parts of the problem.

Those ideological outsiders who brought the notion of a citizen's income to Denmark in the late 1970s and early 1980s – Adler-Karlsson and Gorz in particular -spearheaded a shift of ideas and paradigms. What this involved was – to borrow a term from the American sociologist, Alvin W. Gouldner (Gouldner 1971) – a distinct change of 'domain assumptions', with common agreement to abandon a hitherto dominant economic conception of humankind, and to pursue a new awareness of the limits to human exploitation of nature. With this went also a common concern to diagnose social systems that had got into crisis over their modes of problem solution, to such a point that 'vicious circles' had set in.

The 1980s gave birth to the idea of citizens' incomes as an element to new paradigms in international social science. There were five of these – 1. an ecologically oriented economic paradigm (Herman E. Daly 1990); 2. a paradigm of procedural law (Jürgen Habermas 1996); 3. a paradigm of citizenship (Bill Jordan 1992 and Claus Offe 1992); 4. a feminist paradigm (Nancy Fraser 1994); and 5. a liberal property-paradigm (Samuel Brittan 1995). All of them differed radically from the paradigms of market – and public choice hitherto dominant in social science; and it is on this score that the idea of a citizen's income can be seen as generating a paradigmatic shift.

Despite their diversity of theoretical perspectives, language and traditions, these five new paradigms all have a significant feature in common: they see provision of a citizen's income as a way towards a fairer society and as a breach with traditional conceptions of equality. They also all set their faces against a conventional market-economic understanding of society; and they join the idea of citizens' incomes to an argument that the state has a special part to play, an active role superordinate to that of the market, in creating justice in society.

The emergence and development of the notion of citizens' incomes, in a variety of separate versions during the 1970s and 1980s, can be construed as a shift of ideas and paradigms in relation to the prevailing modes of conceptual and social-scientific understanding. Yet no new common system of ideas, no new single and coherent counter-paradigm to set against that of the economic market, came to fruition in consequence. There was only the germ of a new idea and of a new paradigm about sustainable development.

Citizen's income as a case of 'the unfinished'

My analysis of the Danish debate about citizens' incomes draws on a range of concepts and an approach developed by the Norwegian sociologist of law, Thomas Mathiesen (Mathiesen 1982 and 1992). He has explored the way in which a hegemonic discourse is created by means, on the one hand, of marginalising (excluding) alternative discourses and, on the other hand, of socialising (including) potential alliance-opponents within a mode of perception common to the political public. Inclusion means that efforts are made to absorb opponents into the hegemonic alliance by presenting the common features of deviant action as disadvantageous. Exclusion means that opponents are expelled through presentation of their action as wrong-headed.

Mathiesen lists a series of rhetorical techniques for inclusion directed to erasing disagreement with the hegemonic discourse. The aim is to render potential opponents powerless by presenting them as being in essential agreement with that discourse. But he notes also a series of rhetorical techniques for exclusion, which by contrast underline the disagreement with the hegemonic discourse and characterise it as fundamental. This technique involves labelling the disagreement as Utopian, abstract and dangerous. The aim here is to render opponents powerless by presenting them as being in basic conflict with the system.

The hegemonic discourse is thus maintained by persuading the public at large to perceive and define counter-discourses as being either wholly within or wholly outside the system; and by encouraging opponents themselves to be captured by this imagery, to the point of actually behaving as if they indeed were either within the system or outside it. To establish counter-power, it is therefore essential to avoid precisely such encapture by the imagery of the dominant discourse; and this in turn means demonstrating, in a variety of theoretical and practical ways, that the logic of 'either-or' is spurious and needs to be replaced by a logic of 'both-and'.

The alternative to 'inclusion' and 'exclusion' alike is what Mathiesen calls 'the unfinished'. This involves adopting a stance that is both opposed to the established system and in competition with it. Mathiesen uses the term 'competing contradiction' to describe such a relationship and he calls it 'unfinished', because it offers only a sketch, an outlined prospect towards solutions, not a definitive answer or a final solution. It is unfinished or incomplete in the sense that it has not been tested and that its consequences remain uncertain. The risk to which 'the unfinished' is exposed is either that it may be made 'complete' through incorporation within the system as just a small positive reform; or that it may be wholly excluded from the system as a remote and utopian fantasy.

The idea of citizens' incomes can be taken as an example of an 'unfinished' idea, which has maintained recurrent vitality just because it has served as a mode of 'competing contradiction' vis à vis current welfare society. But the history of this idea has been marked at the same time by tendencies towards both inclusion and exclusion. In the debate on the issue during the 1990s, opponents tended to depict suggestions for a citizen's income as the adoption of an irresponsible line of policy, advocated by theorists remote from real life and hostile to practical short-term measures for improvement. These are typical rhetorical tactics for exclusion.

In fact proponents of a citizen's income have always been faced with a dilemma whether to emphasise the proposition as an idea within a wider context, or to put it forward as merely a technical measure. Technical sketches towards practical implementation of citizens' incomes have in some circumstances helped to give the idea appeal by way of 'competing contradiction'. That was the case to some degree in the 1980s and early 1990s. But there is then a large risk that ideas are quickly downgraded to matters of mere technique, and so lose meaningful coherence. It was in just this way that citizen's-income advocates, in the 1980s and the 1990s alike, came to neglect argument for their cause by reference to the values and concerns with societal context that justified it. There was a shortage of actors who could bring ideas and techniques together and so give the movement that overriding dynamic which the idea of 'the unfinished' implies.

The citizen's income debate as a confrontation between 'reactionary' and 'progressive' political rhetoric

Yet another approach to analysis of the issue is to see politics as a contest between diverse political discourses, in which processes of hegemony formation and exclusion take place. Political discourses arise out of the political process, and have both a rhetorical and an institutional aspect to them.

The American social scientist Albert O. Hirschman (Hirschman 1991) has set out some ideal-type characterisations of the patterns of argument deployed by 'reactionaries' and 'progressives' during the 200-years-long history of democracy. It can be seen in historical perspective that 'reactionaries' have drawn on much the same basic patterns of argument against liberal reformers or 'progressives', in three phases: first, at the time when civil democracy was initiated by the French Revolution; secondly, when political democracy came about through the introduction of general suffrage; and thirdly, when social citizenship made its way through growth of the welfare state.

From this viewpoint it may be said that we are now in a new phase of democratic development, where the issue is how to take the welfare state further, and where the 'progressive' agenda focuses on provision for a citizen's income and sustainable development.

Hirschman identifies three typical patterns of argument against reform: 1. reforms are misguided (the 'perversity thesis') in the sense that they will have consequences other than those envisaged by reformists; 2. reforms are futile (the 'futility thesis') in the sense that they will not change things anyway; and/or 3. reforms are dangerous (the'jeopardy thesis') in the sense that they will destroy features of the present system which are indispensable. As against these, supporters of 'progressive' reform draw on three parallel patterns of argument: 1. reforms will have a synergetic effect, in a process that will lead to solution of not just one problem but a whole complex of problems (the 'mutual support thesis'); 2. reforms are a matter of 'natural' progress or developmental 'necessity' (the thesis that 'history is on our side'); and/or 3. in the absence of reform the system will collapse or produce a totally unacceptable state of affairs (the 'imminent-danger thesis').

The aim of both types of political rhetoric, 'reactionary' and 'progressive', is to persuade recipients of the message by reference to the various kinds of effect that will follow from the implementation and, conversely, the rejection of reform. Reform opponents try to induce negative attitudes to a reform proposal by assertion that there will by no effects to reform at all, or some adverse and even dangerous effects. Reform supporters, by contrast, try to encourage positive attitudes to the proposal by claiming that it will set a virtuous circle in motion towards solution of several problems; or that it constitutes a necessity either by way of the logic of progress or in order to avoid misfortune. Both lines of argument may involve manipulation, more or less covert, unless it is made clear that neither supporters nor opponents are in fact capable of making pronouncements about future patterns of development with any certainty.

In the 1990s' debate about citizens' incomes, opponents resorted to the argumentation-patterns typical of 'reactionaries' in the following ways. First, introduction of a citizen's income will be misguided: as a 'passive' measure, it will create a 'group of losers', 'lead to cuts' or 'send women back to the kitchen sink'. Secondly, it will be useless: for 'it will be fruitless to redefine the notion of work', 'we already have a sort of citizen's income', 'it's just another word for early retirement and disability pension'. Thirdly, it will be dangerous: 'the unemployment funds will be transferred from trade-union hands to the state', the proposal 'is in conflict with the constitution' and/or 'will lead to economic collapse'.

Correspondingly, supporters resorted to arguments typical of the 'progressive' patterns just outlined. First, provision for a citizen's income will solve a number of linked problems: it will tackle 'problems of unemployment, environment and democracy in common context', and 'a series of social dogmas will fall like domino-pieces'. Secondly, it is in line with 'natural' development: it will 'round off the notion of social citizenship', it will finally 'break away from the subsistence logic of capitalism'. Thirdly, it is a necessity in order to avoid danger: 'the choice is between citizen's income and barbarism'.

To a very large extent, situations in the labour market and in society at large can be seen as involving an enforced choice between 'activity' and 'passivity', between 'independence' and 'dependence', between 'wage work' and 'transfer income'. The things usually taken to be 'good' here are activity, independence and wage work; the 'bad' things are passivity, dependence and transfer income. In the dominant dualistic universe of language, opponents of a citizen's income define provision for it in metonymic fashion as a passive transfer income that creates dependency. They adhere to the dualistic contrast between 'activity' and 'passivity', and wish to maintain this because it serves to keep work for wages in dominant place. Citizens' incomes may also be construed in metaphorical fashion, however: as real freedom, as a mechanism to break up the dualisms and double- binds, and to dissolve the enforcements of choice. Seen from that angle, citizens' incomes reflect a shift in frameworks of understanding – a 'framing' of social conceptions – and a challenge to the linguistic and institutional dualism that prevails in society.

Further development of citizen's income as an idea and as a paradigm

The idea of a citizen's income entails a change or shift in the principles by which boundaries are drawn between the different spheres of society – state, market and civil society – because it advances new principles for the distribution of money (of special interest to economists), for the distribution of rights (of special interest to political scientists), for changes in patterns of work and use of time (of special interest to sociologists) and for revision of obligations concerning work and maintenance (of special interest to lawyers).

While the citizen's-income idea has often been discussed and justified by reference only to one of these spheres, whether market or state or civil society, it has been my aim to offer a cross-disciplinary and more rounded portrayal of the concept. I have tried to do so by examining six different modes of approach to interpretation of the issue, drawn from work across the social sciences internationally; and by then setting out a critical analysis of the strengths and weaknesses to be found in a range of diagnoses of the crises of the welfare state, put forward by Danish social scientists. When taken together, the contributions of all these various social theorists help to sketch a fuller and more comprehensive picture of citizen's income as an idea and a scientific paradigm. I conclude on that basis that this idea-cum-paradigm may be seen,

(1) as a further development of democratic fellow-citizenship, more specifically as a full realisation of social citizenship;
(2) as an element in a process of sustainable development, through its contribution to setting a political limit to the exploitation of nature;
(3) as a new form of property right, which will make for a fairer distribution of resources in a market economy;
(4) as a means to creating autonomy vis à vis the market, through its setting of a political limit to the commodification of labour power;
(5) as a means to creating autonomy also vis à vis the state, through its setting of a political limit to client-dependency on the state; and
(6) as an element in the process of creating a new gender balance.

In sum, the conclusion is that citizen's income figures as a prime feature in a narrative about the further development of democratic fellow-citizenship, involving a completion of social citizenship and a step towards establishment of sustainable development. Within those parameters citizen's income also figures in a range of more concrete narratives about the simultaneous creation of greater justice in the distribution of a market economy's resources (a new form of property right); and of greater freedom (autonomy) vis à vis the market (de-commodification), vis à vis the state (diminution of client dependency) and vis à vis the family and civil society (diminution of family patriarchy).

Further development of citizen's income as a feature of a new political discourse about sustainable development

The notion of citizen's income may be seen as a feature of narratives that take the form of ideas, paradigms and political discourses alike. Seen as a paradigm the idea can be so formulated as to figure in a series of narratives that have to do with setting limits: in a narrative about setting limits to the exploitation of nature; in one which concerns setting limits to commodification of labour power; in another which is about setting limits to client dependency on the state; and finally in a narrative directed to setting limits to family dependency.

These narratives about limits may in turn send the ball rolling for a number of discourse-narratives about the need for a range of new social contracts. Welfare society's large social contract between labour and capital needs to be replaced by a multi-dimensional contract which will pose new limits to the exploitation of humankind and nature. This can be expressed as the need for a new version of the contract between labour and capital; and the need simultaneously for a set of other contracts between state and individual, between the sexes, and between generations. A new political contract for a citizen's income satisfies these requirements, because arrangements for such provision will engage with them all and serve towards restoring balance as against a number of the fundamental imbalances of modern welfare society. Provision for citizens' incomes will thus,

(1) help to create a more equal distribution of such work as is essential for society;
(2) allow reinforcement of individuals' legal rights and reduce the problem of client-dependency;
(3) offer the basis for a fairer division of labour between the sexes;
(4) strengthen civil society and democracy;
(5) in conjunction with other measures help towards more sustainable development.

Viewed in relation to the political priorities of the various ideological frameworks of understanding, the idea of a citizen's income should be capable in principle of gaining widespread support: support from those socialists who are particularly concerned to see a more equal division of societally essential labour; from those liberals who especially prioritise a reduction of client dependency; from those feminists for whom a fairer division of work between the sexes is a prime aim; and from those 'greens' on whose agenda a strengthening of civil society is in high place.

It is the function of political discourses to create such identity of feeling and such frameworks for action as will make for a coalition of political actors. At the beginning of the 1990s, the new discourse towards citizens' incomes reflected some attitudes that were widespread in the population, and it helped to sow the seeds of a new pattern of political alliance across a range of familiar political divides.

A further new discourse around the idea, so pitched as to bring together support from among socialists, liberals, feminists and 'greens' on the lines sketched above, is still awaiting its realisation. History seems to show that the idea has a vitality which allows it to re-appear in new shape, even after it has been forgotten for a time. My aim in this analysis has been to offer a firmer and more comprehensive basis for the next debate about citizen's income.

References

Adler-Karlsson, G. (1976), *Lærebog for 80'erne. Et antikonsumistisk manifest,* København: Fremads Fokusbøger.

Adler-Karlsson, G. (1977), *Nej til fuld beskæftigelse – ja til materiel grundtryghed,* København: Erling Olsens Forlag.

Basic Income European Network, *http://www.econ.ucl.ac.be/ETES/BIEN/*

Brittan, S. (1995), *Capitalism with a Human Face,* Aldershot: Edward Elgar.

Christensen, Erik (1998), Borgerløn. Analyse af en politisk ide. Århus: Hovedland (in the press)

Daly, H.E. (1977), *Steady-State Economics. The Economics of Biophysical Equilibrium and Moral Growth,* San Francisco: W.H. Freeman and Co.

Daly, H.E. and Cobb Jr., J.B. (1990), *For The Common Good. Redirecting the Economy towards Community, the Environment and a Sustainable Future,* London: Green print.

Fraser, N. (1994), 'After the Family Wage. Gender Equity and the Welfare State', *Political Theory,* Vol. 22, No. 4, pp. 591-618.

Gorz, A. (1979), *Økologi og frihed,* Viborg: Politisk Revy [English edition, *Ecology as Politics,* London: Pluto Press 1983].

Gorz, A. (1981), *Farvel til Proletariatet – hinsides socialismen,* Viborg: Politisk Revy [English edition, *Farewell to Working Class: an Essay on Post-industrial Socialism,* London: Pluto Press 1982].

Gorz. A. (1983), *Paradisets veje – kapitalens dødskamp,* Viborg: Politisk Revy [English edition, *Path to Paradise: on the Liberation from Work,* London: Pluto Press 1985].

Gouldner, Alvin W. (1971 og 1977, 2nd ed.), *The Coming Crisis of Western Sociology*, London: Heinemann.

Habermas, J. (1996A), *Between Facts and Norms. Contribution to Discourse Theory of Law and Democracy*, Cambridge: Polity Press.

Hirschman, Albert O. (1991), *The Rhetoric of Reaction. Perversity, Futility, Jeopardy*, Cambridge: The Belknap Press of Harvard University Press.

Hoff, Niels (1983), *Borgerstipendiet – den liberale velfærdsmodel.* Forlaget i Haarby.

Jordan, B. (1992), 'Basic Income and the Common Good', in Phillippe van Parijs (ed.) *Arguing for Basic Income*, London and New York: Verso, pp. 155-177.

Kuhn, Thomas S. (1962), *The Structure of Scientific Revolutions*, Chicago: University of Chicago Press.

Mathiesen, Thomas (1982), *Makt og Motmakt*, Drammen: Pax Forlag.

Mathiesen, Thomas (1992), *Det uferdige. Tekster om opprør og undertrykkelse*, Oslo: Pax Forlag.

Meyer, N.I. et al. (1978), *Oprør fra midten*, København: Gyldendal [English edition, *Rebellion from the Centre*, London: Marion Boyers 1981].

Meyer, N.I. et al. (1982), *Røret om oprøret. Mere om midten*, København: Gyldendal.

Offe, C. (1992), 'A Non-Productivist Design for Social Policies', in Phillippe van Parijs (ed.) *Arguing for Basic Income. Ethical Foundations for Radical Reform*, London and New York: Verso, pp. 61-78.

Rhys-Williams, J. (1943), *Something to Look Forward to: A Suggestion for a New Social Contract*, London: MacDonald.

3. Development of work and social (ex)inclusion

HELGE HVID

Work is an essential social category. During this century paid work has been the most important source of livelihood, and work in its different shapes and forms has widely determined values, norms, and relations of solidarity, class belongings and political affiliations. The decisive agents of society have been defined by work positions. Modern society has most of all been a work society. However, in the last one or two decades prominent sociologists such as Baumann, Lyotard and Offe have argued that we are moving away from a work society to a post-industrial or post-modern society, where cultural phenomena with roots outside the world of work are decisive for individual and social development (Rasborg, 1995). This post-modern assumption is founded on the fact that norms, values, political and cultural affiliations do not strictly relate to occupation and class to the same degree as they did before. And this idea is founded, among other things, on the fact that new social movements have arisen from outside the world of work – for instance the environmental and women's movements.

The post-modernists might be right in their observation that occupation and class belonging are no longer fundamental social categories for social orientation and political belonging. But that does not mean that work is no longer a very important factor for the development of individual life, for the development of social life and for the development of society.

The proportion of the population enrolled in paid work is growing and has never been higher. However, the individual person now has a shorter number of years in work. But that is mainly due to the fact that preparation for work, in the form of education, occupies a bigger part of life.

Work is not only a necessary evil, but also a highly appreciated activity. In the case of people actively working, work activities are appreciated most of all – even more than family activities (Gundelach and Riis, 1993, Schmidt, 1990). Work is an important factor for personal and collective experience and development. For many, work creates an important social identity. Work is an important platform from which individuals relate to the rest of society.

And work is, even within the West European welfare states, crucial not least for the individuals' economy, standard of living and individual independence.

But at the same time, there are a lot of risks related to work: the risk of losing one's job, the risk of getting an inhuman job and losing quality of life, the risk of having a job which occupies one's whole life, and the risk of becoming ill because of work. These risks are crucial for individual life and play an important role in social life.

So, even though the post- modernists are probably right in their observation of the reduced importance of occupation and class as social categories, work has not become less important as a social category. What the post- modernists actually observe is that workers' relation to work has become more differentiated and individualised. Occupations and classes are under dissolution. People are individually forced to have their own attitudes to and positions on questions like the meaning of work – what is a good and what is a bad job? What sort of personal career is desirable? What can be expected from employers and colleagues? There are no strong models and norms for answering these questions. Every individual must find his or her answer in a reflexive confrontation with their own desires and the world of reality. Often reality does not correspond to expectations. Some get a less attractive job than they expected. Others do not make the career they wanted and expected – instead of having a work career they perhaps lose their job. Others do not get a steady job at all.

The lack of paid work is the most important factor in labour market marginalisation, and it seems to have a growing significance. Actually, in the EU-countries the proportion of the population over 15 employed has been constant for decades (Eurostat, 1996). But in the 1960s most of the people (women) without a job were provided for via the family – supported by tax and family policies. Now, most of the unemployed are provided for by the welfare state. And 'non-employment', which was concentrated before on the female members of the family, is now concentrated on certain sections of the population – marginalised because of their exclusion from the labour market.

The family was an alternative to work as a means for inclusion. This function of the family has been weakening for a long time. Today there is no other stronger factor for inclusion than work. The development of work, and the development of work policies, is therefore the most important factor for future social (ex)inclusion.

Change of work – towards post-Fordism

Work and production are undergoing vital and comprehensive changes. That is the message we have heard from a wide range of scholars during the last decade or more. The concept of Fordism/post-Fordism has been one important frame for the scientific debate on the changes of work. There are a lot of different ideas within the frame of Fordism/post-Fordism about reasons for the changes, and their consequences (Elam, 1994). Technological change, or the fundamental technological revolution created by information technology, is for some scholars the main reason for the shift from Fordism to post-Fordism (Freeman and Perez, 1988). Others focus on the shift in the global market: a shift from standardisation to non-standardisation, from relatively stable market conditions to unstable market conditions, and to market conditions with increased uncertainty (Piore and Sabel, 1984). Thirdly, some scholars focus on structural and institutional changes (Boyer, 1988, Hirch & Roth, 1986, Jessop, 1994). For them the golden age of Fordism was post war capitalism, founded in an institutional connection and alliance between mass production, mass organisation (trade unions and other organisations) and a national welfare state. This alliance is now breaking down, and a new post-Fordist society is emerging. The characteristics of this are uncertainty and openness. But generally those who see the transmission from Fordism to post-Fordism as a result of technology or market conditions have a predominantly positive view of the post-Fordist society, primarily because working conditions are better here than under the Fordist regime. By contrast, those who see the transition as a result of institutional changes tend to be more pessimistic about the future. They fear the processes they see of individualisation, dismantling of the welfare state, social differentiation and increased exploitation of both human beings and nature.

Outside the debate about Fordism many scholars and observers have argued that we are in a period of transition. The extensive growth of the service sector compared with other sectors in the economy has given rise to the dualism of industrial society and service society (Bell, 1973). It is, however, rather unclear what characterises the service society because of its enormous heterogeneity. Other scholars focus on the significant shift in the objects of work and production – a shift from material things as the dominant objects of work to information and symbols as the dominant objects (Reich, 1992). According to these scholars a predominant section of the labour force in the information society will be employed in highly qualified, highly paid, individualised, flexible jobs. But there will also be a layer of manual workers in routine production and a layer of unqualified workers occupied in personal services. For these two layers the work will be low paid and the jobs will be insecure.

The frames of explanations are many, but there is widespread agreement about the fact that work is changing radically. However this is not new. Work has been under a constant process of change in the last hundred years. But what we see now is a more fundamental shift in the understanding of rationality and efficiency in work and production. Bureaucracy and 'scientific management' as the dominant concepts for rationalisation in this century are being widely replaced by flexibility and inclusion. This shift can be schematically described by a set of dualities.

Table 3.1 Shifts in the notion of efficiency

From	*To*
Centralised management	Centrally formulated goals and local autonomy.
Specialised jobs and a detailed job hierarchy	Broader jobs and fewer levels in the job hierarchy
Standardised qualifications	Development of qualifications starting from the individual
Standardised products	Customer oriented products
Standardised quality	Constant quality development
Utilisation of a boundless nature	Ecology

The impact of this new conception of efficiency is quite diverse. In some companies the work organisation has totally changed, and in others a bureaucratic organisation is maintained with minor adjustments. In the last ten to fifteen years the new understanding of efficiency has crystallised into a range of new principles of management. No company can adopt all these principles, but most companies have adopted some of them.

The new principles of management can be stated as follows (inspired by Sandberg, 1997):

1. *Less hierarchy.* Organisations have fewer levels. Top management and base personnel are strengthened, while middle management is thinned out. What we see is a simultaneous centralisation and decentralisation. Goal setting and the control of results are centralised while operational control is decentralised.

2. *Independent units.* Companies are divided into smaller units with their own economic responsibility. In its full consequence the individual and the production group are made economically responsible, and their contribution to the total economic result is controlled. As it is for each department, so it is for the individual company in the entire concern.

3. *Flow and process orientated production planning.* Boundaries between different functions, departments and occupations are torn down. Specialisation of functions is replaced by specialisation of products (or sub-products), and construction-production-marketing is co-ordinated. This is also the primary purpose of 'Business Process Re-engineering'.

4. *Sophisticated control* is maintained through systems based on information technology. The economic results are closely monitored. The quality of production is recorded and controlled, and so are absence, turnover, job satisfaction, attitudes and commitment.

5. *Result orientated payment.* Efficiency oriented wage systems (piece work etc.) are on the way out. Wages are less dependent on trade and occupation. New wage systems are developed, where quality, cost reduction and the individual employee's contribution to the entire result are calculated.

6. *Management by ideas.* The purpose is to create commitment to the goal of the company. The means can be visible management, quality circles, internal marketing such as campaigns, personal conferences, house organs and so on. If this kind of management does succeed, employees seem to be managed from within themselves.

7. *Flexible conditions of employment.* Part time jobs, employment on fixed contracts, overtime and more flexible rules of working hours are widespread.

8. *New kinds of enterprises.* Companies are outsourcing peripheral activities to independent enterprises. Temporary employment agencies are growing. Franchising is a new form of company formation, where the same centrally developed concept is used in many small enterprises. One-

person companies are established, functioning in networks with other similar companies.

Social consequences of the changes in work

For very good reasons there has been great concern about the social consequences of the changes in work. There has been a tendency to search for definitive answers in relation to this concern and, especially in the public debate, a black and white picture has been drawn. Some commentators have emphasised the development of more skilled, more independent, and more challenging jobs. Others have emphasised the differentiation, the individualisation, the competition, the increasing risk of degradation and/or dismissal. Research in the area has actually shown a more confused picture of the social consequences of the development of work. There are four central dimensions in that picture: the quality of work, labour market risks, work and leisure, and the development of the culture of work. I shall take each in turn.

The quality of work

Here, the central dimensions are the level of qualification needed for the job, the degree of autonomy in the job and work load. A wide range of case studies and surveys have been made in the last decade or more on the development of the quality of work. Kern and Schumann's (Kern and Schumann, 1984) study of the changes in the industrial work in Germany has been a point of reference in the last decade. They found that for a core group in industry the division of labour was reduced and more qualifications were demanded. At the same time, however, there was a growing marginalised group, characterised by small demands for qualifications and low employment security.

This thesis of polarisation has been confirmed and further developed by a range of later studies, and it seems as if there are not only two, but several poles in the development of the quality of work. In a recent Danish study of the development of work in the last five years across the whole labour market (Borg and Burr, 1997), increasing influence on work by the employees and increasing social support in the work have been found. But at the same time the work load has increased with higher demand for concentration, attention, work intensity and responsibility. This development has not reduced repetitive work. The percentage of those employed in repetitive work has been constant.

The development of quality of work is difficult to predict, because no simple determinism seems to be involved. The same new technology implemented by companies in the same market can have quite different consequences for the quality of work. Changes in market conditions and implementation of new management concepts can also have quite different consequences (Nielsen, 1996). The development of work cannot be seen merely as a consequence of technological change and/or changing market conditions. The quality of work is also a result of specific social relations in the enterprises.

Labour market risks

Health risks and risks of expulsion connected to the labour market are probably rising. Some health risks connected to chemicals and physically heavy work tasks have been reduced. On the other hand, risks connected to work stress and psychological problems in work are rising. Stress related illness and illness related to muscular problems are increasing. While the 'old' health risks in work were mainly related to the technical system, the 'new' health risks are primarily related to the social system of work – the work organisation. It has been shown that low degree of influence at the job increases the risk of expulsion, and so has also both a low and a high degree of psychological demands (Borg and Burr, 1997).

Risks connected to inadequate or outdated qualifications are rising because of the speed of change. Life long learning is the main answer to these risks. The educational system is an important factor in reducing risks. But just as important – and perhaps more important – is the possibility of learning on the job (Stahl, 1993). Work organisation – a learning organisation – where employees gain new experiences and have opportunities for daily learning is an important factor in reducing this risk of expulsion from the labour market.

Work and leisure

The demand for flexibility has a great impact on working life. In the EU the number of employees in part time jobs is increasing (see the concluding Chapter Three in this volume). Overtime is increasing and fixed working hours seem to be on the way out. Telework is the next big step in flexibilisation of work. How will this development influence life outside working life? That is also an open question. Will flexibility create polarisation where work occupies the whole life for one group on the labour market, while another group cannot get enough work to live a proper life? Or will flexibilisation give employees better opportunities to organise their lives with higher priority given to family, to the different needs in the life cycle and to personal interests? The answers to these questions will in the main be politically determined.

Work culture

The development of work interacts with norms, attitudes and values related to work. It also interacts with regional or national work cultures and management styles. The organisation of work and participation in change are dependent on the specific cultural context (Hofstede 1994; Hagedorn and Hvid, 1997). It has long been argued that western societies are slowly moving from a materialist to a post materialist culture (Inglehart, 1990). One manifestation of this is a slow change in work ethics. Employment as such does not seem to be a holy duty to the extent it was before. A general trend in the development of the work culture is less orthodoxy and more individualism. That increases the demands for meaning, personal development and experience (Simonsen, 1993; Bild, et al. 1993). This cultural development is a threat both to traditional authoritarian management (Jaeger, 1986), and to the traditional kind of solidarity among workers. It is an open question whether a new anti-authoritarian management can go hand in hand with a new kind of individualistic solidarity (Hvid and Møller, 1992).

To summarise

The social consequences of the development of work are difficult to interpret, because work and the development of work is so diversified. A possible consequence is a significant improvement in the quality of working life, where employees have a high degree of control over their own job, participate in management, obtain security at work through continuous learning, and actively reflect over the content and meaning of their work. Another possible consequence is polarisation in the labour market with a core group, which must live under constant pressure for change, work hard, compete, and neglect the family and private interests. Beside this core group a marginalised group will develop with unqualified and unstable jobs, relatively low wages, little control over their own work and a low degree of participation at their work place and in society.

The actual consequences of the development of work will probably be something in between these two scenarios. Just where, however, it is impossible to say, because determinism in understanding the welfare consequences of the development of work is a mistake. The consequences are determined not only by the development of technology and markets, but also by the culture of work and work policy formed by managers and employees in the companies and by labour market organisations and state agencies.

But at least in a northern European context the current trend in the labour market is apparently characterised by demands for high performance, a high level of effort, a high level of strain and high risk of dismissals and expulsion. And it is a labour market where wage earners want to identify themselves with their work, develop through their work, and create meaning to their lives.

The development of the labour market can be seen as a steep staircase, where every step takes one higher and higher. Those with the shortest legs drop behind, or they are pushed aside by the working masses, who see climbing the steps as a personal challenge and a source of personal development.

Under those conditions the traditional market oriented labour market policy cannot solve the problems of the labour market. Traditional labour market policy has focused on wages, working hours and conditions of employment. This labour market policy cannot solve the problems of increasing work load related to work organisation. It cannot prevent the obsolescence of qualifications. And the traditional labour market policy cannot meet the desire of the employees for challenges and experiences. On the contrary the traditional labour market policy, based on rules and norms, can be an obstacle to challenges and experiences (Hvid, 1990).

To meet the current problems of the labour market it is necessary to develop a work policy. This work policy must be a response to the current development of technology, markets and organisation, and it must be a corrective to most conceptions of management which pay little attention to the welfare aspects of work. And actually, a new work policy is beginning to take shape.

The shift to work policy: Welfare, workfare or work for welfare

Labour market policy is a cornerstone in the politics of the welfare state. A new work policy can become an important renewal of labour market policy and an important contribution to the current transformation of the welfare state regimes. This possibility must be assessed in relation to the general renewal or dismantling of the welfare state that is currently taking place.

Jessop (Jessop, 1994) argues that the national state in the highly industrialised countries is moving from a Keynesian welfare state to a 'hollowed out' Schumpeterian workfare state. The main aims of the Keynesian welfare state was to guarantee market stability, to secure demand for the products of mass production and to secure social stability. The expectations of the Keynesian welfare state were that it could guarantee stability in the demand for products and the demand for labour at the same time. The Keynesian welfare state ran into a deep crisis in the late 1970s, because of internationalisation of the markets and the emergence of new patterns of work and production. From the ruins of the welfare state, a supply oriented workfare state is arising. The main objective of the workfare state is to stimulate innovation and flexibility. The purpose is not to secure market stability, but to stimulate the competitiveness of enterprises on the international markets – and to increase efficiency in the public sector and home based industries.

If we look at the labour market policies and politics related to that, Jessop's characterisation of the current development of the national state seems quite adequate. The core words with regard to labour market regulation are now deregulation, decentralisation, flexibilisation and stimulation.

It is argued that in a global or at least international economy, enterprises (in the highly developed countries) must survive and develop through increased flexibility, high quality and high innovative ability and capacity. Under such circumstances it is very important for the single enterprise to be able to recruit the right person for the right job. This is more important than a fixed national level of wages. It is argued that a flexible economy demands flexible working hours, and the labour market system must adjust itself to this new demand.

Flexible enterprise needs flexible workers who have specific qualifications appropriate for the enterprise. This is illustrated by the discussion about 'the learning organisation' (Bottrup, 1997). The system of vocational training has adopted that point of view, and orientated training away from occupations and trades, towards the specific organisation and enterprise.

The overall change is a shift of focus from regulation of the market to supporting and influencing the development of the enterprise. I shall illustrate this development with examples from Denmark, often similar to the developments in other West European countries.

In Denmark the political institutions remain but the priorities have changed. Labour market policy is increasingly orientated towards the enterprise: much more freedom is given to the enterprise to fix the wages and working hours in local negotiations. The frame for wages and working hours is still set in central negotiations, but all parties at the enterprise level have more room for manoeuvre in the local negotiations about wages and hours. This development has been called 'centralised decentralisation' (Due et al., 1993).

Vocational training is increasingly orientated towards the specific needs of the single enterprise. Standardised courses which qualify workers for a specific trade are replaced by courses related to the specific enterprise.

In the regulation of working environment less importance is given to threshold limiting value and central regulations on occupational health while more attention is given to stipulating the enterprises to improve their working environment. Work place assessment, imposed by the EU-commission is one example of that. The 1993 government programme to reduce repetitive work in Denmark by 50 percent in 10 years is another example.

In recent years, however, government has given high priority to stimulation of enterprises to take social responsibility for people who have difficulties in finding permanent employment. In Denmark social responsibility was until recently a task and a duty for the welfare state. Now the welfare state tries to spread out social responsibility to the individual public and private enterprises. Furthermore, people on social security are increasingly enrolled in job creation programmes – people must work to get social benefit.

It is not only labour market policy that has become more and more enterprise oriented. The same applies to industrial policy and environmental policy. Earlier on industrial policy's main purpose was, in general, to support branches of trade and industry and technological development. Now industrial policy is much more a policy to stimulate enterprises to be more flexible, quality oriented and export oriented. This development is also influenced by the EU. Environmental policy is also oriented towards the enterprises. Until the 1990s environmental policy focused on the emissions from production units and laid down some threshold values for emissions. This is still the case, but environmental policy is increasingly oriented towards stimulating enterprises and branches to develop and use cleaner technology. Experiments involving employees in the development of cleaner technology and cleaner production are carried out.

Simultaneously with the increased public intervention in and support for the development of private enterprises, there is an international tendency in private enterprises to take responsibility for public interests – enterprises take a social and or ethical responsibility on themselves. Although it is quite still uncertain how responsible these forms will prove to be, the change indicates a weakening of the borderline between public and private interests.

Workfare or work for welfare

Jessop and other theorists, who study the institutional development of post-Fordism, are mostly concerned with the making of a new post-Fordist 'accumulation regime', where new relations between state, classes and production are emerging. From a critical perspective, they focus on efforts to create a new stable 'accumulation regime' that allows capitalism to survive.

For the actors in this process of creating the post-Fordist society, the survival of capitalism is, however, not the only perspective. For individuals, the future is not the question of survival of capitalism, but the development of individual welfare and success. In addition, organised interest groups have more diversified and sophisticated perspectives on the future than the survival of capitalism: for employers' organisations reduction of insecurity and maintenance of managers' control over production and work are essential perspectives. For organised labour working conditions and welfare are important perspectives. For the environmental movement an improved relation to nature is the most important perspective. For women's organisations equal opportunities for men and women and room for the family are the main perspectives.

For some people the central question is how the workfare state can be developed to increase welfare – if that is possible at all. According to some trade unions it is possible.

The trade unions in Denmark do not see the current development of labour market policy as a farewell to welfare policy, but as a shift of focus in welfare policy. Focus is moved from *market* to *production* – a gradual shift of focus in welfare policy from the distribution of wealth (from market relations, and especially the relations of the labour market) to the creation of wealth (to production in manufacturing and services and the social relations involved, and to the products). This shift from market to production is evident from the following quotation from an LO (the Danish Confederation of Trade Unions) publication, where a vision of 'the developmental work' is presented (LO, 1995):

> The vision of 'the developmental work' has as its objectives:
> to increase the respect paid to the individual
> to create better conditions in which protection of the environment, contents of work, pay, quality, and good service are at the centre
> to provide meaningful work for all
>
> to enable people to develop their own resources while at the same time respecting the interests of the community
> to create the type of democracy in which everyone would want to participate.
>
> In other words, the concept of Work and Development ('the developmental work') is not just about respecting the individual and his or her personal resources: it is also a factor permitting the undertaking to manufacture a good product or provide a good service. At the same time, .. 'the developmental work'.. is crucial for the creation of a society in which everybody is concerned about protecting the environment and is willing to involve him or herself in social and democratic affairs.

'The developmental work' is the concept most often used in connection with this strategic shift. The chairman of the LO calls the strategy of 'the developmental work' the most decisive issue for the trade unions today.

'The developmental work'

In the 1980s a number of new principles of management and production were imported to Europe and Scandinavia from USA and Japan. At first the trade unions in Scandinavia were very critical of the new concepts of production which were criticised for creating individualised work relations, weakening the position of trade unions and weakening the participation of the employees. After some experiments, in which the trade unions were involved, the labour unions gradually adopted a more positive attitude towards the new concepts of production. They saw some potential for the trade unions in the new principles of management (Sandberg, 1992). In 1985 the Swedish Metal Union published a large report for its congress called *The good work* (Metallindustriarbetareförbundet, 1985). This report focused on the possibilities, seen from a trade union perspective, offered by the new production concepts. The report was a comprehensive and detailed trade union answer to the new concepts of production. This report was a starting point for the strategy of 'the developmental work'.

Around 1990 'the developmental work' was established as a labour market strategy both in Sweden and Denmark. In 1990 the Federation of Swedish Trade Unions, and in 1991 the Danish Trade Unions Federation published congress reports with the title 'The Developmental Work' (LO, 1991). The Swedish report was more comprehensive but in both reports a new strategy to replace the Keynesian inspired active labour market policy was set out. The Swedish report suggested that the solidaristic wage policies, which had been the cornerstone of Swedish labour market policies for decades, should be replaced by a solidaristic work policy. This solidaristic work policy must ensure the development of work, in a manner by which polarisation is avoided, occupational health improved and employment and wage improvement secured.

'The developmental work' as a concept is used only in Denmark and Sweden. It is in Denmark that the concept has been most widely diffused. Here 'the developmental work' is an important strategic concept for the whole trade union movement, in public labour market policies, and the concept is actively used in the modernisation of public institutions. In other countries we see a parallel development. In Norway similar activities are carried out in relation to an agreement established between employers' associations and trade unions about the development of enterprises (Øverland, 1996). Similar intentions were formulated in the EU in relation to the concept of 'antroprocentric production systems' at the beginning of the 1990s (Wobbe, 1991). This concept did not survive, but recently the European Commission has published a Green Paper about partnership in organisational development (EU Commission, 1997). This Green Paper has similar ideas to those of 'the developmental work'.

'The developmental work' is an example of a new kind of welfare policy – a new reflexive welfare policy, founded on life politics (Giddens, 1994). According to the strategy welfare is developed through individuals creating security, self-respect and self-actualisation. To make that possible management, organisation and work must be developed. To secure that development organisations and public agencies outside the companies must stimulate and regulate the development of work, but in a reflexive manner whereby companies are in dialogue with the regulating authorities. The regulating authorities and labour market organisations must not force specific solutions on the companies, but distribute rights, impose some objectives on the company and lay down some procedures for the company.

It is necessary to emphasise that even in Denmark and Sweden 'the developmental work' is not *the* labour market strategy. The concept refers to just one way of modernising labour market policies in competition with other strategies and perspectives, such as regulation through economic incentives or just general deregulation.

The fundamentals of 'the developmental work'

The 'developmental work' can be defined as a project in which the following three considerations are involved simultaneously (Bottrup and Hvid, 1995):

- the employees' desire for good work, individually and for the employees as a group,
- the wishes of the enterprises to develop quality, flexibility and customer orientation, and
- the society's wishes to develop economy, environment and living conditions.

'The developmental work' is based on three fundamental assumptions:

- Good working conditions, marked by security, opportunity, influence and participation, are not an extra burden on the company but an investment with a good yield.
- Improvement of quality, flexibility and customer orientation can be organised so that working conditions are improved.
- Considerations of the interests of the wider economy, living conditions and environment do not necessarily conflict with the goals of the company.

In opposition to most management concepts, the idea of 'the developmental work' recognises that there are different and conflicting interests concerning the development of working conditions. It also recognises that there is overlap between these different interests. The size of that overlap is, however, dependent on whether the focus is on common interests. If it is expected that employers recognise the employees' interests in a good working life, the employers will probably incorporate (some of) these interests in the development of production and make profitable use of them. If employees have insight into and influence on the development of the company, they will use the potentials of the company as a tool to satisfy their own interests. Likewise, the overlap between the interests of the company and the interests of society is dependent on how far companies are expected to recognise social considerations and how far society stimulates the companies to do so.

Characteristics of 'the developmental work'

'The developmental work' contains a range of well known elements taken from modern management theories, theories about qualifications, development of competence and learning, and theories about the development of working environment. Specific features of 'the developmental work' are:

The holistic approach. Flexibility, working environment, education, competence development, quality, use of technology, organisational development and customer orientation are connected. But at the same time it is necessary to maintain the different roles, arenas and institutions at company level to ensure the expression of different interests and considerations.

Focus on the workplace and the single employee. Workplaces and the employees who work in them are very different. Every workplace must find its own way to create 'the developmental work'. And the 'the developmental work' must provide room for the wide diversity of employees.

The work of change most target the employees. The need for change comes mostly from outside as new tasks, new expectations and new market demands. In 'the developmental work', experiences and intentions among the employees are the main ingredient in the management of change.

Just what 'the developmental work' actually comprises is very varied. 'The developmental work' in a school, in a fishing industry, in a market garden, in a nursing home or in a firm of solicitors is not the same. Even at workplaces making the same products 'the developmental work' can differ widely.

Team work for instance can in one workplace be a big step towards 'the developmental work'. It may provide the employees with broader jobs, better possibilities for learning, more knowledge, more influence at the work place and more control over their own work. But team work can also split up the workplace, make things more unclear and confusing, create new conflicts and create a higher level of stress. The same ambiguity applies to other tools to develop the work, like quality management, vocational training, new wage systems, and so on.

Because of that 'the developmental work' is not a tool box to develop the work, but an interrelated set of principles and criteria which must be taken into consideration at company level and imposed on companies by labour market institutions and public agencies.

In the following section the principles and criteria of 'the developmental work' will be presented.

The diamond of 'the developmental work'

As already mentioned 'the developmental work' is a holistic, welfare oriented approach to the differentiated company. This tension between the holistic approach and the differentiation within companies can be illustrated by a diamond. The points illustrate the differentiation and the lines illustrate the holistic approach, see Figure 1.

The problem with the lack of a holistic approach can be observed in many projects for the development of work and organisation. Often the focus is on one spot – on job development or training or new wage systems or better communication or an improved working environment. But because of narrow focus the project will probably create new problems in other arenas of the company. A job development project, where managers and enthusiastic employees with the best intentions create broader and more highly qualified jobs can easily come into conflict with existing wage systems, it can exclude a majority of the employees from influencing the development of their own working conditions, it can marginalise groups of employees, it can increase the level of stress. Without a holistic approach the best intentions with a development project can be undermined and heavy resistance against the project can arise from a neglected arena.

On the other hand, a total integration of arenas in the company level is just as problematic. In modern management literature an almost total inclusion in line management is often recommended. Employees' participation takes place in quality circles, for instance. Here the changes in production, health, environment, training and other things are discussed. This kind of inclusion implies a risk of over-exposing the rationality of production. Training is related only to the actual production and not to furthering the careers of the employees. Health problems which can't be solved without changes of production are very difficult to publicise. There is a risk of undermining formal rights through that kind of inclusion. The development of such an integrated organisation can be inhibited by the lack of contradictions and clashes between different arenas, rationalities and views.

The points in the diamond represents the six most important arenas in the company:

- Goals for the enterprise, developed internally and related to the world outside the enterprise, related to strategy and conflicting interests.
- Work and production, with regard to work tasks, technology and work organisation.
- Management of change, concerning who is involved and how in the process of change, related to employees' participation in the process of management.
- Health, where the purpose is not only the prevention of injuries and known occupational diseases, but to create a healthy working environment, related to occupational health and safety activities.
- Rights, concerning the distribution of formal rights and obligations, related to the formal system of industrial relations.
- Rewards, concerning wages and other kinds of rewards, related to wage agreements and the career system.

These six points all represent important political arenas in the enterprises, and all the points are related to institutions and policies outside the company. Other points could be mentioned, such as gender equality, environment or the integration of disabled people in work. These points don't actually, yet, occupy a central position in daily working life. Hence they are not included here.

In the following each point in the diamond will be discussed, and some principles and criteria for 'the developmental work' at each point will be set out. The relation between the single point and the other points in the company, and the relation to regulation outside the company, will be illustrated. In this way the welfare producing company will be described, and a welfare policy with focus on production outlined.

Here the description of the points will be quite superficial. The purpose is to illustrate the point that 'the developmental work' as strategy actually is a 'a big story' with far-reaching consequences for production, work and daily life. At the same time 'the developmental work' is not a utopian dream, but a practical project, implementation of which can start here and now in individual actions, in experiments at work places and in new forms of regulation of the labour market.

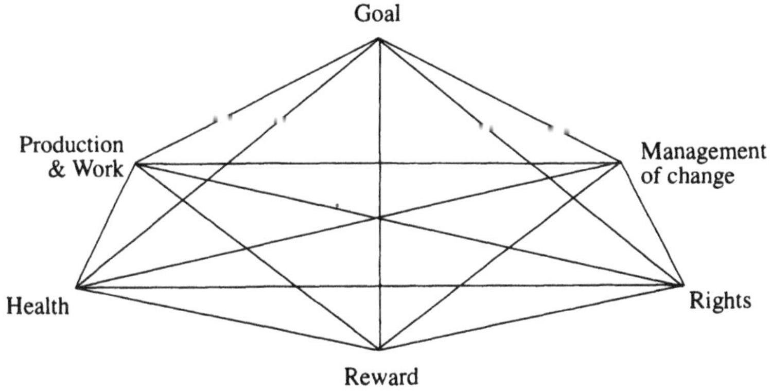

Figure 3.1 The diamond of 'the developmental work'

Goals

The ability of the enterprise to produce welfare depends on whether there is time and room for dialogue about goals and visions of the work carried out in the enterprise. It is critical whether the employees have the necessary background to participate in this dialogue. Do the employees have sufficient information and learning possibilities to participate in the dialogue? And are the voices of the employees heard?

The ability of the enterprise to produce welfare is also dependent on whether the enterprise adopts social goals, expressed by the surrounding society. Society demands increasing social responsibility and environmental sustainability of the enterprises. How far these demands are actually accepted by the enterprise depends on the ability of society to impose the demands and on the ability of the enterprise to adopt them. Public regulation by society and opportunities for dialogue and care of interests within the enterprise are crucial for success in the adoption of social goals.

Relation to the rest of the diamond. Openness and democracy in the development of the goals is dependent, first of all, on the employees' *rights* and participation in the process of *change*.

Regulation. How far it is possible for enterprises to create an open dialogue about goals depends on which rights and duties different agents in the enterprise have imposed: i.e. employees' rights to information, to be heard, to influence and to representation. These rights are regulated from outside the enterprise. Also education and information are a necessity if employees are to be able to influence the goals of the enterprise.

Whether the society around the enterprise can influence the social responsibility and sustainability of production depends on governmental authorities, popular organisations, the policies of institutionalised investors etc.

Production and work

To improve both welfare in work and flexibility and customer orientation in production requires improved opportunities for learning and development of competence for all, through closer relations between customer and employee (user and producer), and through increased responsibility and participation by the employees. Welfare at work will increase if employees acquire 'ownership' of the process of work (Brulin and Nilsson, 1995). And welfare at work is increased if technology and work organisation are developed in a way that allows individual variety with room for different qualifications and desires.

Relation to the rest of the diamond. If the employees are going to have 'ownership' of the process of work, management must be sure they will not abuse their 'ownership' to oppose the goals of the enterprise. A precondition for the employees' 'ownership' of their working process is a high level of trust between different parties in the enterprise. Trust on the other hand implies a good working environment (healthy work). It implies participation – formal rights and influence on the goals of and changes in the enterprise.

Regulation. Collective agreements influence the organisation of production and work, and so do the qualifications available on the labour market. The development of technology, which is influenced by policy, in turn influences the quality of work. Public and private service institutions advise the enterprises, and in that way they influence the development of production and work. Experiments with public support for enterprises which humanise their production have been, and are still being carried out in different countries. These different regulation agencies might influence the development of production and work in a welfare oriented direction.

Change

If changes are to contribute to increased production of welfare, they must come from inside and from the bottom with support from above. This implies among other things that the qualifications and the wishes for change among employees are taken seriously, that sufficient time for change is given, and that the process of change is characterised by dialogue and participation (Svensson, 1991).

Relation to the rest of the diamond. A process of change dominated by the employees implies their identification with the goals of the enterprise – and it implies that the goals of the enterprise have a character that makes such identification possible. A process of change dominated by employees also implies a process of work where new experiences and learning are created. And it implies basic safety, security and confidence based on healthy working conditions and fundamental rights.

Regulation. Education and training in contact with the enterprise is an important factor here. Through education and training employees, hopefully, can keep up with the process of change. Good external institutions for education and training are an important factor. Rights and effective access to vocational training are an other important parameter for regulation. The same applies to job security and active measures of prevention to avoid exclusion. Public guidance in the process of change is also important.

Health

If changes are seen as an opportunity to make the working environment more healthy with reference to a common understanding of the improvements in health most needed at work, and if these understandings are incorporated in the process of change, the production of welfare in the enterprise will increase.

Relation to the rest of the diamond. If the working environment is given a higher priority in the goals of the enterprise, health will presumably improve. Control and social support in production and work will in itself improve the conditions of health (Karasek, 1990). The employees must have the right to strong representation in defence of health at work. And opportunities to improve health can be an active element in engaging the commitment of the employees.

Regulation. Public regulation is crucial when it comes to health at work. To stimulate the production of welfare in the enterprises public regulation on occupational health and safety must be more holistic in its character. Health is an issue everywhere in the enterprise and not only where there are particular readily recognised health problems. Demands must be imposed on the enterprises to improve health but at the same time the enterprise must have room to find its own solutions.

Rights

If formal rights and formal participation can be improved simultaneously with a softening of the detailed rules for organisation of the work, the possibilities for welfare production in the enterprise increase.

Relation to the rest of the diamond. As already mentioned formal rights are a precondition for the dialogue, which is crucial to the diamond as a whole. However, there is a complex relation between rights and the other points of the diamond because a traditional way to take care of the employees' interests might conflict with the development of the rest of the diamond. On the other hand development of involvement and commitment can threaten the collective interests of the employees. How far this contradiction will develop depends, among other things, on the development of regulation of the labour market.

Regulation. Collective agreements and labour laws are the instruments of regulation. Deregulation has been a keyword in the labour market debate of the last decade. Increased welfare production in work does not require deregulation, but a kind of centralised decentralisation, with fewer restrictions and more procedure oriented rights (Due et. al., 1993).

Reward

A system of payment which gives priority to competence and joint performance will (presumably) stimulate a harmonious development of the individual, the collective of employees and the enterprise. It is probably possible to develop systems of rewards, in which concern for enhancement of the working environment, learning, training and education and the development of organisation and work is taken into account.

Relation to the rest of the diamond. The relation between rewards and the rest of the diamond has as yet received only superficial attention, in spite of the obvious relations between reward, rights, health, commitment and participation. The relation between rewards and goals is also of importance, as is evident from the current development of wage systems (i.e. result orientated wages, quality oriented wages and even environment related wages).

Regulation. Collective agreements must be the means of regulation here, where it is necessary to relate the wage system to the quality of work and the production of welfare in work.

Epilogue

With this short examination of the diamond of 'the developmental work' a policy for work has been presented that aims to democratise enterprises, improve working life and enhance the relation between working life and the rest of life. At the same time adoption of such a policy should reduce the risks of expulsion from the labour market.

'The Developmental Work' is a strategy for work and labour market development. It is a strategy with many different but interrelated elements, but no single main element. It is a strategy for which initiatives and responsibilities are distributed among many different agencies. The individual enterprise with its different agents plays a key role in the strategy.

Other welfare considerations such as the inclusion of marginalised groups within working life and care for the environment have been mentioned only peripherally in relation to the goals of the enterprise. It will, however, be possible to relate the diamond to other welfare policies.

In 'the developmental work' the social relations of production and work have the central part but this sort of policy relates to other policies such as social security, family policies, local policies and environmental policies. These are connected through a web of institutions and a web of individual life policies.

For 'the developmental work' the relation to other political spheres is crucial. If welfare were related only to the world of paid work, what then about the unemployed? What about the family? What about the large amount of non paid work carried out in local communities and associations of all kinds?

A policy of work for welfare cannot be confined only to the paid work, but must also cover non paid work, and a fair balance between paid and unpaid work must be established.

References

Bell, Daniel (1973), *The coming of post-industrial society. A venture in social forecasting,* New York: Basic Books.

Bild, T., Jørgensen, H. Lassen, M., and Madsen, M. (1993), *Fællesskab og forskelle,* Aalborg University, CARMA.

Borg, Vilhelm and Burr, Hermann (1997), *Danske lønmodtageres arbejdsmiljø og helbred 1990-95,* Copenhagen: Arbejdsmiljøinstituttet.

Bottrup, Pernille and Hvid, Helge (1995), *Et bedre arbejdsliv og øget vækst,* Copenhagen: Statens Informationstjeneste.

Bottrup, Pernille (1997), *A learning process approach to discussions of working conditions,* in K. Nielsen and C. Clausen (ed.), *Working environment and technological development – positions and perspectives,* Roskilde University: TEK-SAM forlaget.

Boyer, R. (1988), *Technical change and the theory of 'regulation',* in G. Dosi et al., *Technical change and economic theory,* London: Printer.

Brulin, Göran and Nilsson, Tommy (1995), *Arbetets ekonomi. Om arbete och produktivitet i modern produktion,* Stockholm: Tiden.

Due, Jesper, Madsen, Jørgen Steen and Jensen, Carsten Strøby (1993), *Den danske model,* Copenhagen: Jurist- og Økonomforbundets Forlag.

Elam, Mark (1994), 'Puzzling out the post-Fordist debate: Technology, markets and institutions', in Ash Amin (ed.), *Post-Fordism. A reader,* Oxford: Blackwell.

EU Commission (1997), *Greenbook: Partnership,* Bruxelles: DG5

Eurostat a (1996), *Eurostat yearbook: a statistic eye on Europe,* Luxembourg.

Eurostat (1996), *Employment and unemployment,* Luxembourg

Freeman, C and Perez, C. (1988), 'Structural crises of adjustment, business cycles and investment behaviour', in G. Dosi et al., *Technical change and economic theory,* London: Printer.

Giddens, Anthony (1994) *Beyond left and right. A future of radical politics,* Oxford: Polity Press.

Gundelach, Peter and Riis, Ole (1992), *Danskernes værdier,* Copenhagen: Forlaget Sociologi.

Hagedorn-Rasmussen, Peter and Hvid, Helge (1997), 'Management concepts and working conditions – in a Danish context', in K. Nielsen and C. Clausen (ed.), *Working environment and technological development – positions and perspectives,* Roskilde University: TEK-SAM forlaget.

Hirsch, J. and Roth, R. (1986), *Das neue Gesicht des Kapitalismus,* Hamburg: VSA.

Hofstede, Geert (1994), *Cultures and organisations – intercultural cooperation and its importance for survival – software of the mind,* Harper Collins Publishers.

Hvid, Helge and Møller, Niels (1992), *Det udviklende arbejde,* Copenhagen: Fremad.

Inglehart, Ronald (1990), *Culture shift in advanced industrial society,* Princeton University Press.

Jaeger, Alfred (1986), 'Organisation development and national culture: where's the fit?', *Academy of management review,* 1986, Vol. 11, No. 1.

Jessop, Bob (1994), 'Post-Fordism and the State', in Ash Amin (ed.), *Post-Fordism. A reader,* Oxford: Blackwell.

Karasek, R and Theorell, T. (1990), *Healthy work: stress, productivity and the reconstruction of working life,* New York: Basic Books.

Kern, Horst and Schumann, Michael (1984), *Das Ende der Arbeitsteilung? Rationalisierung in der industrielle Produktion,* München: C.H. Beck'sche Verlagsbuchhandlung.

LO (1991), *Det udviklende arbejde,* Copenhagen: Landsorganisationen.

LO (1995), *Work and development,* Copenhagen: Landsorganisationen.

Metallindustriarbetareförbundet (1985), *Det goda arbetet,* Stockholm: Svenska Metallindustriarbetareförbundet.

Nielsen, Klaus (1996), 'How strong are the links between new market conditions, new production principles, and better working conditions?', *The International Journal of Human Factors in Manufacturing,* Vol. 6.

Piore, M and Sable, C. (1984), *The second industrial divide,* New York: Basic Books.

Rasborg, Klaus (1995), *Det sociologiske paradigme – sociologien om det moderne og det postmoderne samfund,* Copenhagen: Forlaget Sociologi.

Reich, Robert (1992), *The work of nations: preparing ourselves for 21st century capitalism,* New York: Vintage Books.

Sandberg, Åke et al. (1992), *Technological change and co-determination in Sweden,* Philadelphia: Temple University Press.

Sandberg, Åke (1997), 'Företagsledning, arbete och fack i förändring', in Å. Sandberg (ed.), *Ledning för alla?,* Stockholm: SNS Förlag.

Schmidt, Erik Ib (1990), *Behøver vi at nå det hele?,* Copenhagen: Spektrum.

Simonsen, Birgitte (1993), *Unges forhold til arbejdsliv og forsørgelse,* Roskilde University: Erhvervs- og voksenuddannelsesgruppen.

Stahl, Thomas, Nyhan, Barry and D'Aloja, Piera, *The learning organisation,* Bruxelles: EUROTECNET.

Svensson, Lennart, Aronsson, Christina and Sten Höglund (1991), *Kan byråkratin förändras?,* Stockholm: Ordfronts förlag, 1991.

Wobbe, Werner (1991), *Anthropocentric production systems – a strategic issue for Europe,* Bruxelles: APS Research Paper Series, Vol. 1.

Øverland, Erik (1996), *Jeg er målløs! Om målsettinger og virkemidler i nordisk arbeidsliv,* Oslo: Work Research Institute.

Part II

Perspectives on new forms of differentiation and inclusion

4. The Portuguese late modernization and the complexities of inclusion through work

PEDRO HESPANHA

The reduced level of unemployment during the last decade in Portugal has concealed the persistence of very diverse forms of work, some of them undoubtedly pre-modern ones. This diversity is partly due to both the character and structure of the labour market (given the relative weight of temporary, part-time, domiciliary, independent or home-based forms of work and the relatively low level of labour qualifications), and partly due to the changes which have occurred in the labour relations of the most advanced sectors of the Portuguese economy (reductions in volume and hours of employment, job insecurity, labour polyvalence).

Employment policies have sought to take into account this double source of difficulties relating to the labour market, but the programmes implemented by the government to solve the difficulties seem to be ambiguous or even contradictory. In fact, along with programmes aimed at including an increasing number of workers within a stable wage system, some others have been developed for the purpose of adapting the wage system to the flexibility sought by firms.

The entry of Portugal into the EU in 1986 also seems to be a factor worth considering in this field, for the effects of the crisis of economic restructuring in the Portuguese labour market during the 1970s and 1980s could have been in part cushioned by the use of European funds for investment and professional reconversion. Nevertheless, these funds have appeared to increase the dualism in the labour markets between the modern, competitive activities they favour, and the traditional activities based on low pay, which the unemployed turn to when the sectors in which they work undergo a crisis.

A brief overview of the recent changes in Portuguese society

Before analyzing the most recent trends in the area of employment which permit us to understand the diversity and complexity of the forms of work in present Portuguese society, it is worth developing the above sketch a little further in order to show in greater detail the extent of the changes which have occurred over the last few decades in every sector of social life, including work and employment.

On the eve of the restoration of democracy at the beginning of the 1970s, Portuguese society showed clear signs of rurality and low indices of modernization. The proportion of the population linked to agriculture and living in rural areas was very high – in 1970 around one third of the active population was working in this sector, and three quarters were living outside the urban centres.

From the middle of the previous decade, emigration to countries of Northern Europe[1] and migration to the developing industrial zones around the biggest cities had initiated a process of rural exodus and littoralization (movement towards, and development of, coastal settlement) by the Portuguese population, which has continued to the present day and has been reinforced by later events, like the democratic reform of institutions after 1974, and entry into the European Community in 1986.

The increase in workers' demands and the appearance of the first autonomous trade unions, at the end of the 1960s, favoured the institution of Fordist labour relations, based on collective contractual agreements and redistribution of part of the productivity gains made by workers in certain more advanced sectors of the economy (banking and insurance, naval construction).

But the political reforms to fit with greater trade union autonomy and with the development of the system of social security only gained significant importance after the revolution of 1974. Important redistributive policies were developed during the following years, whether operating at the level of production (like the institution of the minimum wage) or at the level of reproduction (universalization of social security, control of housing rents, etc.). The purchasing power of the workers rose significantly as a result of the general increase in real earnings during 1974 and 1975. At the same time important sectors of the economy were nationalized (banking, insurance, transport, electricity, etc.) and the extensive landed estates in the south of the country were dismantled by an agrarian reform initiated by the rural workers and imposed by their prolonged occupation of the land. In the area of labour legislation, advances regarding the recognition of workers' rights and guaranteed stable employment[2] were notable in the years following the revolution.

The Portuguese economy, having changed so profoundly and now undergoing the effects of increasing world recession, was unable to regain its balance, and entered a crisis. Not being related to the process of accumulation, a large number of the reforms and redistributive policies failed to be consolidated, and were withdrawn. At the same time inflation reached very high levels (30 percent in 1984) which led ultimately to an erosion of earnings and a decrease in consumption, with negative effects on investment. Although inflation affected all workers, it has been shown that the most severely penalized were those in the lowest income bracket (Almeida *et al.*1992:55).

The country then entered a period during which the Portuguese state was obliged to submit to the conditions of the IMF (the agreements of 1978 and 1983) in order to achieve economic recovery: devaluation of the escudo, cuts in public spending, reduction of consumer demand. The effects of this new policy were a dramatic increase in unemployment, a significant reduction in GNP and, on the other hand, a reinforcement of the peripheralization of the Portuguese economy. Despite resistance from the trade unions and the innumerable strikes, the previously increased power of the workers was weakened again in the face of political changes and the spectre of unemployment.

The economic and political orientation towards basing competitiveness on low pay, which gradually came into effect during the 1980s, made it imperative to lower wages and render the workforce more flexible. This was possible not only because nothing was done to prevent the erosion of real earnings, or even the delays in payment of wages and salaries by companies in crisis, but also because, in pace with the reactions of the market, an active policy was being developed to institutionalize more flexible but more insecure forms of work contract: short term contracts, temporary work, subcontracting, domiciliary work.

Portugal's entry into the European Community in 1986 reinforced this orientation, although causing important changes, particularly at the level of the labour markets, not always convergent with European policy. The structured adjustment which the Portuguese economy was driven to make was accompanied by a progressive harmonization of labour laws and political measures concerning employment, resulting in a strong impulse, in general terms, towards economic and social modernization (Hespanha 1997). The moment of entry into the EU was a turning point for the Portuguese economy, initiating the rise of a new economic cycle, which benefited very well from the new investment opportunities offered by Community aid (Lopes 1996).

In spite of the more favourable prospects for the workers offered by the growing economy, severe inequalities of access to the labour market have been maintained. Newly created forms of employment correspond less and less with the workers' aspirations for security, putting a very significant part of the population at risk of unemployment or in a situation of great vulnerability to social exclusion.

The workers' feelings of insecurity, the competitive weakness of businesses and the reduced scope of state legislation in this area have contributed to the proliferation of these forms of insecure employment, which are frequently associated with practices of circumventing or violating the labour rights recognized by the Constitution and by the labour laws: de facto employment disguised as self-employment, unpaid overtime, abusive dismissals, non-renewal of fixed term contracts, evasion of social security contributions, delayed payment of wages, child labour. In other cases dismissed workers return to their former occupations as independent agricultural workers, small time door-to-door salesmen or artisans in the traditional sectors.

The labour market and social regulation

In this section we will briefly analyse the role of the state and the social partners – namely, trade unions and employers' organisations – in the regulation of labour markets over the past ten years. Attention is paid to the way in which the regulatory policies of different social agents, conditioned by distinct and contradictory interests, are highly sensitive to the pressures of circumstance, and rarely demonstrate a clear logic of intervention.

It is important to emphasise that the state in Portugal (as in other countries that have experienced long periods of authoritarian or dictatorial rule) demonstrates the continuation of a highly centralized regulatory social role compared to the role of civil society (Poulantzas, 1975; Santos, 1993). A bit paradoxically, this enhanced centrality of the state can be seen as reinforced in various ways by membership of the European Union through the associated need to proceed to rapid modernisation and to the adjustment of the structures and institutions of Portuguese society, and, at the same time, through the need to promote the emergence of collective agents that represent the interests of different sectors of civil society.

In the area of macroeconomic policy the state never gave up a moderate Keynesian management of development, and with regard to labour relations it continued tight regulation. Nevertheless, there had not always been so large difference between the extended scope of announced policies and the limited character of their implementation.

In the period following the revolution of 1974, the regulatory role of the state was clearly oriented to the institutionalisation of workers' rights and their unions and to the construction of a public system of social protection that would respond to expectations of an improvement in living conditions of the population governed by the new democratic system. In regard to labour disputes the inability of the social partners to find negotiated solutions, given the weakness of employers caused by the nationalisations of 1975 and the social pressure from workers, led to their resolution by administrative means – by the mediation services of the Ministry of Labour and by arbitration imposed on the parties. We could say that, in this period, the state was forced to assume an increasingly central role by the pressure of events than by the promise to control economic power by means of political power inscribed in the Political Constitution of 1976.

Nonetheless, during the first half of the 1980s the effects of the economic crisis in the Portuguese manufacturing sector, which was weakened and not very competitive, together with the need to control public expenditure imposed by accords with the IMF, required a reorientation of state intervention to restore the confidence of investors and to attract new capital. Previous pro-labour orientations in policies had to be modified so as to favour the emergence of an industrial bourgeoisie capable of adjusting to the new market conditions. In general, these policies operated through the granting of incentives to enterprises, the re-privatisation of a large number of public enterprises, and legislation increasing the flexibility of labour and wage systems. Nevertheless, such a change was only possible because, at the same time, the closing of firms, non-payment of wages, redundancies, and a general rise in the rate of unemployment had dramatically weakened workers' pressure on the state and had reduced their resistance to the deregulatory measures demanded by employers. The creation in 1984 of a system of negotiated regulation by means of a Permanent Council for Social Concertation (CPCS), composed of representatives of the government, management and unions, did not substantially alter the government's room to operate or reduce the regulatory role of the state.

Maintaining levels of employment and, at the same time, reinforcing private capital and improving firms' economic competitiveness were only possible at the price of low wage levels (pay-rise ceilings below the inflation level) and increased job insecurity (an increase in non-standard forms of employment).

Admission to the European Community in 1986 came to consolidate public economic regulatory policies and labour markets. In the improved economic situation due to the influx of capital from community funds, the recovery of markets and the re-absorption of the unemployed, public policies were oriented to enhancing the competitiveness of firms. This objective was achieved by the provision of financial aid or fiscal benefits for industrial re-structuring and modernisation or by means of policies that permitted more flexibility in labour relations and firms' management of labour. In 1989 collective dismissals and, in 1991, individual dismissals of workers were made easier in situations of technological re-conversion or of economic difficulty for firms. Also in 1989, the legislation regarding fixed term-contracts was altered to enlarge the scope for their use as well as to regulate those interim employment agencies whose importance for the management of labour was recognised. More recently, legal provision to encourage geographical mobility and workers' flexibility has been enlarged.

To compensate for the negative effects of these and other forms of flexibility in labour relations, and of unemployment produced by the re-structuring of firms, the state at the same time developed active and passive employment measures.

In the area of active measures for promoting employment, a vast combination of measures was introduced to increase the incentives for firms to create new jobs for young people and the long-term unemployed. Other measures support local development initiatives, encourage the creation of a market for social employment (in the areas of family-aid services and preservation of the natural, urban and cultural heritage), promote vocational training whether at the initial stage of or throughout the career, and provide for redeployment of labour in economic sectors undergoing re-structuring. It is difficult to evaluate the results of these policies. The continued low levels of unemployment and the significant percentage of the labour-force covered by employment schemes and vocational training – 15 percent, according to Mozzicafredo (1997:142) – appear to confirm some success for the policies. Nonetheless, there is a recognised lack of the energy and capacity for initiative on the part of relevant civil society organisations that accompany the implementation of similar measures in other EU countries and, again compared to these, a more decentralised and less integrated pattern of implementation (Figueiredo *et al.* 1997:193).

In the area of passive employment measures, the unemployment benefit created in 1977 constitutes the principal measure instituted by the state. In 1985, the unemployment social benefit, granted to those workers unable to apply for a regular unemployment benefit, was established[3]. Throughout the 1980s and 1990s, the level of the latter was successively raised. Between 1987 and 1996 the proportion of unemployed workers receiving unemployment benefits rose from 22.4 percent to around 38 percent[4] Workers over 55 might in case of redundancy be offered early retirement.

The views of workers and employers on the role of the state are in stark contrast. While employers argue for the liberalisation of the labour market and demand from the state the necessary reforms to guarantee the viability of private economic activity (including the flexibilisation of labour legislation), unions try to maintain employment levels, demanding of the state not only the enforcement of compliance with labour laws by firms but also the development of policies designed to counteract the tendency to increased lack of job security.

For the CGTP, generally considered as a pro-communist workers' confederation, 'unemployment is the main factor in social exclusion and job insecurity is the first step in that direction'. This job insecurity encompasses all work situations which violate human dignity and 'is reflected in (short) term contracts, day wages, temporary work (part of which is clandestine), part-time work, and subcontracted work, which in many cases represent external forms of the exploitation of workers.' In addition, it is considered that, in comparison with Europe generally, the gap between security and insecurity of employment is the wider here because Portuguese workers earn one quarter of the European average, their work hours are much longer, social protection is inferior, there are many more work-related accidents, the level of education and training is much lower, and the level of information and participation of workers in working life is close to zero (CGTP 1996a:3).

With regard to passive employment measures, the CGTP stands in a clear opposition to the policy of subsidizing work that benefits only firms (CGTP 1996b:21) and contributes to discrimination against workers (CGTP 1996c:35).

The other labour union, UGT, more close to the positions of the Socialist and Social-Democratic parties, shares the same idea about the essential need to defend and maintain job security, but has a more open position on the acceptability of specific modes of temporary work and of part-time work according not only to the demands of firms but in terms of the diversity of workers' time requirements, thus allowing them scope for an employment strategy (UGT 1996:7).

According to the UGT active and passive employment policies should complement one another and the union argues that the passive measures should be improved when the active measures do not produce the conditions for the creation of jobs (UGT:1996:22).

Unemployment and insecure terms of labour

Keeping our analysis within the period following the entry into the EU, it has been shown that the civilian labour force has grown continuously throughout the last decade, mainly because of an increased female participation rate. This regular and sustained increase in the active population demonstrates the delayed re-structuring of the Portuguese labour market and the way in which the different categories of the population (according to sex, age, location or occupational sector) have been absorbed into it.

As regards the category of gender, social indicators show that a fairly significant part of the female population has never, or only recently, had access to paid employment. It is worth noting that in periods when employment is in crisis it is the women who are dismissed first.

Young people, by contrast, enter the workforce much too early, bearing in mind the requirements of education and professional training, and the younger they are when they start work, the lower their level of education. A characteristic of the Portuguese population is precisely its low level of education and, according to the most recent data, about half of those employed have only the basic level of education.

In the rural areas part of the population live on family smallholdings, frequently with limited links to the open market, occupying their freetime with a number of activities such as craftwork or small scale commerce and by providing local services, that is, activities which are not recognized in national statistics or accounts. Resorting to off-farm jobs is becoming more and more common as a consequence of the growing establishment in rural areas of labour intensive small-scale industries (principally in the areas of textiles, footwear, light metals and furniture), and the need for agricultural producers to confront the difficulties of competing in the agricultural markets.

Table 4.1 Population and employment

	EU	PT	SP	GR	IT	IRL
1 Persons in employment (1/8)	49,2	55,7	37,4	44,5	42,9	45,0
2 Persons working part-time (2/1)	14,7	7,4	6,6	4,3	5,4	10,8
3 Unemployed persons [3/(1+3)]	10,6	5,3	22,2	8,6	10,3	15,6
4 Persons seeking first job (4/3)	18,1	14,4	19,1	47,4	52,7	16,4
5 Labour Force (5/8)	55,1	58,8	48,1	48,7	47,9	53,3
6 Non-active persons (6/8)	44,9	41,2	51,9	51,3	52,1	46,7
7 Persons in education (7/6)	18,5	23,9	21,8	18,3	19,6	24,7
8 Persons over 15 yrs (8/9)	82,1	81,8	82,1	82,5	84,3	73,9
9 Total population (000s)	341 819	9 801	38 705	10 118	56 115	3 469

Source: EUROSTAT, Labour Force Survey, 1993

In the same way, in the periphery of the big cities, a migratory population poorly integrated into the job market occupy themselves with innumerable informal or clandestine activities, combined with occasional or temporary work, insecure and badly paid.

As noted earlier we can identify a pre-modern component within the economically active Portuguese population, but it would be completely wrong to limit the analysis of Portuguese employment structures to this component. Other categories exist besides these, which appear to correspond more adequately to the contemporary idea of work and employment. These categories, and especially the processes of change in which they are involved, are discussed below.

Unemployment[5]

Analysis of unemployment rates during the last decade in Portugal, when compared with the European average, shows a relatively favourable situation for Portugal. The maximum figure is only a little over 10 percent, and the rate is currently at 7.3 percent. However, this must be viewed with caution, as behind the reduced unemployment rates are concealed low wages and insecure forms of employment. Apart from this, these forms of employment not only represent a high incidence of total employment, but also reflect the enormous instability which characterizes the labour market in consequence of the strategies for survival developed by the workers and of the attempts made by business to succeed under the new conditions of competition.

Table 4.2 Portugal 1992-96; unemployment indicators (percent)

	1992	1993	1994	1995	1996
Total rate	4,2	5,5	6,9	7,2	7,3
Male rate	3,5	4,7	6,1	6,4	6,5
Female rate	4,9	6,6	7,8	8,0	8,2
Youth under 25 yrs rate	10,1	12,7	14,7	16,2	16,7
First job rate	0,9	0,9	1,2	1,4	1,5
New job rate	3,3	4,6	5,7	5,8	5,8
< 12 months job seeking	74,4	68,9	66,1	60,2	57,5
> 12 months job seeking	25,6	31,1	33,9	39,8	42,5

Source: INE, Estatísticas do Emprego

The indicators of the length of unemployment are also favourable for Portugal when compared to her EU partners. The percentage of jobless situations lasting less than a year – 62.1 percent[6] is well above the average (56 percent) while the percentage of unemployment lasting longer than two years, which has a European average of 23.6 percent, is at just 15 percent in Portugal.

In a society still very much dominated by particularistic arrangements the unemployed frequently resort to direct contact with employers via friends or relatives (in about half the cases) in order to obtain a new job. Registration at Employment Centres, although quite high, is not considered to be a very reliable way of finding work, but it figures in the record because it is an indispensable condition for obtaining unemployment benefit. These findings are quite similar to those from Greece, Italy and Ireland.

Self-Employment[7]

The two most outstanding observations when comparing the indicators of self-employment in Portugal with other European countries are their high and increasing levels in Portugal and their proximity to those of other non-core EU countries, that is, Ireland, Spain, Italy and Greece.

At first glance, this seems to result from the higher proportion of small-scale traditional activities in all these countries. In fact, small-scale family farming and other traditional crafts occupy a larger part of the active population in these countries. On the other hand, the classic description of self-employment emphasises the pre-modern character of activities linked to this form of work, stressing the tendency for it to disappear in proportion to the development of industrial economies and the expansion of the system of paid employment.

What is happening in Portugal is that the proportion of self-employment is gradually increasing, rising from 22 percent in 1989 to 27 percent in 1996, and this phenomenon must be interpreted correctly. On the one hand, it shows that this area is also demonstrating the effects of industrial restructuring, in consequence of changes in the system of accumulation which are translated into processes of deconcentration and tertiarization of business, and subcontracting of jobs. The conversion of paid employment to self-employed work constitutes a manifestation of these processes. On the other hand, a new cultural attitude encouraging the search for personal success, fuelled by neo-liberal ideology, is creating a climate favourable to the development of self-employment. In either of these cases, we are dealing with explanations which stress traits in the conditions of labour under late capitalism which are distinct from those of the preceding phase of intensive wage-paid or salaried employment. For this reason, the employment statistics show that the proportion of self-employed is high, not only in certain areas of traditional activities, but also in areas of innovative activity such as real-estate agencies, information technology, consultancy, etc. All this produces a category which lumbs together the very different circumstances of isolated workers, small-scale employers, artisans, self-employed professionals and 'false' self-employed workers (workers obliged to declare themselves as self-employed despite working regularly for and under the direction of firms which refuse to admit them to the workforce as recognised employees, thereby circumventing the regulations protecting wage-earners' rights).

It would appear that in the Portuguese case it is necessary to examine more thoroughly the relationship between the pre-modern and post-modern elements in the economy and the labour markets, in order to emphasise the interdependent and reciprocal nature of this relationship. For example, the fact that the process of professionalization of work is still very limited, and that employees have little autonomy or responsibility at work as opposed to employers, favours the preference for self-employed work. Thus the strategies of self-establishment commonly being developed by hitherto employed workers at the lowest level may function inclusively, as the first stage in a strategy to achieve a status similar to that of an employer. It is because of this that self-employment, far from meaning nothing more than a degraded form of work, may play, at the level of social representation in some groups, a significant role in social inclusion, through increasing intergenerational mobility and by the realization of individual projects (Freire 1995:29).

Nevertheless, it is important to point out that the current Portuguese situation shows that the condition of self-employment is more and more of a kind in which the worker is only formally autonomous in relation to whoever contracts his services. This is the case with workers sub-contracted in the areas of textile production, clothing and footwear, who have a reduced level of manoeuvre in relation to the companies sub-contracting them. It is also the case with workers in a system of exclusivity or franchising for other firms. It is furthermore the case with 'false' self-employed workers. There is, finally, the case of the workers for whom self-employment becomes the only viable alternative, because they are unabble to find any other remunerative work in circumstances of hard pressure for survival.

The job insecurity of the self-employed derives from their not having the right to holidays, working more hours per week, having lower wages, having to pay the full amount of social security contributions themselves, not receiving unemployment benefit and not having any stability of employment.

Over and above enjoying a limited autonomy, the 'ideal type' of a self employed worker is a mature male with low educational and vocational qualifications in a relatively low income bracket[8].

Self-employed workers in Portugal are less well covered by social security than wage earners, owing to the fact that until very recently they were not included in the national contributory system of social security. Today, this system also applies to self-employed workers who declare an annual income greater than six times the minimum national wage[9]. In general, the social security service is very cautious as regards the registration of self-employed workers, barring access to the system for those not earning any income by demanding fiscal proof of income. In this way, many small-scale agricultural producers remain excluded from the system of social security.

The policies directed towards self-employment are designed to facilitate the creation of work for those finding it difficult to enter the job market, particularly young people looking for their first job and the long-term unemployed. Since 1986, financial incentives towards the creation of self-employment for those categories have been deployed, but the results are still not very significant.

Non-permanent employment[10]

In general, limited job duration is related to difficulty in finding permanent employment, and consequently the acceptance of temporary work represents a second best choice for the worker. Since fixed term employment provides flexibility of contracts, there is a close connection between variations in the incidence of temporary employment and the unemployment rate.

In Portugal, the number of fixed term contracts increased considerably during the 1980s along with the process of industrial re-structuring and as a result of an alteration in the labour laws allowing businesses to have recourse to these types of contract[11]. After reaching 19 percent in 1989, the proportion of temporary work has been diminishing subsequently, and was at 12.5 percent in 1996. The figures are higher for women and for workers either in manufacturing or services strongly dependent on market forces (electrical goods, cars, information technology, R & D) or in seasonal work (hotels and construction). In European terms, this situation is very similar to that of other countries in the southern 'variant' of European welfare state regimes, particularly Spain and Greece, where relatively high figures are found. In these countries also, the main reason for taking a temporary job is that the workers are unable to find permanent employment[12].

An emergent type of employment in Portugal, still only a small percentage (0.2 percent of the working population), is that of interim work, involving employment agencies that hire out labour to third parties. Many workers, to avoid unemployment, are obliged to take this type of temporary work, which tends in general to be poorly paid as the agencies only contracy fort unskilled work. On the other hand, many companies and even the state are now substituting interim work for permanent jobs. Given the ease with which the employment agencies are able to take advantage of the Portuguese legislation, and the difficulties of some sectors of the population in finding employment, such as young people and women, a rapid expansion of this type of employment is foreseeable in the future.

In Portugal, temporary workers contribute to social security and benefit equally from it. However, evasion of social security payments is more common in the case of temporary workers given the higher level of dependency of the worker resulting from the unstable nature of the work. When employment agencies are involved they, despite the frequently clandestine nature of the work, the payments to social security are made as for non-skilled workers, which reduces their benefits.

As for the policies actively encouraging temporary work, the most important measures to be mentioned are the occupational programmes for unemployed workers, which provide temporary (less than a year's duration) subsidized jobs under projects promoted by the state itself or by non-profit organizations.

Part-time employment[13]

In countries of late industrialization, part-time work is usually found to be associated with processes of transformation of small scale mercantile production or with the patriarchal family. In both cases, peasants and women in the labour market try at all costs to preserve their traditional occupations, dividing their time between these and their new jobs.

In Portugal, the proportion of part-time work is relatively low – 7.5 percent in 1993 – when compared to the European average (14.7 percent), but similar to that of other southern European countries – Spain (6.6 percent), Italy (5.4 percent) and Greece (4.3 percent) – and also near to that for Ireland (10.8 percent)[14].

The highest incidence of part-time work in Portugal occurs in agriculture (24 percent of agricultural employees). In the case of women a high proportion claim to prefer part-time work because of family commitments (30 percent in 1995). On the other hand, there seems to be a relationship between the level of unemployment and the level of part-time work among Portuguese women. The difficulty in finding secure employment not only inclines women to accept part-time work for their first job (27 percent in 1995), but it also encourages women who have been made unemployed to take on part-time work. It is important to note that in Portugal, as in other countries, there has been an increase observed in the proportion of 'non-voluntary' part-time workers (in 1993, 15 percent of men and 23.2 percent of women employed on a part-time basis); and that part-time jobs are associated with a greater frequency of temporary contracts (36.4 percent in 1993). As a rule, part-time work corresponds to low levels of training and skills[15].

Because of all this, vulnerability to exclusion is quite high in this atypical type of employment, and is manifest in different ways: reduced social security cover, performance of less skilled or less responsible tasks, greater job insecurity and low pay.

Part-time work has been increasing in Portugal over the last few years, from 5 percent in 1989 to 7.5 percent in 1995 and may indicate the presence of the same effects of economic restructuring as in the core European countries. In terms of flexibility of employment, the advantages of part-time work to businesses are innumerable: lower costs, greater productivity of labour, a lower level of unionization, numerical flexibility (to meet fluctuations in productivity), wage flexibility (lower level of remuneration), greater effort per worker, lower rate of absenteeism (OECD 1991).

Added to this there is also the fact that measures actively encouraging part-time employment have been implemented: new opportunities for employment in the public sector, financial or tax incentives for job sharing, opportunities for semi-retirement or incentives to create part-time jobs for young people aged between 16 and 30.

Employment on non-standard timetables

This broad category includes distinct types of work ranging from overtime, through shift work, to work during unsocial hours (night work, weekend work). A common feature of these types of work is that they permit greater flexibility and response to changes related to, for example, new technology, tertiarization and changes in work patterns throughout the career of the worker.

In Portugal, the average number of hours of work per week per worker is very high, although a progressive decrease is observable. In 1996, slightly less than 50 percent of employees worked more than 40 hours per week (Table 3). The persistence of a petty bourgeois ethic of work helps to explain the ease with which companies have been able to mobilize the workforce to put in this overtime, and the paradoxical attitude of workers willing to work more hours[16]. However, the low average wage appears to be the main reason for a long working day[17].

In 1993, compared to other European countries, Portuguese full-time workers had the second highest weekly average, with 41.2 hours per week, following the British (43.4), and immediately above the Greeks (40.6) and the Irish (40.1).

Table 4.3 Employment by weekly labour time

	1992	1993	1994	1995	1996
<10 hours	1,3	1,6	1,5	1,2	1,7
11-20 hours	3,5	3,8	3,9	4,0	4,6
21-30 hours	5,7	5,9	5,8	6,2	6,3
31-40 hours	36,9	36,9	38,6	39,7	40,8
> 40 hours	52,5	51,8	50,2	48,9	46,5

Source: INE, Estatísticas do Emprego

As to the other categories of hours worked, the figures are nearing the European average and are lower than the other countries of southern Europe. In 1995, shift workers represented about 6 percent of the population and workers on unsocial hours represented 12 percent (Vaz 1997:22).

Home working[18]

This type of employment is traditionally linked to small scale production carried out in rural areas and the putting-out system of labour intensive industry[19]. In this sense much home work shades into self-employment and reflects a situation in which rural families – especially women – try to find off-farm work which is compatible with their domestic tasks and family responsibilities. Only a part of home work is carried out under contract, and represented about 4 percent of the employed population in 1995, involving mostly women (61 percent), certain branches of industry (clothing, leather goods), services and relatively low skills.

As in the case of part-time work, this type of work is extremely insecure, mainly through fluctuations of the market and the absence of guaranteed employment contracts. In most cases the firms benefit more from the extended working day of home workers than from the working time put in by their regular employees, on top of which they also have the advantages of lower fixed costs, of minimizing the effects of seasonal or occasional demand fluctuations and circumventing social security and tax obligations[20].

There is also a close relationship between the levels of unemployment and the levels of homeworking. Where work is scarce, and the workforce plentiful, there will be found those who are willing to work for low wages and even without rights, as long as they can add to the total family income[21].

The Portuguese situation in respect of homeworking appears to be very similar to that in other European countries where the same features as those above can be found; homeworking is then a way of escaping unemployment on the part of the worker, a way of minimizing risk and reducing cost on the part of companies, which involves semi-clandestine forms of employment and a notable blurring of the distinctions between self-employment, under-employment and informal work (Meulders *et al.* 1994).

Multiple job holding

Carrying out a second occupation in addition to the principal employment reflects a need to earn extra income, and results in a weakening of the workforce in the principal place of work.

This represents a common situation in countries with a relatively less structured labour market and where it is still possible to combine independent small-scale production in agriculture, industry or the services with wage-paid or salaried employment. This is the case in Portugal and also in other southern European countries, although there the figures are lower. In 1993, about 6 percent of the employed Portuguese population had a second job, in most cases performed regularly, while in the cases of Greece, Spain and Italy the figures weree respectively 3.5 percent, 1.4 percent and 1.3 percent.

In agriculture, pluriactivity has permitted the survival of families at levels of modest or low income on smaller farms, where pluriactivity and farming are relatively stable solutions to the 'income problem'.

In a recent study carried out in a Portuguese rural area of diffuse industrialization it has been shown that 'despite employment figures suggesting a decline in agricultural activity it is in fact as widespread a phenomenon as before but that the proportion of the workforce for which agriculture has remained the *main* [my italics] source of income has decreased. In this respect the structural change which is associated with declining agricultural employment throughout the rest of Europe has not taken place here, but rather family strategies of pluriactivity have been adapted to changing labour market conditions' (The Arkleton Trust 1992:11-21).

Unpaid family worker

Situations in which family members cooperate with each other to operate a business or common activity are very common, particularly in the case of activities compatible with small-scale production, such as agriculture, commerce and some branches of industry and services. The extent to which the statistics reflect this fact depends greatly on the way in which each worker identifies his position in the common undertaking, and also on his recognition of the activity as constituting employment. It should also be noted that, in these situations, the distinction between productive activity and domestic activity (or even employment) is not clear cut in these people's minds. Because of this, the statistics on unpaid family work are not very exact in societies in which the family constitutes an important system of labour force management, and at the same time an important source of income generation. We can assume that the figure of 1.7 percent (1996) of the Portuguese employed population attributed to this category is clearly underestimated[22] and that many family workers (mainly women) were misleadingly classified as inactive persons (or perhaps as self-employed). Similar situations are also observable in other EU countries: Greece, Spain, Italy (Meulders *et al.* 1994:130)

So far as concerns the insecurity and vulnerability of this type of work it is important to stress two points. First, the fact that these workers do not receive any pay and are dependent on the family (almost always under patriarchal domination) in practice means an almost total absence of rights. Also, the choice of these forms of employment generally reflects the absence of other alternatives to employment.

There are no policies which are directed specifically to these situations and which distinguish them from self-employment. As to the benefits of social security, provision for the self-employed also extends to their spouses, but not to any other close relatives.

Informal economy, marginal work and poverty

Some recent attempts to measure the importance of the informal economy in Portugal permit us to confirm its enormous extent and diversity of form.

In very general terms, the informal economy is characterized by the fact that its activities are not recorded in the national accounts and that its workers are not recognized as part of the labour force in the employment statistics. In addition to this, informal jobs are not protected by labour laws or labour policies, which puts the workers in this sector in a position of great insecurity. The clandestine and generally illicit nature of some activities of the informal economy is very often an unintended effect of the solutions found by those unable to enter the formal labour markets. Because of this, the informality of the work is closely related to unemployment and constitutes a common strategy in a society where stable and well-paid jobs are inaccessible to large numbers of people, and in which, on the other hand, the state is relatively consenting or inefficient, which is undoubtedly the case in Portugal. This informal work truly becomes a no-choice option (Baganha 1996:68).

Measuring the share of the informal economy in the Portuguese economy is a particularly difficult and controversial task, given the unreliability of the instruments of measurement. The calculations made by the National Statistics Agency set the figure at 12 percent of GNP, but this estimate has been considered to be very low in view of the results gained from using different methodologies. Thus, comparing the data from the population census with the data recorded by the Ministry of Employment on the basis of company returns, it is possible to estimate the percentage of workers not included in company returns and arrive at figures of 23.6 percent for 1981, and 20.8 percent for 1991 (Baganha 1996). These figures vary greatly from sector to sector, which confirms the wide diversity of situations in informal activity. Because of their importance the following activities deserve mentioning: informal work in house building, part-time farming, small services and child labour.

Although some of the workers in the informal economy choose to remain on the margin of the labour markets for varying lengths of time according to the circumstances, another but not inconsiderable number are forced to remain on the margins of these markets in order just to survive. Such cases are more frequent amongst the long-term unemployed, the elderly, young people and women.

These marginal workers, who do not even feature in the unemployment statistics because they have given up hope of trying to find work, constitute, without doubt, one of the categories most vulnerable to poverty, next after old age pensioners.

According to the most recent data (MQE 1996) poverty affected 18.3 percent of Portuguese families[23] in 1995, and was very irregularly distributed throughout the country, varying from 10 percent in a western central region of diffuse industrialization to 36.8 percent in a southern rural region in demographic decline. The typical profile of the head of a poor family is that of an elderly person (55 percent), with low education and low vocational qualifications (59.8 percent), receiving an old age pension (64.8 percent) and living in very poor housing (65.2 percent). However, there are many families with a younger head of family whose poverty is due to low pay (27 percent), unemployment (16.8 percent), economic crisis (15 percent) and inactivity (6.7 percent).

Modernization, globalization and the risk of exclusion in a semiperipheral European society

Let us first return to our previous analysis of the high incidence of non-standard forms of work in Portuguese society. Bearing in mind the existence of situations in which various forms of employment overlap, a recent study estimated that in 1995, 43 percent of the total labour force were not engaged in full-time permanent employment (Vaz 1997:24).

Secondly, it is important to stress that the diversity of types of employment is associated with unequal degrees of employment insecurity and that the same diversity also carries unequal risks of social exclusion. Some of these types of employment, because of their instability, low levels of pay and absence of guaranteed rights, mask a real situation of unemployment or constitute a lesser evil for the worker relative to a situation of unemployment. Others, as with self-employment or homeworking, give a false impression of independence, which in practice, almost never corresponds to a reality characterized by excessive working days, heavy responsibility and low pay in self- and family employment.

The goal of economic improvement, however, continues to attract a large number of Portuguese workers to self-employment. Other types of employment, such as shift work or work with unsocial hours, do not cause such dramatic problems of insecurity or exclusion and are even preferred by some workers since they facilitate taking on a second job.

When comparing the atypical forms of employment in the different countries of the EU, it is immediately observable that the use made of them differs from one country to another whether with regard to the level of insecurity or to the risk of exclusion. As a rule, the less the organization and bargaining power of the workers in the labour market, the more insecure and risk-prone they become.

The Portuguese case shows that, despite the existence of relatively advanced formal norms of labour, the workers are not in fact able to prevent the erosion of their terms and conditions of employment or to defend their rights[24], and that the state itself is not fully capable of guaranteeing observance of the laws and the application of suitable social and employment policies.

To a large extent, the high incidence of insecure forms of employment which characterizes the Portuguese labour markets is due more to the dominant system of labour relations and the nature of the national economic fabric than to the crisis in the Fordist model of accumulation since the 1970s. The response of a weak capitalist economy to an economic recession is precisely to increase flexibility through insecurity-generating types of recruitment and management of manpower aimed to reduce costs and maintain competitiveness.

As regards the workers, the spread of unemployment, the devaluation of their rights and the emphasis of the political discourse on flexibilization have combined to lower their resistance, decrease unionization and orient the workers more and more towards individualist forms of survival (Ferreira 1996:43).

Thus some workers have taken advantage of increased flexibility, trying to combine activities and sources of income capable of sustaining them in a crisis and assuring the economic reproduction of their families. Homeworking, temporary work, non-standard timetable work, work divided between diverse activities, the use of financial assistance for the unemployed to set up independent enterprises, have all been ways of dealing with the lack of stable and permanent employment. The employment status of a wage-paid or salaried worker has lost its distinctiveness when the role of the subordinate worker became confused with that of the autonomous worker, the role of the subsidized unemployed worker with that of the unpaid family worker, and the role of inactive worker with that of the clandestine worker.

What appears to be important to note is that this blurring of distinctions between the roles of the workers or, more broadly, between the areas of economic production and social reproduction, creates severe impediments to the efficacy of public policies, which generally utilize specialized intervention agencies, in both areas, which are divided among different governmental departments. This is the case, for example, with policies of employment and social security directed towards the unemployed or with policies of health and social security directed towards the aged and handicapped, which are poorly inter-linked and quite often end up pursuing incompatible objectives.

The situation relating to the determinants of the spread and diversification of non-standard forms of employment did not alter substantially when, in the second half of the 1980s, the Portuguese economy started to recover and there was a reduction of the unemployment rate. It must be said that the recovery owed much to the stimulus brought about by Portugal's integration into the European Community, and in particular to policies improving the infrastructure, providing financial support for industrial redevelopment and training manpower, which were implemented with Community support. The creation of new jobs, however, has been occurring without the structural rigidity which characterized the system of employment during the previous decade and under the framework of a competition rationality based on low pay. Because of this, the erosion of security of work conditions became unavoidable.

Furthermore, the particular position of the Portuguese economy within a strongly hierarchical 'world system' and its increasing openness to global trends render more difficult any attempt either to expand the primary labour force or to preserve security of work conditions.

The impact of globalization being uncertain, the probability that it will have detrimental effects on different areas of social life appears to be higher in non-core societies, above all in thosewhich are most open to international interaction and in which the endogenous factors capable of promoting effective responses to global destructuring are weak or non-existent. As Mingione and Pugliese point out, 'in locales left behind by the hypermobility of global capital, the negative consequences are often most evident in terms of unemployment, underemployment, environmental degradation and community decay' (Bonanno *et al.*, 1994: 23).

Portugal constitutes a good example of this type of society. Being semiperipheral in terms of the world context, it has certain characteristics that make for a high vulnerability to penetration by hegemonic forms of globalization, such as the weakness of its regulating mechanisms – economic, social or cultural – and its relatively large degree of social heterogeneity (Santos 1993).

Labour market regulation, in particular, has proved be weak in the sense that the state, though constitutionnally bound to ensuring employment policies, equality of opportunities and improved quality of working conditions, has been unable to fulfil these objectives and to prevent labour force dualization. The lack of a wide social consensus behind employment and social policies, the poor effectiveness of those policies aimed at improving work conditions and modernising working life, the paralyzing excess of corporatism characteristic of the tripartite consultive bodies, and more broadly the high degree of particularism that pervades both culture and institutions, may be seen as distinctive features of the Portuguese social model by reference to the 'softness' of state regulation can be understood[25].

The second characteristic – the high degree of social heterogeneity of Portuguese society – is responsible not only for a particular vulnerability to the processes of globalization, but also for an unequal and contradictory impact of these processes on different sectors of society.

Given the close relationship which exists between the phenomena of globalization and of modernization in societies of intermediate development like Portugal, the differences between the various sectors within the society become particularly relevant to this matter, in that the least modernized sectors of Portuguese society have the least capacity to resist or negotiate in the face of the effects of globalization and, as a result, suffer its most destructive effects.

It is in the light of such a combined perspective on the phenomena of globalization and modernization that the social heterogeneity of work forms seems ultimately best open to analysis.

Notes

1 From 1962 to 1974, more than 1.5 million Portuguese left, legally or clandestinely, to work in European countries, mainly in France, Germany or Luxembourg.

2 The Political Constitution of 1976 imposed on the state the obligation to guarantee the right to work and particularly the prevention of dismissal without just cause, minimum wage, a maximum limit to the number of hours in the working day, a weekend break and paid holidays. It simultaneously recognized the freedom of trade unions, the right to strike, and prohibited lockout.

3 Social unemployment benefit is a means-tested subsidy, the value of which corresponds to between 70 and 100 percent of the national minimum wage according to the size of the family. At present an unemployed worker has the right to unemployment benefit for a period of 10 to 30 months (according to the contributions he has made previously) corresponding to 65 percent of the individual's average earnings during the last year of employment and up to a maximum of three times the national minimum wage, so long as he has worked for at least 540 days over the last two years. Apart from these cases, unemployed workers can still have the right to social unemployment benefit of a lesser amount provided they have worked for at least 180 days during the last year, or if they have used up the period of concession for unemployment benefit.

4 A comparison with other EU countries shows that in 1993 this proportion was below the average; only Greece and Italy, where fi-nancial assistance for the unemployed is very small, had still lower figures.

5 Estimates of unemployment vary according to the source used. Thus, the rates of unemployment calculated on the basis of the Employment Survey by the National Institute

of Statistics are, as a rule, lower (about 2.5 percent in 1995) than by the calculations derived from registrations at Employment Centres. It must be said that the system of registration for work is rather imperfect, since a fraction of those seeking work do not register with the Employment Centres, and also because some who are registered as seeking work are not in fact doing so.

6 The discrepancy with the figures in Table 2 results from the fact that different sources are used.

7 According to the definition used in Portuguese employment statistics, the 'self-employed worker runs his own business or practises independently a profession or trade, with or without employees' (INE 1993).

8 A recent study of self-employment in Portugal concluded that 81 percent of the families of self-employed workers questioned earned a very low monthly income, less than 1000 ECU's (Freire 1995:71).

9 The national minimum wage is revised annually and in 1997 was set at ca. 290 ECU's.

10 According to the definition used in Portuguese employment statistics, non-permanent employment includes 'work under a system of fixed term contracts (the duration limited and defined in writing), or without a permanent contract (seasonal, occasional or temporary).' (INE 1993).

11 The previous legislation of 1976 had established an initial probationary period of not more than six months before the status of permanent employment. This period could be renewed twice more, after which the contract would become permanent. The alteration of 1989 permitted fixed term contracts to be used in cases of temporary replacement of a sick employee, for temporarily increased activity, for a job defined by a specific time limit, and for periods of fluctuation of activity in general.

12 Although in European countries this reason only accounted on average for 36.3 percent of employed workers, in Portugal it applied to 79.9 percent, in Spain to 86.2 percent, in Greece to 74.3 percent, in Ireland to 61.3 percent and in Italy to 50.2 percent.

13 According to the definition used in Portuguese employment statistics, the part-time worker is 'a worker whose total working hours are fewer than those of normal workers employed in businesses, the establishment or in their respective professions.' (INE,1993).

14 The legal status of part-time work takes no account of either the firms' or the workers' preference for this type of work (Ferreira, 1993:238).

15 In 1995 almost three-quarters of the employed population employed in part-time work had a level of education not exceeding 4 years.

16 Significantly, this willingness is greater in the case of self-employed workers employing no employees.

17 A recently approved law reduces the normal working week to 40 hours. Despite having been laboriously negotiated through the established channels for social conciliation, the resistance of owners to its application has given rise to a high level of protest, demonstrating the unfavourable working conditions which the workers are facing.

18 According to the legal definition, home working consists of 'work performed under legal provision, at the home of the worker, or where the worker buys the raw materials and resells the finished product back to the supplier, to such effect that, in each case, the workers must be considered as economically dependent on the party providing the employment' (DI. 440/91 of 14/11).

19 But not all homeworkers fit this pattern of unskilled and degraded employment. In Portugal a growing category of activity is tele-working, linked to developments in information, technology and communications. Recent studies estimate that 60,000 workers (1.4 percent of the employed population) are occupied in this type of work.

20 Homeworking is regulated by the legislation on homeworking of 1991, and includes homeworkers in the system of social security, although with certain exceptions.

21 The presence of child labour associated with homeworking and sub-contracting has been noticed in footwear and clothing industries in northern Portugal. Usually used as unpaid family helpers, children frequently become full-time employees in small firms during periods of increased workload at low wages (Baganha, 1996).

22 The Agricultural Census by the National Institute of Statistics showed, for 1995, that 80.4 percent of the relatives of agricultural producers were involved in work on the family farms. This figure is incomparably higher than that obtained from employment statistics (9.7 percent).

23 In this study poverty is defined as 'a situation of deprivation, persistent and severe, relative to the satisfying of one or more basic necessities as these are expressed in a given society, particularly food, clothing, housing and respective conditions of use of essential services, social support, health and certain unusual services' (MQE 1998:22). To classify a family as poor it is necessary to ascertain, in addition to deprivation in three or more areas, that the indicators exceed a specified level of severity of deprivation.

24 Even before the reforms of labour legislation in 1989, which facilitated individual and collective dismissal and in general made the terms and conditions of work more flexible (temporary work, fixed term contracts, sub-contracting), the workers were not able to prevent delayed payment of wages, or the employers' debts to social security and default of payments due after pay disputes.

25 Most of these features are apparent also in other South European countries which share closely similar peculiarities in terms of modes of regulation and welfare regimes (Leibfried and Pierson, 1992; Ferrera, 1996, Rhodes and Palier, 1997).

References

Almeida, J., Capucha, L., Costa, A., Machado, F., Nicolau, I., Reis, E. (1992), *Exclusão Social. Factores e Tipos de Pobreza em Portugal*, Oeiras: Celta Editora.

Baganha, M. (1996), *Immigration Insertion in the Informal Economy. The Portuguese Case*, Coimbra: CES (mimeo).

Bonanno, A. et al. (1994), 'Global Post-Fordism and Concepts of the State', *International Journal of Sociology of Agriculture and Food*, Vol. 4, pp. 11-29.

CGTP (1996a), *Programa de Acção*, 8° Congresso, Lisboa (mimeo).

CGTP (1996b), *Relatório de Actividades*, 8° Congresso, Lisboa (mimeo).

CGTP (1996c), *Intervenções do Conselho Nacional*, 8° Congresso, Lisboa (mimeo).

Ferreira, A. C. (1996), *Problemas Actuais da Contratação Colectiva em Portugal e na Europa*, Lisboa: Friedrich Ebert Stiftung.

Ferreira, V. (1993), 'Padrões de segregação das mulheres no emprego', in Boaventura S. Santos (ed.), *Portugal: um retrato singular*, Porto: Afrontamento, pp. 233-259.

Ferrera, M. (1996), 'The Southern Model of Welfare in Social Europe', *Journal of European Social Policy*, 6(1):17-37.

Figueredo, A. et al. (1997), *Labour Market Studies: Portugal*, Luxembourg: European Commission.

Freire, J. (1995), *O Trabalho Independente em Portugal*, Lisboa: CIES/ISCTE.

Hespanha, P. (1991), 'Portuguese Rural Society, the State and Farming since 1946. An Overview', in A. Montanari (ed.), *Growth and Perspectives of the Agrarian Sector in Portugal, Italy, Greece and Turkey*, Napoli: Edizioni Scientifiche Italiane.

Hespanha, P. (1995), 'Vers une Société-providence simultanément pré- et post- moderne. L'état des solidarités intergénérationnelles au Portugal', in Claudine Attias-Donfut (ed.), *Générations., Familles, État*, Paris: Éd. Nathan.

Hespanha, P. (1997), 'The Dynamics of Globalization. Social Crisis and Conflict in Portuguese Rural Areas', *International Journal of Sociology of Agriculture and Food,* Vol. 6, pp. 11-24.

Hespanha, P., Ferreira, C. and Portugal, S. (1997), 'The Welfare Society and the Welfare State', in Maurice Roche and Rik van Berkel, *European Citizenship and Social Exclusion*, Aldershot: Ashgate.

Hespanha, P. and Reis, J. (1992), 'Les sociétés semi-périphériques: une regulation multiforme', in Didier le Gal (ed.), *Régulation Sociale et Contextes Sociaux Européens*, Caen: Université de Caen.

INE (1993), *Inquérito ao Emprego. Anos 90. Metodologia,* Série Estudos, No. 66.

Leibfried, S and Pierson, P. (1992), 'Prospects for a Social Europe', *Politics and Society,* Vol. 20, pp. 333-366.

Lopes, J. S. (1996), 'A economia portuguesa desde 1960', in A. Barreto (ed) *A situação social em Portugal, 1960-1995,* Lisboa: ICS.

Meulders, D., Plasman, O. and Plasman R. (1994), *Atypical Employment in the EC*, Aldershot: Dartmouth

Mozzicafreddo, J. (1997), *Estado-Providência e Cidadania em Portugal*, Oeiras: Celta.

MQE (1996), *Caracterização da Pobreza em Portugal*, Lisboa: Departamento de Estatística.

OECD (1991), *Women and Employment Restructuring*, Paris.

Poulantzas, N. (1975), *La crise des dictatures. Portugal, Grèce, Espagne,* Paris: Ed. Seuil.

Santos, B. S. (1993), *Portugal, um retrato singular,* Porto: Afrontamento.

Santos, B. S. (1995), *Toward a New Common Sense,* New York: Routledge.

The Arkleton Trust (1992), *Farm Household Adjustment in Western Europe – 1971-1991*, Nethy Bridge: The Arkleton Trust (mimeo).

UGT (1996), 'Um acordo económico e social para o ano 2000', *Proposta da Comissão Permanente*, Lisboa (mimeo).

Vaz, I. (1997), *As formas atípicas de emprego e a flexibilidade do Mercado de Trabalho*, Lisboa: MQE.CICT.

5. Regulating the unemployed: From protection to participation

RIK VAN BERKEL, HARRY COENEN AND ARJEN DEKKER

Introduction

In this chapter we will discuss and analyze developments in Dutch labour-market and social policies during the last two decades. As we will show, one of the main characteristics of these developments is a paradigmatic shift in those policies from protection (by providing income or services) to (work) participation (WRR 1996). Although it is obvious that these developments involve risks for vulnerable groups on the labour market, we will argue that they entail an emancipatory potential -as far as strengthening full citizenship of these groups in terms of their participation in society is concerned- as well. We will then try to identify the conditions under which this potential can be realized.

In the second section of the chapter, the main changes in Dutch labour-market and social policies, as well as in underlying regulation mechanisms, are described and analyzed. As will be shown, these changes involve new patterns of differentiation among groups of social-security claimants, as well as an emphasis on new types of inclusion. In the third section, the emphasis in Dutch policies on inclusion through participation is analyzed in greater detail. Whereas the main tendency seems to be to decrease protection in order to increase participation, various initiatives directed at specific target groups among vulnerable labour-market groups reveal the importance of finding new balances between participation and protection as a precondition for supporting the participation opportunities of social groups with a high risk of labour-market marginalization (cf. Møller 1997). In the fourth section, we will discuss a new social-policy initiative, called social activation. This new social policy is aimed at the long-term unemployed and is participation-oriented as well, but involves inclusion through unpaid rather than paid activities. This section investigates the significance of unpaid activities for participation-oriented social policies. In the final section, we will draw some conclusions and sketch some prospects for the future of Dutch social policies.

Restructuring Dutch labour-market and social policies

Until the late 1980s, Dutch labour-market and social policies were founded on what has been called a protection paradigm (WRR 1996). Rather than encouraging the growing number of unemployed people towards (re-) inclusion within the labour market and supporting them in finding a new job, these policies aimed at providing relatively generous levels of income protection for those who were the victims of processes of economic restructuring. As Esping-Andersen wrote about the continental welfare states (1997, p.68): 'Rather than boost public employment, as in Scandinavia, their main policy response to "deindustrialization" and unemployment has been to induce labour force exit.' For example, many redundant workers were declared incapacitated rather than unemployed because Dutch disability benefits were more generous than unemployment benefits: disability benefits entitled those who had been declared incapacitated to income-related benefits until their retirement, whereas the entitlement to income-related unemployment benefits was restricted in duration. At the same time, labour-market policies were restrictive (Offe 1994; Therborn 1986). Apart from providing little support in finding employment for those who had become unemployed (or incapacitated), older workers were encouraged to make room for the young by the introduction of early retirement schemes. Furthermore, single mothers on social assistance did not have an obligation to apply for jobs until their youngest child reached the age of twelve; at the same time, this also implied that they would get no support for finding employment until that moment. The same applied for the unemployed older than 57.5 years: they did not have to apply for jobs (and were therefore not included in unemployment statistics), but at the same time would get no support for finding employment.

In terms of differentiation and inclusion, the protection paradigm in Dutch labour-market and social policies implied the following. As far as income protection was concerned, older social security claimants were relatively best off. Their benefits were rather generous, and pressure on them to re-enter the labour market was virtually non-existent. The latter also applied to single mothers with young children, although their benefit levels were lower, since social assistance provided them with flat-rate benefits only. On the other hand, younger unemployed people would receive less protection: they depended on less generous social-security schemes and the pressure on them to accept a job was stronger. At the same time, for those groups that did not have an obligation to apply for jobs, labour-market integration opportunities were quite limited. They could try to find a job, of course, but support for finding employment was absent. Given the surplus of labour-market supply on the one hand, and characteristics of these groups in terms of age, education, work experience, etcetera on the other, their labour-market chances were anything but favourable. Consequently, the labour-market participation of older workers declined drastically. In 1971, 74 percent of men and 13 percent of women between the ages of 60-65 participated in paid work. By 1989, these percentages of labour-market participation had decreased to 30 percent and 11 percent respectively (WRR 1990, p.233). Let us put these figures on labour-market participation of older people in an international perspective: whereas in the Netherlands about 25 percent of people aged 55-65 participated in paid work in 1989, in the OECD countries the average figure was almost 50 percent (WRR 1990, p.63).

The protection paradigm of Dutch labour-market and social policies contributed to an increase in the number of people on social security. Table 1 shows the development of the number of social-security claimants over the period 1978–1996.

In the late 1980s, the protection paradigm met with growing criticism. The most important reason for that was the fact that the social-security system became more and more expensive, which was regarded as a threat to the Dutch position in international economic competition (WRR 1990), although other reasons were mentioned as well, as we shall show in the next section. Gradually, a paradigm shift started to take place, not radically but rather incrementally (Roebroek 1993). An important step in this process was the introduction of an activating labour-market policy (WRR 1987), which was inspired by the so-called 'Swedish Model': the Swedish welfare state was considered to be much more participation-oriented than the Dutch welfare state. A more thorough elaboration of the new paradigm was given in a very influential report by the Dutch Scientific Council for Government Policies (WRR), which was published in 1990 (see also Adriaansens and Dercksen 1993). This report pointed to the low labour-market participation rate in the Netherlands as the most important problem of the Dutch welfare state. With a net labour-market participation rate of 59 percent in 1988, the

Netherlands scored low compared to the OECD-countries (66 percent) and to Western European countries (62 percent), and remarkably low compared to Scandinavia (78 percent) and the Anglo-Saxon countries (71 percent) (WRR 1990, p.59).

Table 5.1 Social-insurance and social-assistance claimants in the Netherlands: most important schemes (in full benefit years), 1978-1996

	1978	1990	1996
Old age pensions*	1,225,000	1,956,000	2,105,000
Early retirement schemes	–	39,000	48,000
Disability	538,000	778,000	737,000
Unemployment benefits	55,000	164,000	388,000
Social assistance for the unemployed	78,000	355,000	329,000 **
Other social assistance (e.g. single mothers)	246,000	192,000 ***	181,000 **

* The increase in the number of old age pensions is partly due to the individualization of pensions which took place during the eighties.
** Figures for 1995, since a new Social Security Act was introduced in 1996.
*** Since 1985, about 100,000 people living in homes for the elderly no longer receive their income through Social Assistance.

Source: Ministerie van Sociale Zaken en Werkgelegenheid 1994; 1996.

Gradually, more steps were taken to transform Dutch social and labour-market policies. In general, these changes were characterized by emphasis on work rather than income, and on participation rather than protection. Work, meaning participation in paid work, was promoted as the royal road to full citizenship. We will now take a closer look at some of these developments.

Social-security policies

The main characteristic of social-security policies under the new paradigm is that living on social security is made less attractive and more difficult to realize. The following developments in social-security policies are illustrative in this respect.

First, the proverbial 'generosity' of Dutch social security benefits has been cut back. As far as income-related benefits are concerned, the income levels assures by these benefits have decreased, and the periods during which people are able to claim them have been shortened. Furthermore, social security payments have not, or only partly, been linked to the increase in the general welfare level over the years. As far as social assistance is concerned, the purchasing power of these benefits decreased by 10 percent between 1979 and 1993, causing 'poverty' to become a policy issue once again in the Netherlands during the 1990s (Oude Engberink and Post 1996; Engbersen, Vrooman and Snel 1996, 1997).

Secondly, claiming income-related benefits has been made more difficult. That is, the requirements one has to fulfil to be entitled to these benefits have been tightened. Against the background of a more and more flexible labour market, one might say that those whose labour market position is most vulnerable are at the same time those who are now least protected by the social security system. Because entitlement to income-related benefits depends on contributions these are workers' benefits rather than citizens' benefits (Twine 1994) and best protect those with strong labour-market positions and with stable and long labour-market careers.

Thirdly, drastic changes have been taking place as regards disability benefits. As we saw before, restrictive labour-market policies contributed to a low labour-market participation rate on the part of older workers, many of whom were on disability benefits. The strategy of offering disability benefits to older workers who were made redundant in recession times as a way out of the labour market, which was encouraged by the organizations of employers and employees and of which the national government feigned ignorance, quadrupled the number of people claiming disability benefits between 1970 and 1991. Some years ago, this social-security scheme was reformed, despite massive protests from the trade-union movement and despite the crisis the reforms brought about in one of the political parties in power, the 'Partij van de Arbeid' (the Dutch Labour Party). The reforms not only made access to this scheme more difficult for new claimants but also forced lots of former claimants onto unemployment benefits or social assistance. For, as a consequence of the reforms of the Disability Act, many people who had been entitled to disability benefits under the old system were medically re-examined under stricter conditions than on entering this scheme. If these examinations revealed that people had still some work capacity left, they were (partly) transferred from disability schemes to unemployment schemes, which obliged them to look for a job.

Fourthly, as a consequence of the social-security reforms described above, a further 'dualization' in income maintenance provision has taken place (Jordan 1996). Nowadays, an increasing proportion of social-security claimants is dependent on means-tested social assistance and is not entitled to earnings-related social insurance (see Vlek 1997), partly because they have exhausted these entitlements, partly because stricter entry requirements exclude them from claiming, partly as a consequence of social security cutbacks in other social arrangements, and, finally, partly as a result of demographic developments. To illustrate this, between 1970 and 1986 the proportion of all social assistance recipients made up by unemployed people increased from 3 percent to 67 percent in the Netherlands (Esping-Andersen 1997, p.75).

Fifthly, according to the new Social Security Act (Algemene Bijstandswet) that was implemented in 1996, single mothers now have an obligation to apply for jobs as soon as their youngest child reaches the age of five; this used to be twelve years. Thus, for single mothers on social assistance whose youngest child is older than five and younger than twelve, motherhood is no longer a legitimate option: these mothers are, at least formally, treated as 'regular' unemployed.

Finally, early retirement schemes are being replaced by flexible pension schemes, and some politicians are arguing in favour of raising the retirement age. Again, these developments will increase the number of unemployed and decrease the possibilities of non-participation in the labour market and of dependence on social security.

On top of these reforms of social-security policies, a debate is going on in which a reconsideration of the responsibilities of the national state in offering social security is being discussed. Although it is too early to predict the outcomes of this debate, current developments might result in the construction of a three-layered social-security system, in which:

- the national state guarantees minimum social security provisions only;
- collective agreements between employers and employees may provide for extra, income-related benefits and other provisions;
- and individual persons may enter into contracts with insurance companies to cover risks on top of those covered by collective arrangements.

This partial individualization of risk protection would change relationships between social security arrangements provided by the welfare state, the welfare society, and the welfare market (cf. Hespanha et al., 1997). Phrased in terms of the regulation models underlying these developments, we would see a curtailment of the role of the state, that is legislation, in the provision of social security whereas the importance of collective agreements and market forces in providing social security and protecting against risks would increase. The recent almost complete abolition, or rather privatization, of the Dutch Health Law (Ziektewet) illustrates these shifts in responsibilities. As a consequence of the abolition of this law, employers have been made responsible for guaranteeing workers 70 percent of their wages during sick leave. If they want, they can reinsure with public or private companies. The abolition of the Dutch Health Law has led to stricter staffing policies, because companies have become much more cautious about employing high-risk groups. In general, this new mode of regulation towards the privatization of social-security provisions may increase workers' rights while weakening citizens' rights, favouring those whose labour-market participation is stable and secure.

Labour-market policies

The developments in social policies outlined above might be interpreted as reducing the 'decommodifying' nature of the Dutch social-security system (cf. Esping-Andersen 1990) by increasing people's dependency on the labour market and strengthening (or, at least, trying to strengthen) their work ethic. In other words, emphasizing participation has increased what Jordan (1996) has called the 'politics of enforcement'.

To what degree are these policies of enforcement or commodification complemented by policies aimed at increasing participation opportunities, of which labour-market policies form an important (but not necessarily the only – see section 4) part? In 1986, Therborn made the following observation in his study of (un)employment policies in OECD-countries: 'Dutch state policy has two basic socio-economic features. On the one hand, a passive economic policy, mainly aimed at diminishing the role of the state still further in order to provide 'space' (...) for the private sector. On the other, a generous social policy, trying to compensate for the failures of Dutch capitalism and Dutch economic policy, by paying social benefits to the mounting number of unemployed and 'disabled' (most of whom are really just unemployed)' (Therborn 1986, pp.160-1). As we have seen, social policies saw their compensation function being reduced. However, economic policies are still passive in the sense that direct interventions to promote employment on the regular labour market are limited. Therborn's description of policies as aimed to provide 'space' is still largely adequate: participation opportunities have been enhanced by deregulation, by providing training and work-experience measures, by introducing wage subsidies to encourage employers to hire long-term unemployed or partly disabled people, etcetera. But the use and implementation of these measures is left to the social partners, particularly employers, who are free to choose whether or not to do so. Thus, the unemployed bear the brunt of the enforcement policies, without there being a similar pressure on the employers.

However, during the decade following Therborn's observations, two important developments did take place. On one hand, the Netherlands have witnessed the creation of a 'secondary' labour market through the introduction of various schemes creating low-skilled, state-subsidized jobs at minimum-wage levels, mainly in the public sector. Thus, after a period of reductions in public employment, the public sector is growing again albeit with low-paid jobs only. On the other, efforts aimed at supporting the unemployed in finding a job have intensified. We will briefly elaborate on some of these developments now (see also the contribution by Beukema and Valkenburg to this volume).

First, nowadays unemployed people under the age of 24 are confronted with compulsory participation in a temporary job scheme after six months of unemployment: the former Youth Employment Act (Jeugdwerkgarantiewet), the Dutch version of the Youth Training Scheme (Spies 1996). These jobs are in the public or private sector for 32 hours a week at the minimum youth wage. Refusal and dismissal deemed to be the employee's own fault are penalised by exclusion from the right to benefit for a period that depends on the individual's work motivation and attitude. In order to increase young people's opportunities to find a regular job after a period of participation in this job scheme, the private sector has been allowed to create jobs in the context of the scheme as well.

Secondly, tens of thousands of so-called additional, state-subsidized jobs are being created. These aim at enhancing participation opportunities for groups of long-term, low-productive unemployed, creating a segment of the labour market offering those who are dependent on it low (minimum) wages and few prospects. In practice, many of the people in these jobs do not manage to make the step from these additional jobs into the regular labour market. Partly because of that trade unions have argued in favour of introducing regular, negotiable labour contracts for workers in these schemes. For some of the workers in these schemes, government has created the possibility of raising workers' wages modestly. This may also reduce the poverty trap some of these workers face when accepting state-subsidized jobs.

Thirdly, measures were taken that sought to stimulate people to find employment. For example, organizations of employers and employees were involved more closely in the administration of the job centres ('tripartization'). Furthermore, job centres have increased efforts to help employment-finding, developing policies targeted at specific groups (the long-term unemployed, women, immigrants, etcetera), and experimenting with more intensive forms of support (see below).

Care

In the context of the paradigm shift in social policies discussed here, we also need to make some remarks on care. Traditionally, people in need of professional care (for example, the mentally handicapped or psychiatric patients) used to be protected against exposure to regular society, for example by being put in institutions where they lived far removed -not only socially but often also spatially- from 'normal' society. However, in this sphere too the same shift from protection to participation is gradually taking place. That is, in order to create opportunities for the people involved to be able to participate in society as fully as their capacities and possibilities will allow them, provisions are being made to facilitate regular living and working conditions. An example of these will be discussed in the next section.

Conclusion

In terms of inclusion, exclusion and differentiation, these developments may be summarized as follows. Some traditional forms of differentiation have made way for new ones. On the one hand, differentiation has decreased since more and more groups dependent on social security are considered as equivalent to the regular unemployed, although some differences remain, for example between the younger and older unemployed. On the other hand, in terms of the 'division of welfare' (Ginsburg 1992), currently existing forms of differentiation may be strengthened or new ones developed, resulting in, for example, greater differences between marginalized groups dependent on state-guaranteed minimum benefits at the one extreme, and strong labour-market groups able to protect themselves individually with generous risk coverage at the other. Furthermore, the introduction of job schemes for the long-term unemployed introduces new forms of labour-market differentiation, creating a large group of low-waged workers with slim prospects of entering the regular labour market.

As far as inclusion is concerned, paid work has become the prescribed inclusion trajectory for more and more people, whereas inclusion within the system of social security is considered less and less desirable. At the same time, next to the regular labour market, which itself has become more segmented than it used to be, a 'secondary' labour market of low-paid, state-subsidized jobs has been developed offering many long-term unemployed second-class inclusion opportunities, for example with regard to income and prospects of paid employment.

From protection to participation

In the previous section, we have analyzed recent developments in Dutch social security and labour-market policies in terms of a paradigm shift from protection to participation. Apart from budgetary and economic motives, this has been advocated for other reasons as well. The influential report by the Dutch Scientific Council for Government Policies on participation in work (WRR 1990) pointed to the important inclusive and emancipatory role of participation in paid work. According to this report, institutions that have traditionally promoted societal cohesion and social integration, such as the church, the working class and its organizations, neighbourhoods and communities, and the family have been eroded as a consequence of processes of individualization. Therefore, the report continues, the importance of inclusion within paid work has increased rather than decreased, as advocates of the 'leisure society', of the introduction of a Basic Income and of 'the end of work-based societies' claim (on this debate, cf. Gorz 1982, 1989; Keane and Owens 1986; Roche 1992; Pixley 1993; Coenen and Leisink 1993). Furthermore, paid work itself has undergone changes that reinforce its inclusive and emancipatory potential. In particular, the report points out that much physically hard work has disappeared.

In emphasizing the inclusive and emancipatory function of labour-market participation, the report points to the significance of work as shown in unemployment research. The functions of paid work as identified by Jahoda (1982) are well-known by now: besides being the main source of independence and income, work structures time, it offers regular activities, it gives people access to social networks, it provides status and identity, and it gives people opportunities to contribute to society at large. In short, paid work is considered to be a necessary condition of full citizenship (Roche and Van Berkel 1997). Thus, insofar as paid work has been removed from its pedestal, it should be put back there, the report concludes.

In evaluating the arguments used in this plea for a revival of paid work, it is not too difficult to point out some weak points used in the argumentation.

First of all, irrespective of one's opinions about the inclusive and emancipatory potential of paid work, it is quite clear that structural unemployment makes full employment very unlikely in the near future, if ever.

Secondly, one may question whether labour-market participation is the only possible road to inclusion and full citizenship. We will return to this in the next section, where we shall discuss the inclusive potential of voluntary, unpaid work.

Thirdly, one may also question to what degree the emancipatory and inclusive functions of work apply to *all* jobs. On the one hand, one might argue that Jahoda's analysis of the importance of paid work primarily refers to the type of job that used to be standard but is no longer so; some theorists of modernization may be inclined to say that Jahoda's analysis applies to 'Fordist jobs', but not necessarily to flexible jobs. On the other hand, it is simply untenable to claim that developments in the quality of work have put an end to poor-quality jobs and have improved rather than diminished emancipation opportunities.

Fourthly, the report does not make any reference to environmental issues involved in advocating a revival of paid work, neglecting the 'ecological risks' (Beck 1986) involved in a 'productivist' design of social policies (Offe 1992).

Nevertheless, we think we should not throw away the baby with the bath-water by interpreting the shift from protection to participation as wholly negative, emphasizing only the increasing labour-market and second-class citizenship risks for those who are already most vulnerable. For it is quite clear that traditional protection schemes have failed to achieve inclusion and full citizenship either. Of course, they provided income for the poor and care for those in need. But at the same time they obstructed rather than stimulated independence and emancipation, as critics of social-security and care systems have argued more than once (cf. Roche 1992; Coenen and Leisink 1993).

Thus, the importance of participation is stressed not only by policy-makers, but by the organizations and social movements of people at risk of being excluded from participation as well (cf. Van Berkel, Coenen and Vlek

1998). These include not only the unemployed, but also other marginalized groups: the (physically or mentally) handicapped, people with psychiatric backgrounds, etcetera. Therefore, the central question is not whether one should emphasize either protection or participation, but first, what mix of protection and participation can contribute to vulnerable groups' independence, autonomy and emancipation as much as possible; and, secondly, how the concepts of participation and protection should be modernized so far as their content is concerned.

It is quite clear that when answering the first question is left to neo-liberals, the result will be unbalanced, overemphasizing participation and neglecting the importance of protection. The analysis of Dutch social policy presented above shows how more and more groups are being made labour-market dependent, whereas efforts to increase participation opportunities and to improve participation conditions (the forms of protection we are mainly concerned with in this chapter) are far less effective, leaving vulnerable groups largely to their own limited devices to realize (labour-market) participation. At the same time, however, experiences with target-group oriented projects to help people in finding employment as well as in keeping their jobs, provide evidence that given the right mix of participation and protection, participation opportunities for vulnerable groups can be increased dramatically. For example, experiments with intensive and tailor-made guidance for the long-term unemployed have succeeded in including them within the labour market whereas regular employment officers at Job Centres would have considered them to be without any prospects on the labour market (Valkenburg 1993). But then, in contrast to most regular support for finding employment, these experiments have been client-oriented rather than institutional, and empowering rather than paternalistic. That is, they have taken clients' wishes and ambitions seriously without raising them to unrealistic levels; and they have been aimed at increasing long-term unemployed people's resources for finding a job (Coenen and Valkenburg 1996). Experiments with Supported Employment go a step further than this. Developed in the United States, these experiments were introduced in the Netherlands to increase the participation opportunities of people with psychiatric backgrounds (cf. Van Weeghel 1995) or mental handicaps (Coenen-Hanegraaf et al. 1994). They offer not only intensive and tailor-made guidance in finding employment, but also coaching and training on the job. In the Dutch Supported Employment programme for the mentally handicapped, for example, people on reinclusion programmes are supported by a (temporary) job coach. These job coaches offer assistance in preparing for and actually carrying out the job, in making employers and colleagues aware of mentally handicapped people's capacities, etcetera.

As to the second question, modernization of the concepts of protection and participation, the following may be observed. A gradual shift towards more empowerment concerned concepts of protection is taking place. Rather than protecting people from participation in 'normal' society (by offering them benefits or putting them in institutions), emphasizing their limitations and lack of capacities and stressing their dependency, these new concepts of protection are directed towards forms of participation in regular society that emphasize the capacities and qualities people have and try to identify the circumstances under which people can be as independent and autonomous as possible. Regarding the concept of participation, the issue is whether we should limit this concept to paid work, that is labour-market participation, or whether unpaid activities or activities that take place in the context of non-monetary exchange systems (for example, LETS; see Williams and Windebank 1997) are a resource for full participation as well. The reasons for raising this issue are various:

- it is important to recognize the useful character of unpaid activities;
- there is a structural surplus on the labour market, raising the issue whether other participation routes are feasible;
- for some groups at least, participation in unpaid activities might match their ambitions and capacities better than labour-market participation.

We will elaborate this issue in greater detail in the next section.

Social activation policies

With the introduction of a new Social Security Act in the Netherlands in 1996, local authorities required a new social-policy instrument to increase participation opportunities for the long-term unemployed and generally to promote their societal inclusion. This Act enabled municipalities to start experiments targeted at long-term unemployed people with few prospects of labour-market participation and aimed at their participation in a range of unpaid activities (Van Berkel 1997; Van Berkel and Brand 1997).

By now, many municipalities in the Netherlands are developing and implementing these so-called social activation experiments. When one compares such experiments, it becomes clear that they may be founded on different views of the content and objectives of social policies. We will illustrate this by comparing the experiments in three dimensions.

First, the experiments differ with respect to how they relate to labour-market participation. For some municipalities, social activation is a labour-market instrument: participation in unpaid activities is considered to have socialization and training functions that prepare the long-term unemployed for subsequent reinclusion within the labour market. For other municipalities, participation in unpaid activities is considered to be a full alternative to labour-market participation. For them, social activation schemes are an opportunity to recognize the social and individual importance of unpaid activities, although current legislation limits this opportunity to the long-term unemployed on social assistance. Participation in paid work may be the result of participation in social activation, but it is not an intended consequence of the schemes, at least not for all participants.

Secondly, the experiments differ with respect to the voluntary versus compulsory character of participation in the programmes. In some municipalities, participation is obligatory. Here, the emphasis in social-policy debates on the obligations of social security claimants takes the form of the introduction of workfare-like measures: participation in social activation programmes is considered to be a first step towards inclusion within the labour market, and hence is considered a legitimate obligation for the unemployed. In other municipalities, social activation is treated as a new arrangement of both rights and obligations for the long-term unemployed. There, participation in social activation is voluntary. The target group for social activation is presented with the following choice: either they opt for the traditional social assistance regime, implying that they have to look for a job in return for their benefits; or they opt for the social activation scheme, implying that they participate in unpaid activities and are released from the obligation to apply for jobs. In some municipalities, participants in social activation receive some remuneration on top of their benefits.

Thirdly, there are differences with respect to which groups of social-assistance claimants are allowed to participate in social-activation programmes. As we saw before, the national government considers social activation as a social policy specifically aimed at those long-term unemployed whose labour-market chances are nil. One might interpret this as follows: the national government does not wish social activation to undermine the primacy of labour-market participation, and considers social activation at most to be a participation safety-net, thus emphasizing the second-class character of participation in unpaid work. Most municipalities stick to this definition of the target group for social activation, partly because they support the national government's point of view, partly because they feel they have no room to act otherwise. However, some municipalities try to broaden the target group for their experiments, for example by including artists or the 'voluntary unemployed'. This way, they try to increase the status of unpaid work, though risking intervention from the national authorities.

To what degree do the long-term unemployed themselves consider participation in social activation programmes a desirable, though perhaps temporary, alternative to labour-market participation? Can participation in unpaid activities be a form of full participation as well? Despite the vanguard role some social theorists have attributed to the unemployed in developing new concepts of work for society, research among the unemployed has concluded time and again that most unemployed want a job, though not any job. Nevertheless, there is some evidence that social-activation programmes are successful, at least for some groups of unemployed people. Some of this evidence comes from a research project we are involved in ourselves. This research project is designed to evaluate the social activation programme of the Dutch city of Rotterdam (see Van Berkel and Brand 1997), which has the largest social activation scheme in the country. In Rotterdam, participation in social activation is voluntary, and the project is not primarily aimed at reinclusion within the labour market. By now, the project has about 2,400 long-term unemployed participants, most of them undertaking some form of organized voluntary work.

On the basis of our research among the participants themselves, we conclude that there is no universal answer to the question to what degree participation in unpaid activities in the context of the social-activation programme contributes to experiences of full participation.

First of all, in some respects unpaid activities do not provide the long-term unemployed with experiences of full participation. Most importantly, participation in social activation does not provide them with an independent income, it does not (or hardly increases) their inclusion within the consumer regime, and it does not make them independent of municipal social services. For those unemployed who consider these to be important aspects of full participation and social citizenship (and many of them do), social activation may remain a second-best option. And since, at least under present conditions, these aspects of full participation can only be realized through labour-market participation, a considerable number of social-activation participants stay focused on finding a paid job.

At the same time, however, social activation does seem to be a viable alternative to full participation through paid work in other respects. Especially with respect to the immaterial functions of paid work identified by Jahoda, unpaid activities also seem to have the potential to fulfil these functions. Most importantly, participants point to the fact that participation in voluntary work provides them with experiences of contributing to society, a sense of being helpful to others, and of being a respected partner in social relations. Furthermore, it widens their social horizon as well as their social networks, and increases their competencies.

Finally, in some respects we may even conclude that participation in social activation contributes to experiences of full participation to a larger extent than paid work would do. This may be so, first, because social activation offers more protection than paid work does, at least under present circumstances: there seems to be no reason why paid work might not be able to provide similar forms of protection as well, at least in principle. This also shows, of course, that it is impossible to give a universal definition of how experiences of full participation can be realized for different categories of people. A second reason why voluntary work may constitute a fuller form of participation than paid work is related to the labour-market prospects of the social-activation participants. Most of them have few formal qualifications, making them dependent on labour-market segments that offer low-skilled jobs, or on the state-subsidized jobs mentioned above. Apart from the fact that such jobs hardly hold out a prospect of income improvement for these unemployed people, some of them also find their present unpaid activities more qualitatively attractive than the jobs they are qualified for. Some of the participants we interviewed turned out to have developed more critical attitudes towards labour-market participation than they had prior to their social-activation participation.

Conclusions and prospects

We started this paper by presenting recent developments in Dutch social security and labour-market policies. We showed that these developments can be interpreted as a shift of paradigms in social policy, towards emphasizing participation rather than protection. Given present labour-market conditions and inequalities, it is evident that this paradigmatic shift involves larger risks for the most vulnerable groups on the labour market. At the same time, however, we argued that emphasizing participation may also offer new opportunities for full participation and citizenship on the part of these groups. Obviously, these opportunities will be realized only if certain conditions are met:

- Social policies should facilitate the definition and implementation of tailor-made mixes of protection and participation;
- the concept of protection should be modernized, to become more concerned with empowerment, to emphasize people's capacities rather than their limitations, and to find new balances between the challenges and the risks of participation;
- the concept of participation should be modernized as well, encompassing both paid and unpaid activities, as well as combinations of various forms of participation.

As far as the latter is concerned, we showed that the Dutch social activation programmes, aimed at participation in unpaid activities, may indeed foster experiences of full participation. For some people, participation in social activation is meant to be (or, where it was not so intended, may turn out to be) a springboard to labour-market participation. For others, it will constitute a protracted or even permanent form of full participation, offering a combination of protection and participation that, at least up until now, cannot be found in labour-market participation.

We will now conclude this paper with an attempt to assess the chances that these conditions may be met in the foreseeable future. Although the ideological debate surrounding the shift in paradigms in the Netherlands may not have been as sharp-edged as in, say, Thatcherite Britain, great stress has been placed on the (alleged) effects of social policy on human motivation. According to the neo-liberal outlook, generous protective schemes have removed the monetary incentive considered to be a necessary condition for claimants' willingness to look for a job. Such incentive should be restored by diminishing the attractiveness of social-security schemes compared to (low paid) jobs. Furthermore, the abundant provision of social security has raised the costs of labour and thereby removed the incentive for employers to create (low-paid) jobs. This incentive should be restored by lowering the costs of labour through control of wages and cuts in the costs of social security. Controlling wages, in turn, necessitates controlling the level of social security benefits in order to protect the attractiveness of paid work.

Defendants of the protection paradigm laid stress on structural unemployment: unemployment is caused by a shortage of job-opportunities, not by unwillingness of the unemployed to look for and accept a job. But by trying to transfer the blame from the victims to 'the system', they made themselves highly vulnerable to the argument that high social security costs remove incentives for employers to create jobs. In the end, they lost the debate, even within the social-democratic party.

Current social policy, dominated by the neo-liberal version of the participation paradigm, focuses to a large extent on these two incentives. Despite clear successes in terms of number of jobs created, which aroused international attention to the Dutch 'polder model', weaknesses are evident. These weaknesses provide some opportunities for change in the direction of a more balanced mix of protection and participation, since the limits of current social policy are now in sight. Leaving the prospects of future job-creation aside, it is evident that the rise in numbers of jobs created does not solve all the problems of a dualized society.

First, quite substantial groups of long-term unemployed remain outside the labour market (even the state-subsidized market), a fact that was pointed out first by local authorities and municipal social services and is now publicly recognized not only, for example, by the trade-union movement (which has thus, for the first time, acknowledged that its full-employment policies cannot provide participation opportunities for everyone, at least not in the short term) but by national government as well. According to government representatives, about 15 years of lowering the costs of labour and strengthening the incentives to find work has contributed considerably to people's employment opportunities, but has failed to create good prospects for the most disadvantaged. Attention therefore needs to be redirected to the need to support these people by increasing both their financial and participation resources.

To a certain extent that is also what is happening now, although hesitantly. Up until now, policy change has mainly been limited to experiments with specific target-groups and experiments like social activation at the local level. These experiments, however, are not without significance. They provide insight into the inclusionary potential of non-traditional forms of work and employment, such as unpaid work or supported employment. The concept of protection is changing into one more concerned with empowerment. In general, these experiments signal a recognition of the partial failure of national social and labour-market policies.

The question whether these experiments herald a more systematic change in social policy cannot be answered positively at this moment, however. On the one hand, one can point out that the government is running out of alternatives. On the other hand, there is a crucial element to these experiments – taking the clients' wishes seriously – which has a potentially devastating effect on the core of current social policy: namely, the assumption that a paid job, virtually *any* paid job, is the ultimate form of social participation, no matter what the target groups of that policy think of it themselves. There are no signs that the national government is willing to enlarge the scope of social activation from a last resort for people who have temporarily or permanently no access to paid labour, into a form of participation which would be as valid for all as is participation in the labour market. Furthermore, recent (but perhaps only temporary?) labour shortages are seized at eagerly to stress the marginality and residuality of new forms of participation.

Secondly, participation in paid work does not necessarily relieve people from poverty, given current wages at the bottom end of the (state-subsidized) labour market. This is now gradually being recognized, and is giving rise to an increase of national and local anti-poverty measures and to an extension of these policies from social security claimants to all low income groups. These anti-poverty-measures, although far from eliminating poverty on Dutch soil, are not as hesitant as the redirection of employment policy mentioned above, and there is growing political support for additional measures. At the same time, one can see a decisive move away from general measures towards target-group oriented and even individually oriented measures. Furthermore, the dualization of income levels and social-security income will not be undone by these measures. Anti-poverty policies can only *soften* the impact of differentiation between people with a secure and stable labour-market position and claims on privatized social security on the one hand, and people on low paid jobs who will be hit hard by a new recession or those already dependent on minimum level state-controlled social security on the other hand. More seriously, this differentiation *cannot* be undone given the current work-income nexus and the reliance of Dutch social policy on the creation of low-paid labour.

To summarize, under present socio-economic and political conditions there is room for new mixes of protection and participation so far as participation in paid work is concerned. However, debates on and experiments with the inclusionary and citizenship effects of participation in unpaid work remain rather marginal. It will probably take an ecological crisis or another employment crisis to create room for a political debate about the validity of the notion of 'paid work at any cost', and to make the experiments described above real forerunners of a modernization of social policies.

References

Adriaansens, H. and Dercksen, W. (1993), 'Labour Force Participation, Citizenship and a Sustainable Welfare State in the Netherlands', in H. Coenen and P. Leisink (eds), *Work and Citizenship in the New Europe*, Aldershot: Edward Elgar.

Beck, U. (1986), *Risikogesellschaft. Auf dem Weg in eine andere Moderne*, Frankfurt a.M.: Suhrkamp.

Coenen, H. and Leisink, P. (eds). (1993), *Work and Citizenship in the New Europe*, Aldershot: Edward Elgar.

Coenen, H. and Valkenburg, B. (1996), 'De Veranderende Betekenis van Arbeid en Zorg', *Tijdschrift voor Arbeid en Bewustzijn*, Vol. 18, No. 3-4.

Coenen-Hanegraaf, M., Van Vliet, K. and Coenen, H. (1994), *Perspectief op Betaalde Arbeid voor Mensen met een Verstandelijke Handicap*, Utrecht: Van Arkel.

Engbersen, G., Vrooman, J.C. and Snel, E. (1996), *Arm Nederland. Het eerste jaarrapport armoede en sociale uitsluiting*, The Hague: VUGA.

Engbersen, G., Vrooman, J.C. and Snel, E. (1997), *Arm Nederland. De kwetsbaren. Tweede jaarrapport armoede en sociale uitsluiting*, Amsterdam: Amsterdam University Press.

Esping-Andersen, G. (1990), *The Three Worlds of Welfare Capitalism*, Princeton: Princeton University Press.

Esping-Andersen, G. (1997), 'Welfare States without Work: the Impasse of Labour Shedding and Familialism in Continental European Social Policy', in G. Esping-Andersen (ed.), *Welfare States in Transition. National Adaptations in Global Economics*, London: Sage.

Ginsburg, N. (1992), *Divisions of Welfare. A Critical Introduction to Comparative Social Policy*, London: Sage.

Gorz, A. (1982), *Afscheid van het Proletariaat*, Amsterdam: Van Gennep.

Gorz, A. (1989), *Kritik der ökonomischen Vernunft. Sinnfragen am Ende der Arbeitsgesellschaft*, Berlin: Rotbuch.

Jahoda, M. (1982), *Employment and Unemployment. A Social-psychological Analysis*, Cambridge: Cambridge UP.

Jordan, B. (1996), *A Theory of Poverty and Social Exclusion*, Cambridge: Polity Press.

Keane, J. and Owens, J. (1986), *After Full Employment*, Hutchinson: London.

Pixley, J. (1993), *Citizenship and Employment. Investigating post-industrial options*, Cambridge: Cambridge UP.

Ministerie van Sociale Zaken en Werkgelegenheid (1994), *Sociale Nota 1995*, The Hague: Sdu.

Ministerie van Sociale Zaken en Werkgelegenheid (1996), *Sociale Nota 1997*, The Hague: Sdu.

Møller, I. (1997), 'Social Integration and Labour-Market Marginalization. The Scandinavian Experience', in M. Roche and R. Van Berkel (eds), *European Citizenship and Social Exclusion*, Aldershot: Ashgate.

Offe, C. (1984), *'Arbeitsgesellschaft': Strukturprobleme und Zukunftsperspektiven*, Frankfurt: Campus.

Offe, C. (1992), 'A Non-productivist Design for Social Policies', in Ph. Van Parijs (ed.), *Arguing for Basic Income. Ethical foundations for a radical reform*, London: Verso.

Oude Engberink, G. and Post, B. (1996), *Grenzen van de Armoede. Risico's en Risicogroepen op het Sociaal Minimum*, Rotterdam: Divosa/SWA.

Roche, M. (1992), *Rethinking Citizenship. Welfare, Ideology and Change in Modern Society*, Cambridge: Polity Press.

Roche, M. and Van Berkel, R. (eds) (1997), *European Citizenship and Social Exclusion*, Aldershot: Ashgate.

Roebroek, J. (1993), *The Imprisoned State. The paradoxical relationship between state and society*, Tilburg: Katholieke Universiteit Brabant.

Spies, H. (1996), 'Workfare: Emancipation or Marginalisation?', in M.P.M. De Goede, De P.M. Klaver, J.A.C. Van Ophem, C.H.A. Verhaar and A. De Vries (eds), *Youth: Unemployment, Identity and Policy*, Aldershot: Averbury.

Therborn, G. (1986), *Why some People are more Unemployed than Others. The Strange Paradox of Growth and Unemployment*, London: Verso.

Twine, F. (1994), *Citizenship and Social Rights. The Interdependence of Self and Society*, London: Sage.

Valkenburg, B. (1993), 'Maatwerk: Tussen Generalisme en Specialisme', *Tijdschrift voor Arbeid en Bewustzijn*, Vol. 17, No. 1.

Van Berkel, R. (1997), 'Urban Integration and Citizenship. Local Policies and the Promotion of Participation', in M. Roche, M. and R. Van Berkel (eds), *Social Exclusion and European Citizenship*, Aldershot: Ashgate.

Van Berkel, R. and Brand, A. (1997), *Social Activation: Policy Instrument against Social Exclusion? The 'Unused Qualities' Project in Rotterdam*, Copenhagen: CID.

Van Berkel, R., Coenen, H. and Vlek, R. (eds) (1998), *Beyond Marginality? Collective Action of Social Security Claimants in Europe*, Aldershot: Ashgate.

Vlek, R. (1997), *Inactieven in actie. Belangenstrijd en belangenbehartiging van uitkeringsgerechtigden in de Nederlandse politiek 1974-1994,* Groningen: Wolters-Noordhoff.

Van Weeghel, J. (1995), *Herstelwerkzaamheden; Arbeidsrehabilitatie van Psychiatrische Patienten*, Utrecht: Lemma.

Williams, C. and Windebank, J. (1997), 'The informal sector in the European Union. Mitigating or reinforcing social exclusion?', in M. Roche, M. and R. Van Berkel (eds), *Social Exclusion and European Citizenship*, Aldershot: Ashgate.

WRR (1987), *Activerend Arbeidsmarktbeleid*, The Hague: Sdu.

WRR (1990), *Een werkend perspectief. Arbeidsparticipatie in de jaren '90*, The Hague: Sdu.

WRR (1996), *Tweedeling in Perspectief*, The Hague: Sdu.

6. Atypical employment in the Netherlands

LENI BEUKEMA AND BEN VALKENBURG

Introduction

Only a few years ago, the regulation of paid employment and the importance of such employment as a basis for participation in society seemed a relatively simple matter. People worked a 40-hour week, Monday to Friday, nine to five, and their pay was sufficient to provide for a family. This standard job also determined the rules regulating terms of employment and industrial relations. Normally, paid work was performed in a regular, direct relationship between employer and employee (private or public sector).

It is evident that this situation has changed fast, and is still changing. On the side of the employers the need for flexibility has grown enormously. On the side of the employees there is a growing number of people (especially women) entering the labour market on top of other important activities (especially care and education). Besides all sorts of flexible work, forms of subsidised work have been developed in an attempt to tackle the problem of long-term unemployment. These jobs also differ from traditional standard jobs in a number of ways. In short, new and varying forms of work are cropping up, and the old standard pattern is subject to erosion. New demands are being made on the regulation of labour: both as to content (regulations can no longer be the same for everyone) and as to development (differentiated regulations have to be developed in practice).

In this contribution we should like to make a closer examination of these problems. After sketching the nature of the problem (section 2), we shall give a general view of three forms of atypical work (section 3), and we review a number of recent developments (section 4). We then go into the background of these new developments. There we shall be concerned in part with the social consequences of atypical employment. This matter has been discussed in detail elsewhere (Valkenburg, Beukema 1996) and this article will give a more limited treatment (section 5). Here we shall dwell more extensively on the consequences for the internal processes of workplace and work organization (section 6). In our final remarks (section 7) we will bring together the social and organizational consequences of developments in atypical employment.

Our central thesis is that the rapid growth of atypical employment leads to new problems about the inclusion of individuals within the field of paid employment and thereby within other areas as well. These constitute problems not only for political and social movements (such as trade unions) that strive for full citizenship, and in doing so rely heavily on paid employment. They constitute problems also for employers (private and public sector), who in relation to their primarily economic objectives are discovering new limitations where atypical employment is concerned.

The nature of the problem

It hardly needs discussion that there has been a rapid growth of atypical jobs. Current discussions focus on the underlying causes and social implications of these developments. In our opinion, there are now sufficient arguments to start this analysis from four basic principles.

First, flexibilization and the resulting rapid growth of atypical jobs reflect a fundamental process of transformation which affects not only economic, but also wider social and cultural aspects of society. At the basis of this process of transformation is the development of flexible (information) technology that can be deployed on a small scale, and the increasingly reflexive nature of modern society. This is to say that economic, social and cultural practice is increasingly based on (the production of) knowledge, which in turn is tested and developed on the basis of such practice (Beck, Giddens, Lash 1994). Economically speaking, this process of transformation implies the decline of the traditional (Taylorist) mode of labour organization, and the rise of complex, flexible logistic chains of production (Lash, Urry 1994). Socially and culturally speaking, the process of transformation results in a process of individualization. Individual identity is increasingly a reflexive project, characterised by change and distinctions between different identities (Valkenburg and Zoll 1995).

Secondly, in its economic aspects this process of transformation is evolving under the traditional relations of power and production characteristic of industrial society. In a climate of high unemployment and a neo-liberal outlook dominant in politics, employers have had a long spell of sailing before the wind. Since only very recently employees have regained some power in consequence of labour shortages. It is doubtful whether this also means any strengthening of the collective power of workers. Due to increased flexibility of work in the past decades such collective power has weakened considerably (Beukema, 1995).

Thirdly, taken especially against the background of the first point, and in spite of the second one, the growth in atypical jobs should not be judged one-sidedly. Of course economic motives and interests (efficiency, competition and optimization of profits) are uppermost, and it can hardly be contested that many atypical jobs in the bottom sector of the labour market are in the best interests of the employer. At the same time it is unthinkable that these economic motives and interests could hold sway at the present rate if they did not also, at least to some extent, reflect ideas people have about the way they arrange their lives and the part to be played by paid labour.

Fourthly, it is hardly realistic to envisage the return of full employment within the foreseeable future. This means that the creation of supplementary, government-subsidised employment, as a form of atypical employment, is likely to remain with us. In short, whether we like it or not, atypical jobs are higher on the agenda of the future than the familiar standard jobs with their full working week, standardised work-time patterns and 'regular' relations between employers and employees.

What is going on?

The standard full-time job is being replaced by new forms of employment in several ways. We distinguish three such forms:

1. Non-standardised jobs with a direct employer-employee relationship
2. Non-standardised jobs with an indirect employer-employee relationship
3. Subsidised employment

Atypical jobs with a direct employer-employee relationship

In the first category, by reference to the size and nature of labour contracts in the Netherlands, part-time work is the most prominent instance. A third of the jobs in the Netherlands are now part-time, filled especially by women as well as by a large number of secondary-school pupils and students. In addition, there are fixed-term contracts which stipulate the length of time during which the employee is in the service of the employer. In many cases this involves an extended period of probation, and the temporary contract is converted into a permanent one in due course. Finally, stand-by contracts also belong to this category: employees here do not have a contract with a fixed number of hours, nor fixed working times but are called upon only when there are peaks in the work to be done. This sort of work is found in retail trade and the care sector. A survey of quantitative developments in the nature of terms of employment is presented in table 1. It should be noted that the data on flexible jobs include temporary staff, a category of employee that will be discussed in more detail in the following paragraph.

Table 6.1 Jobs of employees by type of contract (in thousands)

	full-time	part-time	flexible	total
1987	3646	1211	414	5271
1988	3676	1276	437	5390
1989	3715	1344	476	5536
1990	3780	1414	520	5714
1991	3804	1496	543	5843
1992	3812	1558	558	5928
1993	3752	1648	533	5934
1994	3698	1680	585	5963
1995	3744	1728	611	6083

Source: CBS, 1996

From the table it appears that in the Netherlands, even in absolute numbers, the growth of the number of fulltime jobs over the last 10 years (100,000) has clearly lagged behind the growth in the number of part-time jobs (500,000) and flexible jobs (200,000) in the same period. Analysis by gender shows that the growing number of part-time and flexible jobs are mainly filled by women (400,000+ and 150,000+ respectively). At the moment over a third of the total number of jobs in this country have been destandardised as to terms of employment, with regard to both the nature of the contract and working times.

Beside changes in the scope and nature of labour contracts, an increasing destandardization of working times is evident. This phenomenon has affected employees with non-standardised contracts, as well as employees with fulltime jobs. On the one hand this destandardization is motivated by the desire to adapt working times to peaks and slacks in production and services (e.g. Philips sells more refrigerators in summer than in winter. In the past this was handled by means of stockpiling, but that is now considered too expensive and production and working times are adapted instead). On the other hand this destandardization is also used as a means of increasing worker-involvement in the enterprise.

The two objectives have different results for the employee. In the first instance, it depends on the incidence of peaks in production whether employees have working times they find convenient (peaks in winter entailing longer working hours are generally preferred to peaks in summer).

An example of the adaptation of working hours to peaks and slacks in demand, found more and more often, is so-called 'vari-time'. This is used at DAF, one of Holland's largest motor works. Workers there have an average working week of 36 hours, distributed over 4 9-hour days. The maximum working week is 45 hours (5 days), the minimum is 27 hours (3 days). Workers can run up a maximum of 198 hours of slack, meaning the number of hours worked less than the average working week. During peaks they can run up a maximum of 80 supplementary hours. In practice this leads to 27-hour weeks in quiet times; but when the tide turned and DAF's market position strengthened, most workers had a six-months stint of 45-hour weeks. Because of the vari-time agreement this was not rewarded by overtime supplementary pay, which would have been the case in the past.

In the second instance, positive assessment of working hours is an explicit policy objective. New ways are being explored of fitting hours to workers' differing life styles.

The cafeteria model is one where employees are given the choice of 'spending their credit' in time or money. The insurance company *Centraal Beheer* has taken the lead in this respect. The company, which employs 2600 people, officially has a 40-hour working week and 13 days of statutory reduction of working hours. This averages out to a working week of 38 hours. The system of working hours offers the options of adherence to collective agreements, of buying extra free days (to a maximum of 13 annually), or of selling them (to a maximum of 16 annually). When selling free days, the money must be spent on fixed projects (mortgage, health insurance, annuities etc.). Employees are required to state in advance what their options are for the coming year.

About a third of the employees participate in the system of buying or selling extra time, the others prefer the collective agreements. It appears that participants in the system buy more leisure time than they sell. Expressed in jobs, this has grown from 5 jobs in 1992 to 10 jobs in 1994. Employees at all levels participate. In addition, it appears in this case also that women especially, as well as part-timers, are more inclined to buy leisure time, while at higher levels of the staff hierarchy more time tends to be sold than bought.

Quantification of the number of employees in full-time work involved in atypical working hours is not yet feasible. But it is known that in most of the collective agreements of 1996 and 1997, working hours were an issue in negotiations, which often lead to agreements on more flexibility.

Non-standardised jobs with indirect employer-employee relationships

For decades temporary work has been regulated in the Netherlands. Temporary workers are covered by a specific collective agreement, cf below. Many collective agreements commit the companies concerned to maintain primary terms of employment that are equal for permanent and temporary staff. There has been a substantial growth in the deployment of temporary staff in the past few years, and a remarkable extension of the services offered by agencies over the past twelve to eighteen months has taken place. For instance, in about 150 companies 'in-house' offices have been opened by temping agencies on the companies' sites. The intermediary employed by the agency arranges for the supply of flexible workers to one plant twice daily, selects a number of temps who are eligible for company certificates and arranges in-company training programmes. In fact, part of the work of the personnel department is taken over by the temping agency.

Another example is the increasing number of 'pools': employees in a certain region rotate between a number of companies where they perform comparable tasks, but where peaks in production occur at different times. Examples include two companies producing photo-copiers and a company producing fencing. The employees concerned perform core tasks in all three companies at different times of the year, and they are employed by the agency.

Another kind of pool is where employees no longer find employment in their present jobs. They are taken on by the agency for three years, and the agency tries to get them employed in other companies in the region. The original employer supplements wages to the old level for these three years.

Such pools seem to be thirteen to the dozen in several regions and branches of industry. In practice, temping agencies are taking on the entire cycle of provision of employment (a public sector concern until recently), with the proviso that they will limit themselves to people for whom employment seems reasonably feasible.

These forms of flexibilization involve not only temporary staff, but may also explicitly aim to organise the work of permanent employees on a more flexible basis. A striking example which attracted a lot of attention is 'Stork Mobiel': a temporary agency called 'Start' and the metal enterprise 'Stork' set up together a new company, Stork Mobiel. The task of this company has been on the one hand to streamline recruitment and selection of temporary workers for the whole enterprise. On the other hand some of the permanent workers have been transferred to this new firm in order to work in different plants of the enterprise. In the long run Stork aims at transferring all their employers to this new firm. Workers will then no longer be tied to particular activities but can be distributed according to the shifting needs for labour in varying numbers and skill-mixes in different activities.

Subsidised employment

In a European context, the Netherlands is regarded as a country with a very large element of state-subsidised, supplementary employment. The oldest form of subsidised employment is that of sheltered workshops. These have a very long history (Coenen, Hens, Vroomans 1985). Their main aim is to provide sheltered employment for those who have insufficient productivity to participate in the regular labour market, as a result of physical and/or mental handicap. Sheltered employment is offered in two forms: subsidised jobs within a special organization, and so-called secondment (where employees are leased to a company or institution). The provision originated at a time when there was little structural unemployment. In the present situation, where that is no longer the case, sheltered employment is being deployed as an instrument of wider labour market policies, so that it now also employs job-seekers outside the original target group (e.g. unemployed without a handicap).

From the latter half of the nineteen-eighties, two new forms of subsidised employment have come into being: the *Jeugd Werk Garantiewet* (JWG) and the *Banenpool*-scheme. The aim of the JWG is to offer young people, at present up to 24 years of age, who are not enrolled in regular education and are without paid employment, training or a place of work in which to gain experience. In the latter case, this involves jobs created in the public sector, where the youngster concerned is placed (on secondment) by the institution implementing the scheme. The young people are not employed by the enterprise they are working for, but by the implementing institution.

The *Banenpool*-scheme was set up for older long-term unemployed people, whose chances of getting regular paid employment are slim (because of age, lack of training and experience, and any other factor). Subsidised jobs are created for them in the collective or subsidised sector (health care, welfare work etc.). They too are employed by the implementing institution, on the basis of secondment. Their employers pay a hiring charge.

In the early nineties it was recognised, also in politics, that in spite of all measures and the large number of the above mentioned schemes, there remains a hard core of long-term unemployed. For this reason a 'new' offensive was launched including two new schemes for creating supplementary, subsidised employment. The first scheme aimed to create within four years from 1995 on a total of 40,000 subsidised jobs, in the lowest segment of the labour market (Miedema, Valkenburg 1996). These jobs were to be created in the public sector (surveillance, maintenance of public property, etc.) and in a number of subsidised sectors like welfare, child and health care. People under this scheme are employed by the actual employer, whose wage costs and overheads will then be met in full by subsidies. These so-called *Melkert-1* jobs (named after the minister who introduced them) are structural, meaning that subsidies will be continued in the long term.

The second is the so-called *Melkert-2* scheme. Under this scheme the public or private sector employer, who creates a new job and employs a long-term unemployed person, is reimbursed for half the wages (at minimum wage level) for a maximum of two years. The expectation is that the worker after this period will have enhanced opportunities in the regular labour market.

Recent discussions and changes in the social mode of regulation

It can be safely concluded that major changes are taking place in the development of atypical employment. As a consequence we have reached consensus on the point that new regulation is necessary to keep the process of flexibility socially acceptable. At the same time consideration of such regulation has widened discussion about the practical implementation of new forms of flexibility. In the field of subsidised employment, too, major changes are becoming visible.

The next section will take up some of these discussions about policy and new social modes of regulation. We will first describe the general framework of social-economic policy and show how the issue of atypical jobs is strongly connected to the issue of (long term) unemployment. Then, within this general framework, we will elaborate a little more on some specific developments.

The general framework

In the Netherlands the general framework of social policy throughout the eighties and the first part of the nineties, can be characterised as in process of a paradigmatic shift from protection (by providing income or services) to participation (see elsewhere in this volume the contribution of Van Berkel, Coenen and Dekker). Priorities in socio-economic policy since that time have been set to three themes: a very moderate rise in the level of wages, cuts in collective finances and spending, and deregulation of the labour-market. These regulations are supposed to serve the central goals of stimulating economic growth and, as a result of that, creating new jobs.

Restraint on wage increases is strongly stressed in government policy. If necessary, Dutch government can impose such restraint by law on the social partners. In practice it has not used this option, because there was no need to do it. In particular Dutch trade unions have negotiated wages in a 'responsible' way, which means that they have put moderate demands on the bargaining table in exchange for shortening working hours. The underlying argument was that moderate wages and shorter working hours were necessary conditions for growth of employment. In this situation government did not formulate demands about the kind of investments to be made, nor about the kind of jobs to be created with them. In this respect the argument, again, was that this sort of regulation would not stimulate but hamper economic growth. Trade unions did not resist the growth of flexible jobs but stressed that new investments should result in 'full and fulfilling' employment. They stressed this, however, on a very general level. No translation was made (or could be made) to the level of specific companies. In practice in this situation employers were free to create the forms of employment they thought best, which in many cases meant creating atypical jobs.

The second priority is cuts in collective finances and public spending. In this respect the argument is that these cuts reduce the burden on the economy and thus contribute to more favourable conditions for new investments. This argument is strengthened by Dutch acceptance of EMU requirements. This means that the state itself, as an employer, has become one of the major motors behind the rapid growth of atypical employment. Many organizations in the public sector have for years been forced to try to maintain their level of services with shrinking financial means. As a solution to this they have relied heavily on cheap atypical jobs.

The third new type of regulation is the deregulation of the labour-market which has occurred in two ways. First, employers' scope to introduce flexibility has been enlarged. Traditional procedures for firing employees have been changed in favour of employers. Other forms of regulation, like a legally based minimum wage, are under heavy pressure. Second, the rules of social security have been tightened. This means that more people than ever are forced to look actively for a paid job. In the past, for example, single mothers with young children were not obliged to do this. Recently this has been changed. In relation to the growth of atypical jobs the most relevant change concerns the rules for a 'suitable job'. In the past people on social benefits had a right to say 'no' to a particular job, if this job was below their level of qualification and/or less skilled than their last-former job. This rule has been changed too. Under the new regulations people on welfare benefits have to accept almost any job that is offered to them and can be penalized if they do not. These changes in regulations have strengthened the possibilities for employers to offer inferior jobs and get employees to take them.

The three priorities mentioned above are still very strong influences on general socio-economic policy. At the same time, however, there are other and countervailing social modes of regulation: some people and some fractions within the government coalition of social-democrats and liberals are beginning to realise that there has to be a certain level of protection for people who work in atypical jobs. The same goes for the social partners, employers and trade unions. Below we will mention a few of these recent changes in more detail.

Specific developments

In the Netherlands it had long been commonly assumed that the number of flexible *contracts* would not exceed 10 percent. Should this happen, companies would disintegrate to an undesirable degree, and employees would not be able to fulfil their economic contribution to the enterprise to a sufficient degree. This 10 percent was a national average. In a number of branches of industry, with largely unskilled labour and easily divisible tasks (as in health care and retail trade) the percentage was much higher; in a number of others with highly-skilled, specialist jobs, as in the chemical industry, it was much lower.

Meanwhile, we have long passed the 10 percent mark and flexible work is on the increase, not only in semi- and unskilled work, but also in the latter more specialist sectors. In our view that is mainly the result of the changing nature of flexibilization. Permanent staff get flexible working hours and highly skilled personnel are put on flexible contracts. Flexibilization is thus penetrating into the core of the production process.

Besides those for whom temporary employment was previously 'normal' a new group of flexible contract workers is emerging, which also enjoys more protection than the old group of temporary employees. This enhanced protection has materialized especially with the collective agreement for the job agencies. In 1996 national collective agreements were made between unions and employers in the job agency industry. These agreements comprise a number of improvements for temporary staff such as permanent contracts including some pension rights, etc. The improvements are especially favourable for those who work on a temporary basis for fairly long periods of time.

In addition, employer organizations and unions have reached a national 'flexi-accord', which on the one hand provides for simplification of the laws governing dismissal, and on the other hand protects the rights of flexible contract workers in line with collective agreements in the job agency industry.

At the same time temping agencies – no doubt as a result of the innovation of collective agreements – are also experiencing spectacular growth so far as initiating and implementing new forms of flexible work is concerned. The agencies are coming up with one proposal after the other for 'flexipools', 'mobilitypools', 'elderlypools', aimed at management of companies (cf. section 3). Moreover, for the first time banks have offered mortgages to people employed by temping agencies for more than three years, thus enhancing an important element of social participation in this country.

New regulations are also being implemented concerning working times. At the national level the new *Arbeidstijdenwet* (Law governing working hours) was introduced on 1 January 1996, which makes further flexibilization of working hours possible. This law replaces regulations dating from 1919 on the eight-hour day and which in the course of time had accumulated detailed regulations for all kinds of different sectors. The new law has a standard regulation which applies to everybody. Companies can deviate from this with the permission of the works council or staff representative body. In the latter case the law provides a maximum norm for specific agreements. Introduction of the new law has led to adaptation of collective agreements in several sectors of industry, with respect to working hours. Unions have tried to combine these agreements with arrangements for shorter working hours. In a number of cases this has indeed led to experiments in which shorter working hours have been introduced in exchange for more flexibility. Recently, employers have announced that they want to scrap some collective agreements on shorter hours. Arrangements have now been made where employees can opt for a shorter working week of 36 hours for the same pay. Should they want to maintain their present 38-hour week, they will receive a 2 percent lower wage increase than the equivalent in time with a shorter working week.

In many sectors there is a growing tendency towards agreements which represent a minimum provision. In individual companies or for groups of workers special arrangements can then be made. In fact this follows the system of the new law: the standard arrangement applies, unless there is agreement to diverge.

Especially the women's movement and the unions have put pressure on the minister of Welfare and Employment to come up with a law to provide for long-term leave. The idea is that such a law should cater for the needs of employees to perform care tasks, for education and for the improvement of 'employability' (=mobility on the job market).

In the field of subsidised employment three changes are imminent. The first has to do with pay levels. The government a few years ago adopted the principles that 'work is more important than income', and furthermore that subsidised jobs belong to the lowest sector of the labour market. On the basis of these two principles, low levels of pay are now common. An employee in a Melkert-1 job can earn a maximum of 120 percent of the minimum wages per hour. Combined with a maximum working week of 32 hours, that yields a frugal income. At this moment there is a strong movement (in which trade unions, local authorities, but also the minister for Welfare and Employment himself, participate) for raising levels of pay. Secondly, though only tentatively, there have been arguments for changing the present basis of funding. Funds made available for creating supplementary employment in the public sector (especially for the Melkert-1 scheme), should be budgeted directly (and not through subsidies) by the (government) institutions concerned. That would mean a substantial de facto extension of the public sector, and thus a break with the dominant neo-liberal tendency of current political thinking. Thirdly, serious research is going on into the possibility of reducing the traditional divide between the public and the private sector, when deploying subsidised labour. Implementing institutions (sheltered workshops, for instance) are increasingly behaving like regular entrepreneurs who compete with 'really' private enterprises by using their grants. The latter category are slowly coming to see the advantages of using certain forms of subsidised labour. In places where cooperation arises between these two (and several examples can be given), a new phenomenon arises at the interface between the public and private sectors, the so-called 'public enterprise'.

Social participation and full citizenship

The developments in the types of regulation described must be seen partly against the background of the problematic consequences of atypical employment for the security and social participation of citizens.

In pursuit of protection, security and full participation in society by wage-earners, trade unions and policy makers have traditionally given great importance to paid labour and, more especially, to the standard job as a norm and a policy basis. In their own sphere of activity trade unions implemented this through collective bargaining, which meant that collective protection was equal to collective arrangements based on the standard job. In the field of politics it was implemented through the system of social security. In this system too the precondition for building up full entitlement to insurance against unemployment, illness and old-age pensions was a standard job. It hardly needs argument that the growth of atypical employment is eroding this basis for collective protection and social security.

In current economic and social conditions, making a secure living is still primarily based on employment in a standard job, or in comparable jobs in the core of the labour market. In general, this also holds true for entitlement to social security.

Under present circumstances, atypical jobs in the bottom sector of the labour market mean a high level of insecurity for many people. The income they make is uncertain and insufficient to provide for basic needs. In order to make a living, a substantial number are dependent on the larger family to supplement their income. However, if this family-network is lacking, people depend on supplementary benefits, which usually offer only a minimum livelihood. And they may remain dependent on these supplements, because on the basis of their atypical jobs they do not accumulate entitlement to social security provision. Being dependent on benefits not only entails a lot of bureaucratic paperwork (and invasions of privacy). It also means that income from work is deducted from the benefit payments, which in turn makes it hard to rise above the minimum level of income.

The consequence of this is that the problem of modern poverty, recently rediscovered as an issue in national politics, arises not only for people without any form of paid work, but also for people with flexible jobs in the lowest bracket of the labour market. The position of those who depend on forms of subsidised labour also turns out to be problematic in many cases.

The JWG (Youth work guarantee plan) is meant to be an all-encompassing solution (all young people who are neither in education nor in paid work are intended to be covered by this scheme and helped by it), but in practice it does not work that way. Many youngsters drop out at the bottom, because they are unable to follow a course of education or to work, for all sorts of reasons. Their social position deteriorates because when they drop out of the scheme they are no longer entitled to social security payments. At present preparatory courses have been developed for these young people (to prepare them for schooling or work). A large number of people, especially in the job-pool or the Melkert-1 scheme, are faced with an insoluble debt problem. This is partly due to the fact that they were already in debt when they took up a subsidised job. It is also, however, due to the ironical fact that their new status as working persons leads to a rise in their aspirations towards social participation, whereas their actual jobs offer insufficient basis for realising these aspirations. From being on the dole, they become more or less regular employees. This can mean that they are faced with new expenses, or that they think they can afford to spend money on new things. Sometimes these higher expenses are a result of pressure from the social surroundings, because they are regarded as having ample resources available since they are in work. In reality their financial means have increased by very little indeed.

Inclusion within the work plant

Atypical work in the Netherlands is growing rapidly, as we have sketched above. We have seen a growth of atypical jobs not only on the bottom of the labour market, but also by way of new forms of atypical contracts and working hours for permanent workers. To understand the impact of these developments on the inclusion of the individuals into society at large, it is not sufficient to point out the (problematic) consequences of atypical employment for social participation and citizenship. It is at least as important to describe the consequences of atypical employment at the level of work organizations, where many of the processes relevant to social inclusion or exclusion through work take place.

From the point of view of management, employees have to make their contribution to the economic process in the work organization. Social relations within the work place and work organization should enable people to make this contribution. Social relations change when flexibility is introduced in the organization, not least when activities and workers become more separated from each other (see section 3). In a situation in which Human Resource Management is the buzz word in management circles, it is a delicate question which human resources are within, and which are just beyond, the limits of possible deployment. This is not just a question of what demands can be made on people in respect of their direct contribution to the economic production process, but also of their position in the social relations of an enterprise. The question we discuss in this section concerns the requirements atypical employment has to meet for the purpose of socially including employees within the work plant.

Social scientific investigations into the consequences of flexibilization have focussed on segmentation of the labour market (Atkinson 1989; Kluytmans et al. 1992), where a separation is seen between core-workers and the peripheral workforce. The above sketch of the developments in atypical employment makes it clear, even though only by way of a very rough sketch, that this notion of segmentation is too simple.

Harvey (1996), following Rubery, proposes to drop the distinction between core and periphery as the basis of analysis. In his view it is better to analyse the position of the employee with the aid of the concepts of continuity and discontinuity in the employment relationship. Consequently, the employment relationship is analysed by reference to its degree of a continuous connection between employer and employee. Concepts have been sought that will allow unambiguous analysis of the position of employees in relation to the employer. This line of thought can be followed through to useful effect, in our view, not least because the concept of employment relationship then includes the relations which result from their (dis)continuity.

Harvey's analysis is aimed especially at developments on the labour market. In order to analyse also the level of organization adequately, it appears of importance to take not only the employment relationship as such into account, but also its varying character in terms of qualifications, working hours and terms of employment (cf. Huiskamp,1992). The line Harvey draws between continuity and discontinuity may then be complemented by lines between autonomy and control.

With the aid of these concepts we can identify a number of areas where the differentiation of the employee group could become problematic for adequate management of organizations. These problems arise over the degree of (dis)continuity in employment relationships, as well as over variations in such relationships by reference to qualifications, working hours and terms of employment.

A first point concerns the effects of discontinuity of *the employment relationship* itself. This affects communication and information structures in the company. Information technology will play a larger role here in the future. Teleworking is growing fast. The social and cultural aspects of operating a company grow in importance and have to be considered from a different angle. Relationships between colleagues, between executives and leadership, and indeed also the involvement of people in the corporate identity, will have to find new forms. It is difficult to tell where the limits of involvement in the company will be drawn. There is a growing interest in management circles for ‘self-driving teams’, which usually involve permanent staff in working flexible hours: the organization of work within the team is left to its members. One of the aims of such teams is to increase the involvement of employees.

An important question that arises as a result of the changing nature of flexibilization has to do with developments in the *qualifications* of employees. As flexible employees perform more core functions they should be retrained regularly, especially in industries where technological development takes place at a high rate. Enterprises do not just become more flexible, they also need to turn themselves more into ‘learning organizations’ and that requires learning on the part of employees. There may be a new limit to flexibilization here. There is growing emphasis, also in trade unions, on employability of workers: people need to keep up-to-date, so that they increase their versatility in the labour market. Training courses are often too expensive for individuals, and companies will be loath to invest in people who are going to apply their knowledge elsewhere via their agency’s workpool. In this way differences are created between groups of employees in respect of their opportunities to develop their qualifications.

Analysis of the development in *working hours* seems to indicate that differences between groups of employees are diminishing rather than growing in this respect. Permanent workers also need to adapt their working hours to peaks and lows in the production process. For them too, standard hours are losing currency. The limits to transferring the burden of flexible hours onto stand-by workers and the like are well within sight in some places.

Differences in formal participation in decision taking about working hours are still very much in place for workers on short contracts. It is still the case that it is works councils which have the power to approve or reject changes, while people who are with a company for a period of under six months are not eligible for these councils, nor can they elect representatives to them.

The next point we wish to discuss is the regulation of *terms of employment*. Especially where workers work in pools shared by companies in different branches of industry, this can become a complicated matter. In the Netherlands there are different collective agreements for different branches of industry, and a separate collective agreement for the temping agency workers. Workers in agency pools will be employed on the terms in the agency agreement. That raises a number of practical problems (for instance, concerning overwork, supplementary pay, breaks), but when such employment relations become established, this will meet with opposition from the unions because it will lead to the hollowing out of existing agreements in favour of the temping agency collective agreement.

The problems for employees working in subsidised schemes are essentially similar to those for people working on flexible contracts. Here too, inclusion within the work plant is a central issue.

Final remarks

As in many other countries there has been a rapid growth of atypical jobs in the Netherlands. This growth is the result of structural changes and has been stimulated by significant changes in the social mode of regulation, the general framework of socio-economic policy.

Atypical work in the Netherlands is growing not only at the bottom of the labour market. New forms of atypical contracts and working hours for permanent workers are emerging. Enterprises are beginning to separate activities and workers more and more. These developments are giving the labour market a new look. The working situation in the core is showing parallels with that of the periphery, as a result of changes there too in working hours or contracts. Peripheral workers (for instance those employed in a pool operated by the temping agency) nowadays work in jobs formerly reserved for core workers. And some temporary staff now have perks which offer protection comparable to that offered to permanent staff.

On the one hand there is no reason to believe that this development will stop or fundamentally change course in the foreseeable future. On the other hand, however, there are modest, but relevant countervailing changes. New forms of regulation are beginning to come up. So far as employers are concerned, these new forms of regulation are not only and perhaps not even primarily inspired by social considerations, but rather by economic ones. Yet they do give grounds to argue that the process of flexibilization is reaching certain limits of economic rationality. On the one hand this potentially gives new scope for trade unions to introduce social considerations into the process. On the other hand, however, there is also the danger of widening the gaps between different groups of people who work in atypical employment. The fact that new forms of regulation are primarily inspired by economic considerations means that they are so far mainly confined to people who work in relatively 'good' atypical jobs. If new regulations are developed, they will have to be widened to those people who really are in the lower part of the labour market. There is still a long and hard way to go to achieve this.

References

Atkinson, J. (1989), 'Flexibilisering van de arbeid in de Engelse industrie en dienstverlening', in *Ter Elfder Ure 41, Het ontwerpen van arbeidsprocessen,* Nijmegen: SUN.

Baglioni, G. and Crouch, C. (1990), *European Industrial Relations; the challenge of flexibility,* London: Sage.

Beck, U., Giddens, A. and Lash, S. (1994), *Reflexive Modernization,* Polity Press, Cambridge.

Beukema, L. (1995), 'Differentiatie van belangen als uitgangspunt voor nieuw beleid', in H. Coenen (ed.), *De vakbeweging na 2000,* Utrecht: Van Arkel.

CBS (1996), *Figures on 'jobs of employees by type of contract,* Den Haag: CBS.

Coenen, H. (ed.) (1995), *De vakbeweging na 2000,* Utrecht: Van Arkel.

Coenen, H., Hens, H. and Vroomans, L. (1986), *De WSW gewogen,* Groningen: Konstapel.

Van Dijck, J.J.J. (ed.) (1995), *Baas over eigen (loop)baan,* Houten: Stenfert Kroese.

Ferner, A. and Hyman, R. (1992), *Industrial Relations in the New Europe,* Oxford: Blackwell.

Harvey M. (1996), *Varieties of continuity and discontinuity,* paper presented in working group 'Arbeid en Participatie', University of Utrecht.

Huiskamp, R. (1992), 'Arbeidsverhoudingen en sociotechniek: een nieuwe benadering', in *M&O, Tijdschrift voor organisatiekunde en sociaal beleid,* Alphen a/d Rijn: Samson Bedrijfsinformatie.

Kluytmans, F. and Meeren, W.Vander (ed.) (1992), *Management van human resources. Stromen, stimuleren, structureren,* Deventer/Heerlen: Kluwer Bedrijfswetenschappen /Open Universiteit.

Lash, S. and Urry, J. (1994), *Economies of Signs and Space,* London: Sage.

Leisink, P., Leemput, J. van and Vilrokx, J. (1996), *The challenges to trade unions in Europe; Innovation or Adaptation*, Cheltenham: Elgar.

Miedema, F. and Valkenburg, B. (1996), *Melkert-I onder de loep,* Onderzoeksrapport, Rotterdam.

Ormel, B. (1986), 'Thuiswerk in de marge van de arbeidsverhoudingen', in *Tijdschrift voor Arbeid en Bewustzijn*, Vol. 10, No. 1.

Timmer, J. and Doorman-Vreugdenhill, A. (1992), *Vrouwen en flexibel werk; achtergronden en afwegingen,* Paper, Amsterdam.

Valkenburg, B. (1995), 'Participatie in sociale bewegingen', Utrecht: Van Arkel.

Valkenburg, B. and Beukema, L. (1996), 'Atypical jobs as a challenge for the modernization of trade unions', in *Transfer,* Vol. 2, No. 4.

Valkenburg, B. and Zoll, R. (1995), 'Modernization, Individualization and Solidarity: Two perspectives on European Trade Unions Today', in *European Journal of Industrial Relations,* Vol. 1, No. 1.

7. Non-standard employment, social exclusion, and the household: Evidence from Britain

ROSEMARY CROMPTON

Introduction

In this paper, we will examine the broad outline of recent British employment trends. These trends have been accompanied by increasing social exclusion and polarisation – that is, the widening of the gap between the poorest and the better-off members of society. In part, this is because relative wage rates have declined amongst the lowest paid (Rowntree 1995), but polarisation has also taken place because the distribution of paid employment amongst men, women, and households is itself undergoing a process of change with the gradual decline of the 'male breadwinner' model. Women's employment has not only shown a steady increase, but as the levels of their qualifications and employment experiences have improved, an increasing number have begun to move into higher-level jobs. This trend has contributed to a growing gap between 'employment-rich' and 'employment poor' households – and in the case of the latter, neither adult may be in employment.

These developments have been accompanied by the growth of 'non-standard' – that is, not full time and/or permanent – employment. The expansion of 'non-standard' employment reflects not only the shift to services and the increase in women's employment, but in the British case, has been positively encouraged by government policies which sought to deregulate the employment relationship – a process which included the removal of many labour market protections (such as Wages Councils, which once regulated wages in the lowest paid industries). 'Employment rich' households, it will be suggested, have played their part in generating 'non-standard' employment in Britain. Thus it may be suggested that although material improvements for some women have been achieved, this has been in a context of increasing inequalities overall. However, it is argued that the answer lies not in a return to the 'male breadwinner' model, but rather, through a combination of both positive employment regulation and the increased breaking down of the gender division of labour.

With the election of the Conservative Government in 1979, 'de-industrialisation' in Britain proved to be particularly rapid. Although it is true that industries such as steel and coal would probably have declined in any case, they provided an arena for disputes between the Government and the Trade Union movement which were not only an important background to the erosion of employment rights and protections, but also resulted in a very rapid 'shake-out' of traditional industry and rising levels of unemployment. Unemployment rose through the 1980s, but then declined towards the end of the decade, rising again in the early 1990s (after the end of the consumer-led Lawson boom). At the moment, employment in Britain is on an upward trend. However, under a half of new jobs created in recent years have been for permanent, full-time employees, and the majority are 'non-standard' jobs.

Non-standard employment

'Non-standard' employment relates to casual, part-time, and short contract working, as well as self-employment and outworking. Such employment has served to increase the flexibility of the workforce and, it is argued, economic competitiveness. It has therefore been, to varying degrees, positively encouraged as a policy option by governments and indeed has been endorsed in the EU White Paper (1993). More negatively, however, non-standard employment is also associated with low wages and job insecurity and its increase may therefore contribute to rising levels of social exclusion. It is important to recognise that the increase in non-standard forms of employment is not only a consequence of deliberate policy initiatives. Indeed, some would argue that policy changes in this area are themselves but reflections of deeper structural changes in productive activity associated with the relative decline of manufacturing industry and the growth of services, together with changes in the social and economic status of women.

In Britain, employment in services has grown from 53 percent of total employment in 1971, to 73 percent in 1993 (Employment Gazette 1994). The growth of service employment has run in parallel with the crumbling of the 'social settlement' associated with 'Fordism', in which 'standard employment' was full-time, relatively well protected (e.g. dismissals could not be arbitrary, extra and/or unsocial hours had to be paid for), and relatively secure. These jobs were also usually occupied by prime age males. The major power bases that secured the social settlement were the Trade Unions, and Trade Unionism was strongest in manufacturing industry. As we have noted, such industries have been in rapid decline in employment terms, and number of factors make the (re)development of old-style trade unionism in services not very likely. These include the 'people work' nature of much service employment (where industrial action would be likely to have more of an impact on [potentially] vulnerable clients than the employer), and extensive working of shifts and unusual hours. Working hours have been extended by the growth of 'just-in-time' systems, and extended opening hours in both retail and leisure services. None of these conditions provides the homogeneous employment conditions, and physical proximity, which contributed to the growth of 'old style' unionism.

The crumbling of the social settlement in Britain, and the growth of employment flexibility and non-standard employment were associated with a political swing in a neo-liberal direction and a corresponding emphasis upon the 'marketisation' of society. Social protections have been dismissed (and removed) as bureaucratic impediments to economic performance, 'rates for the job' replaced by individualised payment systems, flexibility promoted as a means of maximising the use of labour power. In some contrast to the rest of Europe, the political promotion of these trends has been most extensive in Britain.[1] The most important developments have been:

- Part-time work. The number of part-time jobs in Britain increased from 3.3 million in 1971 to 5.9 million in 1994, and the proportion of part-time workers increased from 19 percent in 1978 to 28 percent in 1994. Part-time workers are predominantly women, and in 1994, 78 percent of part-time jobs were held by women (Beatson 1995). Britain has the lowest level of state-provided childcare in Europe, and as we shall see, many women work part-time in order to accommodate childcare. However, part-time work for men is actually increasing faster than for women, as in 1978, women were 82 percent of part-time employees. The extent of part-time work in Britain is higher than in other European countries, and the hours worked by part-timers tend to be shorter. This is believed to be a consequence of British employment legislation (or rather, the lack of it). Part-time workers who work for less than 16 hours a week have to have 5 years continuous employment before they are eligible for employment protection legislation, and employees who work less than 8 hours a week are not covered at all (a recent European-level decision means that this legislation will be amended). In practice, part-time employees do not seem to be more insecure than full-time workers despite their lack of legislative protection. Salary levels, however are lower. In addition, employers do not have to pay National Insurance contributions for part-time workers earning less than £57 per week (in 1995).

- Self-employment. In contrast to part-time employment, self-employment is predominantly male, and in 1994, 75 percent of the self-employed were men (nevertheless, the proportion of self-employed is rising amongst women as well). Self-employment fell during the 1970s before growing rapidly, by 88 percent, between 1979 and 1990 (government inducements such as 'business start-ups' were in operation during this period). Figures for small business failure suggest that 60 percent are wound up within a decade (Observer April 13 1997). Over the period 1979-90, self-employment has increased from 7 percent to 13 percent. However, measuring self-employment is difficult, as people's perception as to whether they are self-employed does not necessarily correspond to their status in law (e.g. in the building trade and leisure industry, 'casual' self-employed workers may work for the same company for many years or even decades). This will affect figures given by, e.g., the LFS (Labour Force Survey), which is a household survey.
- Temporary employment. LFS data suggests that the number of temporary workers changed little between 1984 and 1991. From 1992, however, there has been a very rapid increase in the incidence of temporary work (it may be noted that one historic reason for the low level of temporary work in Britain is that employment protection for permanent workers is extremely weak). Much of the growth in temporary work has come from the more widespread use of fixed-term contracts. Another form of temporary work which is on the increase, however, is the use of agency workers (Forde 1997). Workers are hired out to firms from the employment agency on a temporary basis. Roughly 10 percent of the temporary workforce are agency workers (i.e. under 1 percent of the employed workforce). The numbers are small, but as suggested above, this is one of the fastest growing types of non-standard employment, and has more than trebled in the past ten years. Some major companies undergoing restructuring – for example, Natwest bank – now has most of its counter staff drawn from agency workers. Fiftytwo percent of agency

workers are women. In contrast to the situation with regard to part-time workers, a majority of agency workers sampled by Forde (1997) said that they would prefer a full-time job.

Thus over the last four years, in Britain, only 38 percent of new jobs created have been for permanent full-time employees. It might be argued that this development is a positive one. Besides the economic benefits of increased flexibility (this issue will not be discussed in this paper), the growth of non-standard employment might be seen as making it easier to combine paid work and family life.[2] However, the New Earnings Survey shows that in the case of part-time work rates of pay in non-standard employment are considerably lower than in standard employment. As we shall see, the distribution of paid employment between households – including non-standard employment – has also contributed to growing inequality.

Women's employment

Women constituted 29 percent of the labour force in Britain in 1911, and 29 percent in 1951, but this had risen to 34 percent by 1966 and 43 percent by 1991. Women's employment levels have been rising whilst men's have been in decline. Amongst women, it is employment amongst mothers that has been rising the most rapidly. Between 1984 and 1994, the economic activity rate for mothers (i.e. women with dependent children under 16) increased from 55 percent to 64 percent, compared with an increase from 66 percent to 71 percent for all working women (Sly 1994). Indeed, the greatest increase in labour market participation since 1984 has been amongst women with children under five; from 37 percent in 1984 to 52 percent in 1993/4. The proportion of women in employment goes up as children get older, and over three quarters of married women whose youngest child is aged between 11-15 are in employment. There has been a small decline in the number of women working full-time – reflecting the decline in the number of full-time jobs.

The pattern of the increase in mother's employment has been moulded to the contours of the existing structures of household inequality. Thus mothers in couples are more likely to be economically active (67 percent) than are lone mothers (48 percent). Whereas a half of mothers in couple relationships with children under five are working, this is true of only a quarter of lone mothers with children of the same age. The unemployment rate of lone mothers is 20 percent, as compared to only 7-8 percent for mothers in couples. Lone parent families (and we should remember that 20 percent of all children in Britain live in lone parent families) are much more likely to be families in which no-one is employed than are two parent families. Both parents are unemployed in only 11 percent of two-parent families with children under sixteen, but 61 percent of lone mothers and 46 percent of lone fathers are not in employment. A similar pattern of cumulative disadvantage, reflected in women's employment, is also to be found in couple families. Mothers whose husbands/partners are unemployed are less likely to be in employment (24 percent) than are those with employed husbands (68 percent).

Employment amongst mothers, therefore, is more likely to be found amongst women with partners or husbands than women who are lone parents, and amongst the wives of men who are employed rather than the wives of men who are unemployed. A similar pattern of inequality-reinforcing employment amongst women is to be seen in the relative rates of mother's employment by qualification level. In 1993/4, 82 percent of mothers with higher (i.e. above degree level) qualifications were in employment, as compared to 65 percent of mothers with qualifications at or below A level, and only 40 percent of mothers with no qualifications. Mothers with higher levels of qualification are also more likely to be in full-time employment.

Mothers, particularly mothers of young children, are, therefore, the fastest growing section of the labour force. Within this group, however, employment is rising most rapidly of all amongst well-educated women living in a partnership (Harrop and Moss 1994), and these women are more likely to work full-time, rather than part-time.

Rubery (1994: 345) has argued that in Britain, there is a 'social norm' that it is appropriate for women with children to work part-time but not full-time. One consequence of this norm is that British men work the longest hours in Europe (i.e. to 'compensate' for the short hours worked by British women and make up the family budget. See Rubery et al. 1997). However, this norm is not universal but is cross-cut by social class. Higher-educated, higher earning women are more likely to work full-time even when they have young children. Together with the fact that deregulation has resulted in very high incomes at the top of the range, and that persons earning these incomes are likely to be sharing households, then the increased employment of women has widened inequality at the level of the household (Rowntree 1995).

In the next sections, therefore, we will discuss two factors associated with these trends: (i) household inequality, and (ii) the growth of domestic, childcare, and related employment to replace the household labour once carried out by middle-class women. This latter development might be seen, potentially, as an important source of paid work and thus new jobs. However, as we shall see, domestic service and related jobs tend to be, on the whole, both relatively low level and poorly paid.

Household Inequality

The major factor associated with growing household inequality in Britain has been the rise in the proportion of households in which no-one is working. In this respect there are also significant geographical variations (reflecting variations in levels of unemployment), and the number of workless households is greater in the older industrial areas of the Midlands and North, as well as in Scotland and Wales. In 1990, the same number of *individuals* of working age did not work as in 1975, but twice the number of *households* had no income from work (Rowntree 1995). The number of individuals in workless households has risen as follows:

Table 7.1 Numbers of People Living in Workless Households

1975	1984	1988	1992	1995
1,687	3,481	3,648	4,043	4,477

Source: Rowntree 1995

As noted above, social polarisation has not only been a consequence of the growing gap between 'work rich' and 'work poor' households, but also the growing dispersion of wages. From 1966 to 1979, median, top decile and bottom decile male wage rates rose gradually and more or less in tandem. After 1978, however, the experiences of the three parts of the distribution diverged: wages for the lowest paid hardly changes, and by 1992 were lower in real terms than in 1975; median wages grew by 35 percent; but high wages grew by 50 percent (data to 1992, source Rowntree Report 1995). The impact of fluctuations in employment levels and declining real wage rates has also been exacerbated by other trends – most notably, an increasing rate of family breakdown. Britain now has one of the highest rates of divorce in Europe. These trends have led to a widening dispersion of household incomes (see Table 2).

The growth of 'work rich' and 'work poor' households, together with wage disparities, is exacerbated by the fact that more of the 'economically active' in 1994 will be in non-standard employment than in 1978, given that, as we have seen, it is this kind of employment that has been on the increase, rather than permanent, full-time, jobs.

Table 7.2 UK Household Average Disposable Income (£1995 prices) and Economically Active

	Quintile group 1	2	3	4	5	All household
1971	4603	7613	10297	13477	20763	11352
1978	5309	8561	12151	15768	24050	13171
1994	5515	9089	12773	18195	32293	15572
Real Increase 1971-94	£912	£1475	£2476	£4718	£11530	£4220
Annual Growth	0.8%	0.8%	1.0%	1.5%	2.3%	
Economically Active per Household (number)						
1978	0.2	0.9	1.3	1.7	2.1	1.4
1994	0.3	0.6	1.1	1.7	2.1	1.2

Source: Froud et al. 1997

Domestic Service Employment

To summarise our argument so far: a combination of social and political, as well as economic and technological, factors have contributed to increasing social and economic polaristion, and thus exclusion, at the level of both labour force and household in Britain. It might be argued, however, that the present situation represents merely a period of transition, rather than an end state. Technological change means that industry now employs fewer people, social change means that more women are both in employment, and in independent households. This latter change, however, will ultimately lead to the creation of more jobs to replace women's unpaid household labour. Thus this kind of argument suggests that we should see the total amount of work required by societies not so much as having declined, but rather, as having been shifted around – in particular, from the household to the market sphere. In this section, therefore, we will examine both the manner in which women in Britain combine employment and family caring, as well as the kinds of jobs which have emerged to supplement or replace women's domestic labour.

As Moss has argued: 'Working parents (in Britain) with children under three must rely almost entirely on either the private market or their social networks' (1991:125). Another way in which mothers combine paid work with childcare is for them to work from home. Mothers of older children may be able to find work which takes place only during school hours, and of course, older children do not necessarily require permanently-available care – maternal or otherwise. Table 3 summarises the pattern of childcare arrangements amongst working mothers in Britain today (more than one form of childcare may be used by working mothers, so the percentages in the table add to more than 100).

Table 7.3 Child care arrangements of all working women with dependent children, 1994 (multiple response, percentages)

Childminder or nanny	13
Nursery, crèche, nursery school or playgroup	11
After school or holiday playscheme	4
Partner	33
Parents/parents in law	32
Other relatives and friends	18
Children old enough to look after themselves	24
Only works when children are at school	22
Works at home	8
Number of mothers	3438

Source: Adapted from Finlayson, Ford and Marsh, 1994.

It can be seen that by far the greater proportion of childcare relies on networks of families and friends (including partners) and may be described as 'informal'. The proportion of mothers paying for individual childminders or nannies is very small (indeed, only 2 percent of all working mothers in the survey said that they employed nannies), and nearly a third of mothers avoided the cost of childcare by only working when children were at school or working from home. The paid employment of these mothers, therefore, would obviously be 'non-standard'. Most importantly, however, it would appear that the amount of paid employment *directly* generated as a consequence of the increase in women's paid work is in fact rather low.

Childcare arrangements, however, will obviously vary considerably according to the age of the child. Table 4, therefore, gives details of childcare arrangements for children of different ages. 'Professional' childcare denotes childcare that is paid for – that is, childminders, nannies, nurseries, crèches, nursery school or playgroup, 'informal' childcare includes partners, parents, and friends, and double counting has been avoided by identifying mothers using a combination of professional and informal childcare separately. 'Avoid child care' includes mothers who only work school hours, or who work from home.

Table 7.4 Child care arrangements of working mothers by age of their youngest child, 1994, percentages

	0-4	5-10	11-15	16+	All
Professional only	24	10	2	*	12
Combination	23	10	3	-	11
Informal only	48	54	40	8	45
Child old enough	*	*	28	78	14
Avoid child care	5	26	28	13	19
Numbers:	1016	950	896	213	3087

Source: Adapted from Finlayson, Ford and Marsh, 1994.

Table 4 shows that the use of paid childcare is heavily concentrated amongst mothers of children under school age – this group of mothers, it will be remembered, is the most rapidly expanding section of the labour force, and is most likely to be highly educated and in good jobs – but nevertheless, nearly a half of these mothers rely on childcare help from partners, parents, and friends. Paid childcare drops off steeply as children get older, as might have been expected.

Surveys of childcare arrangements similar to that used in Tables 3 and 4 were also carried out in 1991 and 1992, so some idea of recent trends can be given. The proportion of mothers using any professional childcare has risen from 20 percent to 23 percent – reflecting the increase in employment of mothers with young children, the group most likely to use paid childcare. The costs of childcare have also risen, from a mean of 110p per hour worked by the mother in 1991, to 154p per hour worked in 1994. Employment amongst mothers of young children might be rising, therefore, but these figures suggest that mothers have to buy themselves back in to the labour market, and that the costs of this buy back are on the increase.

The increase in the level of paid childcare, of course, means that the numbers of employees – usually women – providing this childcare is increasing as well. The British government's policy has been to encourage the growth in the market for private service provision, rather than to organise public provision of these services. Thus not only childcare, but also a range of other caring services once provided within the household (i.e. by women) are now a source of paid employment.

It is difficult to be precise about the numbers of people who are now employed to carry out work once done by women in the home. For example, one of the fastest growing parts of the service sector is the 'hospitality industry' – hotels and catering. Although some of this work might be a substitute for home cooking, most of this expansion will reflect changing patterns of consumption. Table 5 gives details of more specifically 'caring' occupations:

It may be seen that, as might have been expected, caring jobs are overwhelmingly 'women's work'. Only 10 percent of paid carers in these categories are men, and in some categories e.g. childcare and related – men are only 1 percent. The extent of this kind of paid work has been increasing in the recent past, but still only represents less than one percent of all paid jobs. With the exception of nursery nurses (who will be professionally qualified), it can be seen that rates of pay in domestic and caring occupations are low, particularly in the case of men (note that the hourly rates of pay given in Table 5 are for full-time employees, hourly rates for part-time workers are even lower). These figures suggest, therefore, that in Britain, the kind of employment generated as a consequence of mothers' paid work is relatively low level and poorly paid.

Only a minority of households, of course, will actually employ paid domestic workers directly, but this minority is on the increase given the growing proportion of well-qualified mothers who are returning to work whilst their children are young. Gregson and Lowe (1994) have estimated the pattern of increase in demand for paid domestic workers by analysing the advertisements for such jobs (in magazines such as *The Lady).* The advertised demand for such workers increased very rapidly – in fact, more than doubled – throughout the 1980s, but fell off with the onset of the economic recession in 1990. They found that the kinds of jobs advertised changed over the decade. In the early 1980s, the demand for paid domestic labour was mainly for housekeepers and mother's helps, whilst by the end of the 1980s, the major category of demand was for nannies to care for young children – reflecting the increasing number of mothers of young children staying in work. Childcare is obviously very important, but their interviews with employers of domestic labour also found that very often, working couples paid for domestic help in order to give them more 'quality time' with each other, as well as to resolve conflicts over who did the domestic work. It was the most unpopular tasks – in particular, household cleaning – which led to conflict, and it was men's refusal to clean (or rather, their inability to 'see' household dirt) which had led to the employment of a cleaner.

The wages of paid domestic workers are low. Actual pay levels for cleaning reported by Gregson and Lowe in the early 1990s (p 208-9) range from £2.50 to £4 an hour (usually 'cash in hand'). Many nannies live in and may receive benefits 'in kind' but even taking this into account, salaries are low. In the North-east, 88 percent of nannies did not have a signed contract of employment. The average gross annual earnings of nannies in the families they studied were £4800 in the North-east, and £7200 in the South-east.

We have seen, therefore, that employment is rising fastest amongst the mothers of young children, and that there has been a corresponding increase in the demand for childcare. Most childcare is arranged through informal sources – partners, families or friends – or the mother adjusts her own paid work to accommodate childcare – but the level of professional (i.e. paid) childcare has been increasing, as has its cost. In Britain, there is very little by way of publicly provided childcare, and families must make private arrangements – either paid or unpaid. Such employment is on the increase, but is largely unregulated and poorly paid. Gregson and Lowe suggest that as long as such caring is left to 'private' arrangements, this situation will persist.

Table 7.5 Domestic Caring Occupations

	Total	Men	Women	Hourly rate (including over-time): pence Men	Women
644 Care assistants	28276	1705	26571	514	449
650 Nursery nurses	5925	72	5853	*	550
651 Playgroup leaders	1957	66	1891	*	*
659 Other childcare and related	19211	196	19015	*	369
670 Domestic housekeepers	3082	347	2735	*	*
958 Cleaners, domestics	77860	11784	66076	466	417
Total %	100%	10%	90%		
All manual workers				670	481
All workers				934	751

* Insufficient numbers in LFS

Source: 1991 census; 1996 Labour Force Survey

In summary: in Britain, many women with children take up flexible and/or non-standard employment (such as homeworking) in order to manage childcare. This strategy will not be likely to generate more jobs, it is more likely that the labour intensity of individual women will be increased. Other women (most usually, those in full-time jobs), will seek to supplement or replace their domestic labour with that of paid workers (either privately, or through bought-in services). However, the employment generated by the increased demand for paid caring would seem to be likely to be both non-standard and low paid.

Discussion

This paper has focused on the links between non-standard employment, the expansion of women's employment, and its impact on the household. In Britain, these issues are closely related. One reason for this is the virtual absence of state-provided childcare. The expansion of deregulated, non-standard employment, and its distribution within households together with the emergence of 'work rich' and 'work poor' households, has led to growing economic and social polarisation. As many commentators have noted, children are major losers. Children are disproportionately represented in work poor households, and many of these children will live in poverty, growing up in households in which paid work is virtually unknown. At the other end of the spectrum, parents of young children working very long hours (particularly fathers) find it difficult to give sufficient attention to them. Indeed, as far as children and young people are concerned, something of a moral panic seems to be opening up, sometimes accompanied by calls for women to return to the home.[3]

However, (in most countries), the increase in the status of women, of which the expansion of women's employment is but one manifestation, is unlikely to be put into reverse. It is no doubt the case that many families are two-earner families out of necessity. However, a growing number of women are signalling the extent of their commitment to employment by gaining qualifications and taking up higher level jobs (Crompton and Sanderson 1990). For example, in Britain, men were 80 percent of higher-level employers and managers in 1981, but only 71 percent by 1991. Men were 90 percent of professionals in 1981, but 87 percent of self-employed, and 82 percent of employed, professionals by 1991 (Crompton 1995). In particular occupations, the recorded rate of increase in female participation is even more dramatic (Hakim 1992). In the UK, the percentage of women lawyers, judges and solicitors has increased by 13 percent between 1981-91, the percentage of female accountants by 12 percent and the percentage of doctors by 7 percent.

Classification difficulties make cross-national comparisons problematic, but a similar pattern of female entry into higher-level occupations seems to be taking place everywhere. In the US, between 1983 and 1995 the percentage of women lawyers and judges increased by 10 percent, accountants by 15 percent, and doctors by 9 percent. In France, between 1982 and 1990 the percentage of women in legal professions increased by 8 percent, accountants by 9 percent, and doctors by 9 percent (Crompton

1997). In Spain and Italy, women have made rapid inroads into jobs in higher education, and in Spain and France, women are an increasing share of computer professionals. Women have increased their share of higher-grade jobs in public administration in Belgium, Germany, Spain, Italy, the Netherlands and the UK, and they have also improved their relative levels of employment in Banking. Rubery and Fagan (1993) argue that underlying this general tendency for women to improve their occupational positions are changes in recruitment policies supporting the direct entry to higher-level positions of the well-qualified – and women are everywhere improving their formal educational qualifications.

We have noted above the concern which is being expressed as to the impact of parental employment on children. Even more dramatic in the long run, however, might be that children do not get born at all, and one of the most striking consequences of the increase in women's employment is the declining birth rate. Although rising levels of women's employment are obviously not the only cause of declining fertility, it is clearly a contributory factor to the decline in the birth rate, which is taking place all over Europe. The EU as a whole has seen a decline in fertility from a rate of 2.61 in 1960 to 1.48 in 1992, and in all European countries (with the exception of Ireland) fertility is now below replacement level. Indeed, it has been suggested that 'Below-replacement fertility has emerged as a characteristic feature of post-industrial society' (Sporton 1993). In Belgium, Denmark, Germany, France, Luxembourg Netherlands and the UK the decline in fertility rates began in the 1960s and slowed after the mid 1970s (although still remaining below replacement level). In Greece, Spain, Italy and Portugal, there was no corresponding decline in fertility from the 1960s, but an even more rapid decrease from the mid 1970s. In 1991, fertility rates in these Southern countries had reached their lowest ever: 1.30 in Spain, and 1.28 in Italy (Social Portrait of Europe, Luxembourg 1996). As we have seen in our discussion above, these are also the countries in which women's entry into higher-level positions appears to have improved very recently. Recent commentaries suggest that there will be no significant reversal in fertility trends in the future. Demographers attribute these trends to greater opportunities for female labour force participation, and the fertility-reducing practice of cohabitation (Sporton 1993:61).

Our review of non-standard employment in Britain has been a largely negative one. We have argued that its expansion has contributed to growing economic and social polarisation at the level of the household, together with increasing insecurity. It should be stressed, however, that this situation is not inevitable. As we have argued, the expansion of services, and the growth of women's employment, (two major features which we have associated with the expansion of non-standard employment) reflect social trends which are not going to be turned back. Traditional manufacturing methods are not going to be revived, married women are not going to return to domesticity – in short, the conditions which originally generated the pressures towards a standard male breadwinner wage will not return. Longer retail opening hours, the need to buy caring services, space for leisure as a consequence of the sharing of market work between men and women together with shorter working hours – all of these are features which might be associated with a 'family friendly' employment mix. Properly regulated caring jobs could provide security and careers. Employment flexibility might be achieved via investments in skills training and supported by social insurance, rather than via the development of a chronically insecure workforce. However, the deregulated expansion of non-standard employment in Britain has contributed to a vicious spiral of household polarisation (Rubery 1994).

Two major factors might serve to interrupt this downward spiral. First, as feminists have argued, we should seek to deconstruct the gender coding generated by the 'male breadwinner' model of employment, in which a single ('family') wage was held to be sufficient to support a 'breadwinner' and his family, whilst women were held responsible for caregiving and domestic labour (Fraser 1994). Thus one development which might help to check current trends in the direction of increased polarisation would be for men's work to become more like that of women, rather than *vice versa*. Since the Second World War, increasing numbers of women have combined 'breadwinning' (i.e., paid work) with caregiving. If men, as well as women, were expected to provide care (that is, take up their proportionate share of domestic labour) as well as earning a wage we might begin to see changes in the organisation of paid employment, as well as unpaid care. Working hours (in employment) might become shorter, and the status of caregiving given due recognition.

Thus secondly, it is important to develop forms of caring and paid domestic employment, in both the public and private spheres, which provide reasonably regular, secure, and well-paid work. Changing this situation would require a much higher level of bureaucratic state intervention than has come to be seen as acceptable in increasingly 'marketised' societies. The example of Britain, however, might be seen as evidence for raising, rather than removing, the level of state intervention in respect of employment, although it is of course necessary to keep the nature of this intervention under constant review. There can be no return to the past, but we should be thinking beyond the market as far as the future of work, of all kinds, is concerned.

Notes

1 It is as yet too early to judge whether the election of the Labour Government (1997) will substantially reverse these trends.
2 Hakim (1996) has argued that this is the main reason why 'uncommitted' women take up part-time work. There are, however, a number of problems with her argument. See Crompton forthcoming.
3 For example, press features emphasizing the superiority of 'stay-at-home' mothers, which are a regular occurrence in such papers as the *Daily Mail.* Paradoxically, such outlets would also favour deregulated employment and the market determination of wages – which is one of the factors which has led to pressures for two incomes within the household.

References

Beatson M. (1995b), *Labour Market Flexibility,* London: Department of Employment.
Crompton R. (1995), 'Women's Employment and the "Middle Class"', in T. Butler and M. Savage (eds) *Social Change and the Middle Classes,* London: UCL Press.
Crompton R. (1997), *The Gendered Restructuring of the Middle Classes,* ANU Canberra, August.
Crompton R. and Sanderson K. (1990), *Gendered Jobs and Social Change,* London: Unwin Hyman.
Finlayson L.R., Ford, R. and Marsh, A. (1996), 'Paying more for child care', *Employment Gazette* July, pp. 295-303.
Forde C. (1997), *Temporary employment agency working: issues and evidence,* Paper given at the Labour Process Conference, Edinburgh.
Fraser N. (1994), 'After the Family Wage', *Political Theory,* Vol 22, pp. 591-618.
Froud J. et al. (1997), *From social settlement to household lottery,* Paper given at the Labour Process Conference, Edinburgh.
Gregson N. and Lowe, M. (1994), *Servicing the middle classes,* London: Routledge.
Hakim, C. (1992), Explaining Trends in Occupational Segregation: The Measurement, Causes, and Consequences of the Sexual Division of Labour, *European Sociological Review,* 8(2): 127-152.
Hakim, C. (1996), *Key Issues in Women's Work,* London: The Athlone Press Ltd.
Harrop, A. and Moss, P. (1994), Working parents: trends in the 1980s, *Employment Gazette,* October, pp. 343-51.
Joseph Rowntree Foundation (1995), *Inquiry into Income and Wealth.* York.
Moss P. (1991), 'Day care for young children in the United Kingdom', in Melhuish and Moss (eds), *Day Care for Young Children,* London: Tavistock/Routledge.
Rubery J. (1994), 'The British production regime: a societal-specific system?', *Economy and Society.*

Rubery J. and Fagan, C. (1993), *Occupational Segregation of Women and Men in the European Community,* EC Brussels.
Rubery J. et al. (1997), *Explaining working-time patterns by gender: sociatal and sectoral effects,* Paper given at the Labour Process Conference, Edinburgh.
Sly, F. (1994), 'Mothers in the Labour Market', *Employment Gazette,* 1994, pp. 403-413.
Sporton D. (1993), 'Fertility: the lowest level in the world', in D. Noin and R. Woods (eds), *The Changing Population of Europe,* Oxford: Blackwell.

8. Employment and social exclusion: The policy context and the policy response in the United Kingdom

PETE ALCOCK

Labour market change

In the last quarter of the twentieth century profound changes have been experienced in social structure and social policy in the UK, as they have in all other advanced industrial countries. These changes have been characterised by regulation theorists as the collapse of the Fordist model of production and accumulation, leading to the end of the period of socio-economic development associated with the expansion of mass manufacturing production and the move towards a regime of fragmented and flexible production, sometimes dubbed 'post-Fordism'. In fact the shift to post-Fordism is a complex and disputed process of socio-economic change, as discussed by Lind and Møller in the introductory chapter; and the existence of a post-Fordist regime of regulation is itself disputed (see Tickell and Peck, 1995). Nevertheless the changes are real and they have resulted in very different patterns of labour market participation in the UK in the 1990s; and these have led to very different welfare and policy needs, perhaps resulting in a shift in the model of welfare too, as we shall return to discuss later.

Many of the changes to labour market participation in the UK have been summarised by Crompton elsewhere in this volume, so I will not repeat them here. In short they have resulted in the development of a wide range of non-standard work patterns – a move away from the employment model of the full-time male breadwinner and towards a wider mix of employment types and a different balance between male and female participation in the labour market[1]. These changes have been driven largely by the forces of production rather than the employment preferences of men and women, although they have of course had important positive consequences for some, especially women employees able to balance part-time or temporary employment with caring commitments at home.

For many, however – and particularly for the male breadwinners with experience only of full-time manufacturing work – these changes have had significant negative consequences.

- Unemployment has grown in depth – and length.
- Levels of economic inactivity have grown significantly.
- Pay differentials have widened and low paid work increased.
- Insecurity and lack of legal protection at work has spread.
- Trade union membership and participation has decreased.

Within the labour market in the UK in the 1990s therefore there has been experience of exclusion and marginalisation, rather than inclusion and social solidarity.

It is this exclusion and marginalisation of the male breadwinner which has been taken by many politicians and policy-makers to be the most important problem flowing from the socio-economic restructuring of the late twentieth century. This is clearly a partial, and politically biased, picture; but it is based on evidence of significant, and probably irreversible changes in the labour market relations of male workers.

British government statistics reveal growing levels of unemployment in the 1980s, with a decline towards the end of the decade followed by a further rise in the early 1990s. These figures have been subject to numerous technical revisions (mainly seeking to reduce the overall count) and their validity, especially on a comparative basis, must be treated with some caution. Nevertheless they show a gradually worsening picture. What is more this picture varies significantly on a geographical basis throughout the country. Some regions, notably the older industrial areas of the North and Midlands, have experienced much higher levels of unemployment than others, such as the more prosperous South-East. At a more localised geographical level differences are also stark. For example, in many larger cities unemployment levels in the poorer wards have risen much more rapidly than in the more affluent ones[2].

Moreover, formal unemployment has been accompanied by a major growth in economic inactivity especially amongst male ex-workers. In practice recorded unemployment is only a small part of a broader picture of social exclusion and marginalisation within the labour market. A closer examination of the statistics reveals large numbers of working age men also in education and training, on long term sickness benefits or in effect early retired. These people are not included in the unemployment count; but they may be more than willing to take employment if it were available (Beatty et al., 1997).

The growth in both unemployment and economic inactivity has further been compounded by a massive rise in wage inequality, which was revealed in some of the research carried out as part of the Rowntree Inquiry into Income and Wealth in the UK in the early 1990s (Hills, 1995). One consequence of this has been that wages in entry and re-entry jobs at the bottom of the labour market have showed no real rise in value over the 1980s and early 1990s (Gosling et al., 1994). Thus for those seeking to make the return to employment the prospects of a secure and adequate income from work have been much reduced; and for those in work receipt of wages is frequently completed by dependency upon means-tested benefits – a point to which we will return later. Growing unemployment and labour market marginalisation have thus contributed to increased social exclusion within the UK.

Social exclusion

Changes in labour markets have been accompanied by other changes in British society in the 1980s and 1990s, however; and these changes have coincided to accentuate the problems of social exclusion. There have been changes in family structure and demographic trends. These have resulted in higher levels of family breakdown, increased numbers of lone parents and more complex child/parent relationships. There has been a gradual decline in the birth-rate and a rise in longevity and in the overall gerontic ratio. The results are fewer two parent/two child households, and more lone parents, reconstituted families and lone pensioners – groups often associated with higher levels of poverty and benefit dependency.

Community structures also have been changing. This does not mean a collapse of community support, indeed in many ways support within communities remains a major feature of social inclusion, as I shall return to discuss below. However, some forms of community organisation, such as trade unions and workplace social clubs, have been declining in significance, and this has compounded the exclusionary effects of labour market absence for some. Furthermore geographical polarisation has resulted in greater social distance between the communities living within deprived estates or inner city neighbourhoods and the local population around them. More generally, as Jordan (1996) has recently argued, the exclusive impact of community and group membership has operated to marginalise further those who are not members of, or participants in, community affairs or support networks[3].

A recent study by Paugam (1996) examined the links between labour market disadvantage and social exclusion within EU nations. He argued that these could combine to accentuate a process of 'social disqualification' in some countries. The process was not experienced in all, however, with Denmark and the Netherlands, for instance, showing support from family and friends for people facing social problems. But in Britain unemployment and job insecurity were compounded by more generally impoverished social relations.

Social disqualification can also extend to problems with access to and use of public and private services. Public services are an essential means of meeting welfare needs and enhancing quality life for people of all income levels (they have been referred to in Britain as the 'social wage'). Those who do not or cannot use them will experience deprivation and probably long term disadvantage – for instance, low educational qualifications. Yet access to and use of public services in the UK varies significantly across individuals and groups and can be a significant aspect of inequality. In Britain in the 1990s public and private services are often closely linked (for instance, in pension provision or some aspects of health services); and these new private welfare services operate to exclude from protection most of those in society who cannot afford to insure themselves against future risks. More generally private services dominate the provision of most consumer services and goods. Yet access to these private services too is grossly inequitable, and not only because of inability to pay. For instance, many new shopping and leisure centres are built outside of local areas of population and are inaccessible to those who have to rely on public transport to reach them.

Social exclusion is a phenomenon closely related to the discrimination and disadvantage which flows from other social divisions in society. This is not just about changes in social class to which we shall return shortly, it is also true of the major divisions of gender and race. For instance, it is women who constitute some of the most marginalised and deprived groups such as lone parents and single elderly pensioners; and for black people in Britain the experience of racism can lead to fear and isolation even where monetary poverty may not be so severe. It is also true of other social divisions such as that between the disabled and the able-bodied. For instance, disabled people in Britain are more likely to be excluded from regular participation in the labour market, because of their disability they may also find that they cannot get access to many public and private services, and although they are entitled to social security benefits for some special needs many do realise the need to claim these (Dalley, 1991).

The 'drawbridge mentality'

The socio-economic trends which have been accentuating social exclusion in Britain in the 1980s and 1990s have been accompanied by policy changes which have pushed further the forces of social polarisation. Most obvious here has been the deregulation of the labour market which has facilitated the process of labour flexibilisation, but has also sharpened its most damaging effects. Job insecurity is a product of reduced employment rights as well as alterations in the forces of production. Deregulation in the UK has extended much beyond the labour market, however. Housing rights have been reduced, especially in the rented sector, leading to increased costs and diminished tenant protection. More generally deregulation, or reduced government 'interference', in private markets has contributed to a range of social problems from BSE to broken down buses[4].

Alongside deregulation has gone privatisation. The high profile privatisation measures in Britain over the past two decades have been the sell-off of state industries and utilities, but there has also been significant privatisation in the welfare sector. Most well-known here is the sale of public rented houses to sitting tenants, and this was followed in the late 1980s with measures to transfer whole estates into private hands – although in practice this power has been little used. Private provision has been encouraged, and subsidised, in education, health and social services; and these areas too have seen significant moves towards 'quasi-privatisation' in the 1990s with the introduction of direct funding and purchaser/provider splits (Le Grand and Bartlett, 1993).

One of the most important consequences of privatisation of public services has been the residualisation of those services which have remained in public control. The implicit policy agenda here is to use private provision to expand and improve services (for some) and to restrict public provision to low level support for those who cannot afford to protect or insure themselves. Residualisation is a gradual process of decline in public service therefore, although its consequences can clearly be seen, most starkly in the housing field where public housing is now associated many of the key features of social exclusion. In most British towns and cities in the 1990s the better quality public housing has in many cases been sold to the more secure public tenants (who since 1980 have had a right to purchase their home), and the public housing that remains is that on large estates and tower blocks where levels of unemployment and economic inactivity are high and where the vast majority of tenants are in receipt of means-tested supplements to cover the cost of their rents.

Deregulation, privatisation and residualisation have changed the character of welfare provision in Britain over the 1980s and 1990s. There has been a move away from a notion of collective welfare for all with standards being maintained through joint investment in services from which all expect to benefit towards a fragmentation of provision in which high quality protection is frequently only reserved for those who can afford to pay high prices for it. One of the key indicators of this is the substantial growth of means-testing within welfare provision in the UK. Compared to other OECD nations the UK relies extensively on social assistance (Eardley et al., 1995) with 10 million people dependent upon the major social assistance benefit (Income Support) in the mid 1990s and many of those in paid employment relying upon regular means-tested supplements to increase their low wage levels. Means-tests also increasingly govern access to a wider and wider range of social services, such as home care, adult education and leisure pursuits, as a result of the spread of charges for such services which are then rebated for those with low incomes.

This growth in both charging and means-testing as welfare becomes more residualised also accentuates the divisions created within British society as a result of the growing inequality revealed by research such as the Rowntree Inquiry (Hills, 1995). For those who can afford to pay, a wide range of consumer sensitive welfare services can now be found. For those who cannot, state services are much reduced and are more readily seen as the preserve only of the poor and excluded – and access to such services is frequently mediated through the application of means-tests which require proof of poverty to precede access to support. These forces reinforce a stigmatised vision of state welfare, and yet through the operation of the 'poverty trap'[5] serve to extend and reinforce continued dependency on it.

Taken together with increasing deregulation, privatisation and residualisation in welfare, the growth of means-testing in the UK can be seen as part of a gradual ideological drift within social policy. This ideological drift was referred to in the late 1980s by Labour MP, Frank Field, as the *drawbridge mentality* (Field, 1989). Field was making an analogy here with the medieval castle in which some were protected (behind the drawbridge) and others were left to fend for themselves outside – in such a context concern is directed at making sure you are inside the castle rather than caring what happens to those who are not. It is the mentality of a polarised society in which social exclusion has become an endemic feature of social structure. This drift has prompted some commentators, including Field himself, to suggest that it might even be evidence of a more fundamental change in class formations resulting in the creation of a new social class in the UK at the end of the twentieth century – the underclass.

The underclass phenomenon

In his book in 1989 Field referred to the development of the drawbridge mentality in the context of a discussion of the emergence of an 'underclass' within British society in the 1980s. Following similar references by well-known commentators such as Dahrendorf (1987), Field was concerned that these policy changes has led to the creation of a new social class below the traditional social order, characterised by insecurity, welfare dependency and social exclusion. Field's concern for this underclass was a sympathetic one – he viewed them as the victims of policy change. But at the same time others were also debating the emerging British underclass in more pejorative terms.

This most notably true of the American social scientist Murray (1990), invited over to the UK in 1989 by the *Sunday Times* newspaper to assess the extent to which the country was following American trends in social dislocation. Murray did identify an emerging British underclass in 1989, and he confirmed that it had been getting worse when he came back in 1994 (Murray, 1994). Unlike Field, however, Murray saw the causes of the underclass phenomenon not in the changing structure of public services but in the changing attitudes of certain social groups. Murray's underclass was composed of groups like the long term unemployed and lone parents who in his view had rejected traditional values of work and family responsibility and had opted instead for a life of idleness and isolation – what he, and others, have referred to as a benefit *dependency culture*.

Now in practice the debate about the possible emergence of an underclass within British socio-economic structure in the late twentieth century is a much more complex one than arguments of commentators like Field and Murray at first sight suggest[6]. Research by Morris and Irwin (1992) has revealed that the unemployed and those on the margins of the labour market are far from being a homogeneous group and in practice have been moving in and out of employment rather than opting for idleness. Drawing on a major social survey from the 1980s[7], Gallie (1994) also found that vulnerability to unemployment was not related to social attitudes. Research from the British Household Panel Survey (BHPS) looking at longitudinal changes has revealed that large numbers of people are moving regularly in and out of the lower social categories (Jarvis and Jenkins, 1995) – the underclass is not therefore a separate social class. And this is supported by similar research examining movement into and out of employment (Gregg and Wadsworth, 1997).

Quantitative analysis thus provides us with no evidence that there is a separate social category emerging below the working class as a result of recent trends towards social exclusion. This is complemented by a review of qualitative research by Kempson (1996) which concluded that people who were poor had the same aspirations for jobs, homes and incomes as others in society and in no sense constituted a detached social group. In seeking to understand the impact of social exclusion and social polarisation in the UK, therefore, the underclass phenomenon is something of a diversion.

Despite this, however, concern about the dependency culture and the growth of new class forces continues to receive high profile in popular media coverage of social change. More importantly it also appears to have operated indirectly to inform the policy responses to the problems of unemployment and social exclusion which have been developed by government over the 1980s and 1990s. The underclass approach (falsely) directs analytical concern to the victims of social changes rather than their social context; policy responses in the 1980s have similarly directed social action onto these victims in the (mistaken) belief that with help they can themselves escape from the forces which excluded and isolated them. In particular this has resulted in a response to the problems of labour market change which focuses upon the availability (or not) of workers for work rather than the availability of work for workers – a focus upon labour market supply rather than labour market demand.

Promoting labour supply

Escalating unemployment and labour market marginalisation have been a major concerns for policy action by British governments in the 1980s and

1990s. Despite their repudiation of earlier post-war commitments to the promotion of full-employment, high unemployment levels were a political embarrassment, at least, even for the Thatcher governments of the 1980s; and hence they became a focus for policy initiative. Of course, one significant – but disingenuous – policy initiative was the continuing attempt to reduce the employment count through changing the technical definition of unemployment, thus creating the hidden unemployment mentioned earlier. However, the Thatcher and Major governments did more than merely fiddle with the figures.

Throughout the early post-war years the government commitment to full employment in Britain was underpinned by a Keynesian economic strategy based loosely on demand management through public spending and investment, supported by a more or less comprehensive liberal Anglo-Saxon welfare state. In the 1980s Keynesianism was abandoned, and in its place public policy shifted to support for private market leadership in the pursuit of economic growth. In the employment field this meant a shift from management of demand to the stimulation of supply. Inadequacies in labour supply were promoted as the cause of unemployment and therefore the focus for policy action. New policy initiatives were therefore developed directed at individual workers and claimants rather than broader economic investment. They included positive measures to improve employability and negative measures to encourage job search.

The positive measures included the development and expansion of a wide range of state-supported 'opportunities' for training and work experience for the unemployed, which have now become common in many other European countries. In the UK the most important examples date back to the late 1970s although they were altered and much expanded in the 1980s. Most measures are targeted especially on the long term and youth unemployed where problems of exclusion from the labour market are felt to be higher. Early measures included a joint training and work experience package for unemployed school leavers providing an income just above benefit entitlement levels (initially called the youth opportunities programme) and a programme of support for temporary employment in community-based enterprises for the long term unemployed (initially called the community programme). These were managed by a new QUANGO (Quasi-Autonomous Non-Government Organisation), the Manpower Services Commission (MSC), established by the Department of Employment with representatives from government, employers and trade unions.

In the 1980s and 1990s these programmes were reformed and retitled. Youth opportunities became youth training and later the modern apprenticeship. The community programme became employment training and later training for work. In general the quality of placements deteriorated and the support for trainees or workers declined. Later placements were also largely in the private sector, whereas the early schemes had used public sector and community-based organisations for both training and work experience. Management of provision also shifted from the national level, through the MSC which was disbanded, to the local level, through newly established Training and Enterprise Councils (TECs), which were largely controlled by local business interests. Nevertheless the overall approach remained the same – to use state intervention to equip the workers for employment. This was completed by increased pressure within the social security system to persuade them to look for jobs, at any cost.

The negative dimension of the supply-side approach to training and enterprise was exemplified in the ever stricter conditions imposed on the unemployed claiming state benefits requiring them to seek work. Throughout the 1980s and 1990s a number of changes in the conditions for receipt of unemployment benefit were introduced resulting in a gradual drift from a passive concern with employment availability to an active concern to encourage, and police, job-seeking. In addition to the standard requirement to 'sign-on' as available for work unemployment claimants were expected to take steps to seek employment on a regular basis, and they were also subject to direct 'encouragement' to look for jobs through 'restart' interviews with 'claimant advisers' and more or less compulsory membership of 'job clubs', which facilitated positive attitudes towards work and active search for employment. This direct pressure was supplemented by indirect pressure to take any employment or training on offer with the threat of benefit penalties or withdrawal of entitlement if these were turned down. In the mid 1990s the change in emphasis in social security provision for the unemployed received symbolic representation in a change of name. Unemployment benefit is now called the Job Seeker's Allowance (JSA), and this change also introduced substantive new measures such as the requirement of all job-seekers to enter into a 'contract' with the Employment Service (who now deliver the benefits) detailing their plans for finding employment.

The next step after inducement and threat, of course, is the compulsory enforcement of some form of work or contribution in return for benefit entitlement. Such compulsion is often dubbed *workfare*, and it has been used in many continental European countries (see Møller and Berkel, Coenen &

Dekker elsewhere in this volume) and to a limited extent in the US to force unemployed people into the labour market, including groups such as lone parents who have not been a target of such negative pressures in the UK. The merits, and demerits, of a workfare regime for the UK have been debated in a number of policy circles, including some surrounding the new Labour government, as we shall discuss briefly below (see Deacon, 1997). As yet, however, no direct policy commitment to introduce compulsory work as a formal requirement for receipt of benefit payments by the unemployed has been made.

Of course workfare moves beyond supply-side promotion of labour market participation towards the provision of work experience, and perhaps therefore real work, for the unemployed. As the experience of the Revenue Minimum d'Insertion (RMI) in France has revealed, however, this can have significant strategic and resource implications; and in the 1980s and 1990s it seemed that the British government had neither the commitment nor the resources to make such a dramatic policy shift.

With the advent to power of the new Labour government, however, the supply-side approach to labour market policy has taken a new turn. One of Labour's earliest and most prominent policy priorities was its new programme for 'Welfare to Work'. The principle behind this new initiative is similar to the supply-side measures of the previous twenty years or so, based as it is on the belief that workers need to be provided with the skills and experience to access the labour market. But, partly funded by a major 'windfall tax' on the country's new privatised utility companies, the government have provided significant extra resources to improve its practical impact and to secure improved training and job placements for the unemployed. The welfare to work programme is focused particularly on the youth unemployed, as was the first opportunities scheme in the 1970s, but there are supplementary schemes for other groups, including lone parents and disabled persons. For these groups the offer of work or training is compulsory in all but name, making it more or less a workfare scheme, albeit one with positive commitments to using state support to equip people to achieve independent access to the labour market after the expiry of their period of work and training (see Deacon, 1997).

Whether the welfare to work scheme will succeed where past schemes have failed in creating new employment opportunities in the UK, or whether it will experience some of the operational difficulties encountered by the RMI in France remains to be seen at the time of writing. However, it continues to be based upon the supply-side assumption that workers create jobs, rather than the other way round. In Britain at least this assumption is hardly supported by the evidence of unemployment and labour market change in the 1980s and 1990s when fluctuations in jobs and joblessness have appeared to reflect broader trends in economic growth and decline rather more closely than they have the development and implementation of policy initiatives for the unemployed. And this is true more generally of problems of poverty and social exclusion, where similar trends towards the targeting of policy initiatives onto the victims of social forces have been underway.

Targeting welfare

Targeting welfare has been a major theme of social policy in the 1980s and 1990s across a number of dimensions. This can be seen in the increased emphasis on means-testing in social security and the shift from investment subsidy to rent subsidy in housing. Of particular interest in this context, however, has been the growth of locally-based initiatives to combat poverty and social exclusion by working with people to promote inclusion and empowerment. This local 'anti-poverty' action has been supported by local government on a rapidly expanding scale in the 1980s and 1990s. It has been supported by the EU, most notably via the three 'poverty programmes'. It has also been supported since the 1970s by central government, both directly and indirectly, for instance in the 1980s through Urban Aid and in the 1990s through the Single Regeneration Budget.

Local anti-poverty activity covers a wide range of ideas and activities. Recent trends within the local authority area have been reviewed by Alcock at al. (1995). European initiatives have been subject to formal review through the Commission (see Room et al., 1993; Robbins et al., 1994). Central government regeneration activity was recently reviewed by Robson et al. (1994) for the Department of the Environment, although this review focused more on economic regeneration than anti-poverty action. The conclusions of all show some common ground. Locally-based activity for community and economic development can provide a range of benefits for the local people involved.

Benefits in particular flow when activity is developed in conjunction with local people and representatives of local communities – *bottom-up* as well as *top-down*, to use the policy jargon. In practical terms local action has secured additional welfare benefits for local people, led to improvements in housing repair and housing management, encouraged the development of new service initiatives more closely geared to the needs of local people, and much more. In process terms many initiatives have sought to promote:

- Community capacity-building – assisting local citizens to establish and run organisations within their local neighbourhood. This has resulted in the development of community advice and advocacy projects, adult education programmes, child care projects, crime prevention forums, and other initiatives.
- Inclusion policies – encouraging local people to join and participate in these organisations or other local activities. Membership of groups and organisations has reduced isolation and exclusion and given people access to other members of their community and have includede people into those local and national agencies who influence or control their lives.
- Empowerment – promoting self-belief and transferring control to local people. Engaging in social action empowers people to take more control over their own lives and life course decisions. The active challenge from local people also encourages those with power to review their relations with local citizens, and even to share power with them.

This is a very different emphasis within policy making and policy delivery to the paternalistic approaches which largely underlay the implementation of the modern liberal Angle-Saxon welfare state in the early post-war period in Britain. In these modern post-war welfare services the emphasis was on national service provision, basic standards for all and control by providers and professionals. In the 'post-modern' welfare projects the emphasis is on local initiative, variation to meet particular needs and control by users and citizens. Modern welfare was *collective, centralised and controlled.* Post-modern welfare is *fragmented, focused and flexible.*

There is therefore much of value in the new targeting approach to welfare in Britain. Many of the restrictive and bureaucratic practices of old state welfare services have been challenged and changed by local action, and in many successful cases a different relationship has been developed been services and citizens. Nevertheless there are some serious problems and contradictions at the heart of these post-modern approaches to welfare. In similar fashion to the employment policies discussed above, by directing policy towards the individuals and communities experiencing exclusion rather than the social or economic policies which create and recreate this, they are dealing only with victims of the process. Social exclusion therefore becomes a problem for those who are excluded only.

Thus the targeting approach imports into policy development an element of the pathologisation found in some of the underclass literature – these people are excluded from economic life and social services, this must be because they have not developed the appropriate means of participating in society, therefore we will provide extra support to help them to develop their capacity and become more included. Whilst capacity building and ininclusion can be promoted by local action, however, there are obvious contradictions within the targeting approach here. The focus on working with the local people who are the victims of social exclusion directs attention away from those agencies who have contributed to their exclusion, both locally and nationally, and from the broader socio-economic forces within the agencies operate. Combating social exclusion requires changes in the forces of exclusion as well as changes from the people who are excluded.

There are other problems and contradictions in the targeting approach to welfare, however. For a start the process of targeting is in itself necessarily an exclusionary process. If resources are targeted on some, then inevitably others will miss out. Boundaries have to be drawn, and boundaries operate to exclude those outside of them. In the anti-poverty and regeneration field this has frequently meant that resources and activity have been targeted onto deprived inner urban areas, missing out entirely the poor and socially excluded who live in rural or suburban areas – and yet for these people the processes of exclusion may be doubly debilitating. Targeting, especially geographical targeting, can also have negative as well as positive consequences. In effect it can contribute to a process of negative labelling in which neighbourhoods, and their inhabitants, become identified as poor and deprived – even perhaps as members of an 'underclass'. This can lead to a downward spiral of disinvestment and outward migration, rather than an upward spiral of capacity building and empowerment.

The use of targeting and flexibility in the distribution of welfare resources can also have both a direct and an indirect effect in contributing to the process of residualisation in broader public services. In a direct sense the resources allocated to targeted activity may be diverted from other mainstream service budgets; and this has been the case in the UK both with central government programmes, such as Urban Aid and more recently the Single Regeneration Budget (SRB), and with local authority initiatives to develop anti-poverty action within existing service commitments. More generally the indirect effect of targeting welfare can operate both to undermine the rational for maintaining high quality services for all (for those in need service deficiencies can be supplemented by targeting and those not in need can supplement these themselves) and to remove the political support for such services throughout society (if the middle class have to supplement services will they still wish to pay for improved basic provision for all?). Targeting can therefore accompany, and encourage, residualisation; and again this has happened in the UK, for example, with declining general investment budgets for house building and maintenance being replaced with targeted housing improvement projects in a small number of areas[8].

Targeting welfare has developed in the UK in the 1980s and 1990s as a post-modern response to the growth of social exclusion and failings in the national welfare state. There is a danger, however, that the development of new public commitments to capacity building, inclusion and empowerment for some can operate at the same time to reduce the scale and scope of public welfare provision for others. As with the supply-side responses to unemployment, the effect of this process of integration through targeting has been to exaggerate the importance, and the potential, of *agency* in the process of social and policy change at the expense of the maintenance and development of a concern with *structure*.

Full employment and the welfare state

It is certainly true that much of the political philosophy which underlay the development of the post-war liberal Anglo-Saxon welfare state and its accompanying policy of full-employment did assume that structural change in work and welfare would be sufficient to generate social integration. The economic pressures of the last quarter of the century and the broader impact, and understanding, of social exclusion which is now widely shared have revealed significant limitations in this approach – and not the least because the emphasis on structure resulted in a paternalism and a bureaucracy in which the concerns and activities of agents became relegated or ignored.

The shift to targeting and flexibility within post-modern welfare has challenged this. The skills and capacities of individuals and communities have displaced the powers and responsibilities of the state as the key foci of policy design and development. This has been characterised by writers such as Jessop (1994) as constituting a shift from a Keynesian welfare state to a Schumpeterian workfare state in which supply-side innovation and the promotion of competition shift the focus of state intervention onto the agents of social change.

These have been important changes, and they are changes which have been felt by many to be welcome and necessary. But where they have replaced or undermined state commitments to the promotion of employment and the provision of welfare – as has been very much the case in the UK – they may have resulted in a situation where the medicine has endangered the patient more than the original disease. A focus on job-seeking when there are no jobs to be sought, does not reduce unemployment or stimulate labour market growth. The diversion of resources into targeted initiatives to combat social exclusion does not restore the welfare services which have excluded so many people.

The legacy that the new Labour government in Britain has inherited in this context is thus a complex and conflicting one. Labour is pledged to the maintenance of social development through economic growth and to the continuation of a low taxation, high flexibility labour market to achieve this. At the same time Labour is committed to promoting a more strategic response to the promotion of labour market participation, through 'welfare to work', and is committed to increased support for welfare services which might promote greater social solidarity and social integration, such as state education.

In such a context it is unlikely that the new government would be able to challenge the dominance of the Schumpeterian workfare model and seek a return to the paths of full employment and universal public welfare that characterised the Keynesian settlement of the post-war era. Nor indeed is it at all clear that they would wish to do this. They recognise only too readily the limitations of reliance on a structural approach to welfare through state action. Flexible labour markets, characterised by insecurity, part-time working and wage subsidisation, are therefore likely to remain the focus of employment policy initiatives. Continued reliance upon means-testing and targeting of resources onto areas or groups of those in need are likely to dominate the delivery of welfare services. However, the development of a more strategic response to labour market restructuring and a more positive approach to the potential role of public provision within a new welfare mix could result in the gradual promotion of improved social solidarity and declining social polarisation in the early part of the twenty-first century.

It is to be hoped, perhaps, that the late twentieth century concerns with *agency* now dominating the policy agenda in the UK which Labour have inherited and largely incorporated, can be balanced with a maintenance of past commitments to *structure*. The prospects both for promoting employment and combatting social exclusion within the country may lie in their ability to secure something of a balance between the two.

Notes

1 We should be aware of course that this 'traditional' model of employment never accurately represented the work and family relations of many men and women, with women often occupying essential roles as joint breadwinners with their partners in many low paid families.
2 Statistics from Sheffield show a rise of 2 to 3 percentage points in affluent areas compared to a rise of between 15 and 20 percentage points in deprived wards between 1977 and 1994 (Sheffield City Liaison Group, 1995).
3 For instance, credit unions, co-operative organisations providing cheap loans to their members, sometimes exclude from membership the very poorest because they are unable to make contributions in the first place.
4 Deregulation of public transport has resulted in competition between private providers who reduce costs by cutting staff wages and vehicle maintenance standards.
5 The poverty trap is the incentive effect of means-testing on those in receipt of such support. Because the support received is conditional upon low income then any increase in income reduces the level of support, thus trapping recipients in poverty and dependence and, perversely, encouraging further reliance upon means-tested welfare.
6 For a useful review of debates on the underclass see Morris (1994) and for a review of some of the research evidence see Smith (1992).
7 The ESRC's Social Change and Economic Life Initiative (SCELI).
8 This is the case, for instance, with the Housing Action Trust (HAT) initiative of the late 1980s.

References

Alcock, P. et al. (1995), *Combating Local Poverty: The Management of Anti-Poverty Strategies by Local Government*, Luton: Local Government Management Board.

Beatty C. et al. (1997), *The Real Level of Employment*, Sheffield Hallam University: CRESR.

Crompton, R. (1997), *Non-Standard Employment, Social Cohesion, and the Household: Evidence from Britain*, Paper to 'Work and Social Integration Seminar', Lund, Sweden.

Dahrendorf, R. (1987), 'The Erosion of Citizenship and its Consequences for Us All', *New Statesman*, June 12.

Dalley, G. (ed.) (1991), *Disability and Social Policy*, London: Policy Studies Institute.

Deacon, A. (1997), 'Welfare to Work: Options and Issues', in M. May, E. Brunsdon, and G. Craig (eds), *Social Policy Review 9*, London: Social Policy Association.

Eardley, T. et al. (1995), *Social Assistance in the OECD Countries*, Department of Social Security Research Papers 46/47, London: HMSO.

Field F. (1989), *Losing Out: the Emergence of Britain's Underclass*, Oxford: Blackwell.

Gallie, D. (1994), 'Are the Unemployed an Underclass? Some Evidence for the Social Change and Economic Life Initiative', *Sociology*, Vol. 28:3, pp. 755-56.

Gregg, P. and Wadsworth, J. (1997), 'The Changing Nature of Entry Jobs in Britain', in P. Gregg (ed.) *Jobs, Wages and Poverty: Patterns of Persistence and Mobility on the New Flexible Labour Market*, London: London School of Economics.

Gosling, A., Machin, S. and Meghir, C. (1994), *The Changing Distribution of Wages in the UK 1966 to 1992*, London: Institute for Fiscal Studies.

Hills, J. (1995), *Joseph Rowntree Foundation Inquiry into Income and Wealth – Vol. 2*, York: JR Foundation.

Jarvis, S. and Jenkins, S. (1995), *Do the Poor Stay Poor?*, University of Essex.

Jessop, B. (1994), 'The Transition to Post-Fordism and the Schumpeterian Workfare State', in T. Burrows and B. Loader (eds), *Towards a Post-Fordist Welfare State*, London: Routledge.

Jordan, B. (1996), *A Theory of Poverty and Social Exclusion*, Oxford: Polity Press.

Kempson, E. (1996), *Life on a Low Income*, York: JR Foundation.

Le Grand, J. and Bartlett, W. (eds) (1993), *Quasi-Markets and Social Policy*, Basingstoke: Macmillan.

Morris, L. (1994), *Dangerous Classes: The Underclass and Social Citizenship*, London: Routledge.

Morris, L. and Irwin, S. (1992), 'Employment Histories and the Concept of the Underclass', *Sociology*, Vol. 26, pp. 401-20.

Murray, C. (1990), *The Emerging British Underclass*, Institute of Economic Affairs.

Murray, C. (1994), *Underclass: the Crisis Deepens*, Institute of Economic Affairs.

Paugam, S. (1996), 'Poverty and Social Disqualification: a Comparative Analysis of Cumulative Social Disadvantage in Europe', *Journal of European Social Policy*, 6:2, pp. 287-303.

Robbins, D. et al. (1994), *Observatory on National Policies to Combat Social Exclusion, Third Annual Report*, Brussels: European Commission.

Robson, B. et al. (1994), *Assessing the Impact of Urban Policy*, London: Department of the Environment.

Room, G. et al. (1993), *Anti-Poverty Action Research in Europe*, University of Bristol: Policy Press.

Sheffield City Liaison Group (1995), *Shaping the Future: Plans for Social Regeneration*, Sheffield Liaison Group.

Smith, D. (ed.) (1992), *Understanding the Underclass*, London: Policy Studies Institute.

Tickell, A. and Peck, J. (1995), 'Social Regulation *after* Fordism: Regulation Theory, Neo-Liberalism and the Global-Local Nexus', *Economy and Society*, Vol. 24, No. 3, pp. 357-87.

9. Trends in the Danish social mode of economic regulation

IVER HORNEMANN MØLLER

Introduction

The basic assumptions underlying the last decades' Danish discourses on the social mode of economic regulation are the centrality of the work norm and of social inclusion.

The social mode of economic regulation (SMR) is conceived as an ensemble of norms, institutions, organisational forms, social networks and patterns of conduct which sustain and 'guide' a given economic regime (Jessop 1994). The purpose of any SMR is to cope with capitalist contradictions, i.e. the crises which cannot be avoided and which prevent the economic regime from ever achieving a stable equilibrium. So the SMR tends to be concerned with institutional dynamics which are not limited to the state and other forms of top-down regulation but encompasses a broad spectrum of institutions of both political and social character, organisations, ideologies, norms and rules.

There are, of course, different opinions among the classes, the political parties and groups as to which type of SMR is most appropriate when dealing with questions of unemployment and non-standard work. The present article deals with the last decades' Danish SMR, with a focus on how ideas imbedded into and furthering the main types of SMR regarding unemployment and non-standard work compete with each other, and on disputes about which problems shall have priority and about how to deal with them.

The work norm and the importance of individuals' inclusion into the subsystem of income-creating employment are both seen as basic assumptions common to the last decades' various Danish discourses on SMR[1]. The norm that every adult, within normal working age, shall be doing paid or other income-creating work, and will thereby contribute to their own and the society's reproduction, is deeply rooted in Danish society (Madsen 1992 and Graversen 1992). Partly as a consequence of this, the status of housewife as well as of household work in general is, in today's Denmark, generally low and may decline further until it is materially recognised that household and caring work *is* work. The work norm is not seen to be in conflict with the view that work, as pointed out among others by Offe (1984:20), has undergone significant changes in the last decades. The point that changing industrial structures and altered organisation and contents of work have not challenged the work norm is clearly illustrated by the Danish debates in the early 1980s and again since the early 1990s about Basic Income Systems (BIS). The proposals for BIS are, so far, the most elaborated and popular attacks on the work norm and on the other normative relationship about 'food for work', i.e. workfare, and the fierceness with which BIS proposals have been repudiated by society's dominant interests and their spokesmen is a fine illustration of the still fundamental importance of the work norm (Lind & Møller 1997).

The notion of inclusion is here inspired by Niklas Luhmann and seen as a matter of individuals' having or not having a role from where they can communicate and act. The role will often be in more than one of the sub-systems into which the society is conceived to be differentiated (work, family, culture, network, education, income, politics, etc.) Those individuals who do not have such a role are seen as excluded[2].

Inclusion within the sub-system of income-creating employment is a fundamental basis for all main Danish discourses on SMR: the *liberal discourse* sees market forces as a crucial means of including the unemployed and the under-employed people within the labour market and thereby of maintaining societal coherence – a high degree of social integration; the *solidaristic discourse* proposes to share out the 'limited amount of paid work available' as a main device for redistribution and equality, expected to be followed by declining social conflicts and increasing social integration; and the *discourse on compulsory workfare and education* seeks to enhance social integration by compulsory state-steered inclusion of people on public support in 'activities' and thereby to reduce the amount of tax money spent on public support. As it can be seen then, within all three discourses there are close links between the work norm and inclusion of individuals within the sub-system of income-creating employment.

The background

In the 1960s a hegemonic project was established in Denmark[3]. To a very high degree the formative context was an unprecedented economic growth mainly promoted by what can be termed 'the second Danish industrial revolution'. The growth in manufacturing industry was the primary dynamo for capital accumulation, and unemployment fell to 2-4 percent. The prospects were viewed optimistically, and the employers and their federations often preferred to accept workers' demands instead of open conflicts. The two main classes expanded their cooperation to all levels from the top organisational one down to the shop floor level. With the exception of the unions' demand for 'economic democracy' which was never accepted by the employers, the two main classes also extended their cooperation around unlimited growth to cooperation on the development and expansion of the welfare state, in which endeavours they were joined by all political parties, including the centre and right wing parties, but with the social democrats in the leading role (Møller 1986). Thus the hegemonic project, characterised by active and clear consent also from society's exploited and less privileged classes and groups, consisted of ideas of unlimited growth, class co-operation in several dimensions, and improvement and expansion of all sides of the welfare state, including education where a 'new principle' of equal opportunity was introduced[4].

Classical Keynesian economic policy instruments were the dominant SMR, and neo-liberal discourses and workfare discourses were totally absent. Labour market policies instead emphasised an almost unlimited period of access to unemployment benefits and policies for more or less universal coverage of people by the unemployment funds (Lind 1998). It was not until the debate about the voluntary early retirement act in the late 1970s that a new discourse – the solidaristic discourse – saw daylight. By this time the hegemonic project from the 1960s had, however, been breaking down for several years.

The 1960s were also the heyday of 'negotiated economic governance', based on the principle that economic success, social solidarity and institutional pluralism can be combined within an overall policy context in which the state assumes a strategic and developmental role in the economy (Amin & Thomas 1996). These authors, however, also claim that in presentday Denmark 'compared to other countries, the general system of economic governance is highly institutionalised and associative'...'based on negotiated decision making'(ibid 278-279). Although they may be right in their overall characterisation of Danish governance, they severely underestimate the prevailing conflicts about the welfare state in general and about labour market policies in particular. Furthermore, they seem to ignore the point that the present society differs from the full employment society, among other things, by a growing deficit in both democracy and governance. This stems from the fact that the increasing number of people who are labour-market marginalised (Møller 1997) do not have any organisation to represent them. They also take less part anyway in the governance of the society (Hansen & Hansen 1997). Empirical data indeed confirm that they feel, 'less than those on the labour market', that they or their interests are at all represented by any organisation (Andersen et al.1993).

During the heyday of class co-operation and political consensus critics of the welfare state were extremely rare and consisted mainly of Marxist critics of class cooperation and its part in sustaining of the capitalist economic system. The fast growth of the public sector – taxes increased in the 1960s from 25 percent of GNP to more than 40 percent – the high rate of inflation and a large and increasing deficit in the balance of payments, however, slowly convinced not only the centre and the right wing parties but also a growing number of social democrats about the need for a new economic policy and a halt to the welfare state's growth. The electoral success of the right wing populist Progress Party, in 1973, was manifest support for reducing taxes and for critics of public bureaucracy. At almost the same time the emerging economic crisis began to be felt through increased unemployment. Both events were important for the final breakdown of the hegemonic project.

From the end of the 1970s and the beginning of the 1980s, when it became still more clear that the economic crisis was not a temporary phenomenon, *three still more visible trends* in the Danish discourses on SMR can be traced[5], which will be outlined below.

The three trends gradually became clearer, lubricated by the *continuation of the crisis* (still fewer people believed that the crisis could be overcome by traditional economic means only; public opinions polls, today, indicate that sceptics as to the effectiveness of traditional Keynesian economic means to establish full employment amount to around 90 percent of the population).

The three trends were also accentuated by the often heated debates about the *'dependency culture'*. The empirical basis was the observation, valid already from the early 1950s though commonly unnoticed till later, of a steady growth in the number of people, within working age, permanently or temporarily receiving public support (Møller 1997). The growth was accompanied by fast increasing public expenditure on unemployment support to people who 'normally' should have been in employment. Thus growing public expenditure again contributed to increasing deficits in the state's finances. 'Money gushes out of the treasury'...'a nation-state on social assistance'...'burdens for future generations'... were some of the more colourful headlines about the issue in the debates which followed on the 'dependency culture'.

From the beginning of the 1990s governmental reports revealed remarkable disagreement between central ministries on the issue of a continuation of high unemployment as well as on the importance of the 'dependency culture'. On the one side, we find the most powerful Ministry of Finance whose evaluations tend to downplay the devastating effects of the growing number of people receiving public support. The Ministry claims that the prevailing strong Danish economy with high growth rates, low inflation, a positive balance of payments and a declining deficit in the state's finances can rather easily provide for those on public support until unemployment, in the not so distant future, is significantly reduced. This counter-intuitive optimism on the part of the Ministry of Finance can partly be explained by the fact that the social democratic Minister of Finance is a leading person of the party's right wing, which upholds somewhat traditional Keynesian points of view.

On the other side, we can observe that the less powerful though far from insignificant Ministry of Business and Industry points out two types of related threat to social integration. First, the Ministry claims that a 'long lasting marginalisation of a large group of people may lead to social polarisation of the Danish population'. Secondly, it argues that if growing marginalisation is followed by growing public expenditure this may, in the long run, lead the tax payers to revolt – to refuse to pay the public transfers to those on public support. Such a refusal may again imply 'a threat to society's social coherence'(various ministries 1995:289).

Another, substantially different, debate is running parallel to the debate between the two Ministries. This is the debate going on between 'the economists' and 'the sociologists' around the economic and social consequences of increasing labour market marginalisation. While the economists point to the growing public expenditure for people on public support and the subsequent and unacceptable increase in tax burdens, the sociologists are more inclined to pay attention to the adverse consequences for the marginalised people themselves and society's social integration. So contrary to the Ministry of Finance's rather unconcerned attitude towards labour market marginalisation, these two approaches express much more worry over the issue though from different perspectives.

Both these disagreements are reflected, in various ways, in the three main discourses presented below, most clearly in the demand of the liberal discourse for lower public expenditure and reduced taxes.

The three main discourses[6]

The liberal discourse

At the general level the liberal discourse centres, from its intensification at the beginning of the 1980s, around the classic concepts of freedom, initiative and responsibility. It builds on the classical paradigm that institutional and politically determined barriers inhibit free expansion of market forces and limit economic growth and welfare – among those barriers at present especially trade unions' influence on wage formation/differentiation, and the welfare state's safety nets. Solving both problems is seen as the strategic challenge and essential for avoiding welfare stagnation in the future.

So far as the public sector is concerned several elements are proposed to pursue renewal: de-centralisation of governance and responsibility; more market steering; greater consumer freedom; more privatisation; higher consumer charges; better service and a more efficient human resource management policy. These were all elements in the new bourgeois government's programme for the modernisation of the public sector (Ministry of Finance 1983). It was most important for the liberal discourse that it made a good start through wide dissemination of the belief that growth in the public sector was the main cause of the nation's economic difficulties. This 'crowding-out' theory asserts that the welfare state was not a victim of economic decline in the early seventies but was actually the cause of the crisis. Growth in public expenditure 'crowded-out' industrial investment in the market sector. The political counterpart to the economic 'crowding out' theory is the 'overload theory'. Growth of the welfare state is seen as a result of an overload of the state to such a degree that it acts ineffectively. Social security benefits render the population dependent on the system and lock them into a dependency culture where they lose the initiative and incentives to become self-supportive (Andersen 1997)[7].

More specifically in respect of labour market policy, the liberal discourse, supported most strongly but not exclusively by the right wing parties and the most powerful sections of the business and financial community, argues for wage restraint, widening of wage differentials, in particular lower minimum wages, cuts in the unemployment system and a general de-regulation of the labour market, as means of 'prising' people back into work.

Although some of the inspiration can be traced back to Thatcherism and Reaganism, the specific Danish version of the liberal project has a relatively 'human face': social considerations have often played a greater role which, combined with a tradition of cooperation between the liberalists and the social democrats, has resulted in less comprehensive reforms than usually recommended by the economists (Lind 1997). Not only were the liberal parties and their spokesmen more moderate, but the social democratic version of liberalism also contributed to the 'human face'. Already in 1980, while that party was still in government, it stated that it wanted to stop the growth in public expenditure. It was, however, not until the SAMAC report in 1989 that more specific policies were formulated by authoritative social democratic leaders: certain ancillery services, e.g. cleaning, catering and laundering, could be privatised, but, it was underlined, not education, health and social security which had to remain public. More choice should be given consumers to choose between different public and private services. Wage incentives should be introduced into public employees' wage systems; decentralisation of public services should be increased; and there should be higher consumer charges for certain types of public service (but still not for health and education).

Some of the most important parts of the labour market side of the liberal discourse have, so far, been politically 'shelved'. This is so with the Zeuthen Commission's suggestion, from the early 1990s, for a financial reform of the unemployment insurance system. In summary, the commission stated that the unions could chose between, on the one hand, high wages, high unemployment and high member contributions to the unemployment funds; and on the other hand, low wages, low unemployment and low member contributions. The recommendations of the parallel Social Commission were also shelved. This commission had recommended greater wage differentials, including lower minimum wages to make entrance to the labour market easier for youth and different categories of non-skilled labour. What happened was that the social democrats, the unions and the small centre parties found that now the liberal discourse was going too far!

And when the liberal proponents claimed that to reduce unemployment, below the level of structural unemployment, would fuel inflation, the social democrats turned to the 'traditional' active labour market policy remedy, education. A better educated/trained labour force would increase functional flexibility, which together with other parts of the active labour market policy, e.g. improved employment service, would reduce unemployment, they claimed, without inducing inflation. Education became a 'key answer' for the social democrats not only within the liberal discourse but also in the two other main discourses on SMR.

Other parts of the liberal discourse, for example the de-regulation of shops' opening hours to increase employees' time-flexibility, are striking examples of liberal success. To some extent the same is true of the so-called social chapters. These are paragraphs, included in collective agreements between the unions and the employers' organisations, whereby it is officially approved that elderly workers as a consequence of their lower productivity may be paid less than normal wages. This way of arguing is, however, cunningly cushioned by the 'intention to care for the elderly workers' as part of a general 'senior policy' for the elderly to postpone their retirement from the labour market. Last but not least, the liberal discourse has been very influential on revisions of the labour market's collective agreements in spring 1997. Comprehensive wage differentials, to be set by de-centralised negotiations, shall be fixed according to wage-earners' qualifications, their work performance and their leader-functions. These differentials have been included in both private and public employees' wage systems.

To a lesser extent the liberal sub-discourse on privatisation, a part of the main discourse from the beginning of the 1980s, has also lept lasting traces. This particular discourse was fuelled by the then bourgeois government, which in several public reports advocated the transfer of governmental tasks to private enterprises, on the assumption that market steering would be more effective and cheaper than public management. The social democrats on their side often agreed about both effectiveness and costs but often preferred a restructuring of the public sector rather than a transfer to private enterprise. The discourse, so far, ended up with a predominantly social democratic influenced compromise to set up joint ventures with continuing state control, through majority (or major) public shareholding in previously exclusively state owned firms: this combined, however, with provisions that the firms should now operate more on market conditions (profit optimizing, effectiveness and cost-minimising) and more in accordance with consumer demands. Most recently, however, the sub-discourse on privatisation has re-emerged and is now, with the social democratic government in a new and leading role, intensifying transfers of public enterprises to private hands.

The solidaristic discourse

This discourse on SMR was, from its outset, strongly related to schemes whose aim it is to share income-giving work in new ways. It was argued that the individual's work load, for example, could vary over the lifecycle and between different periods through movements in and out of the labour market, depending on the family situation, the need for personal development and the desire/need to upgrade educational or training levels.

The discourse in its more radical variants, the BIS (Lind & Møller 1997) and the sabbatical leave scheme – the latter offers a temporary paid leave from work to do whatever one wants – challenges the work norm 'that every adult should do paid work'. In its less radical versions, e.g. the educational leave scheme, the discourse is, however, fully in line with 'traditional' active labour market policy which provides economic support for temporary leave for educational and training purposes.

As mentioned earlier, however, the solidaristic discourse opened in the mid 1970s from a slightly different angle. The major unions of unskilled workers demanded legislation to provide early retirement for work-exhausted members. This, it was argued, would both free these from onerous work and establish job openings for youngsters. The discourse was fuelled by a widespread fear that fast growing youth unemployment would lead not only to social unrest but also to loss of a whole generation for production and reproduction of society (Møller 1979). Later came other schemes, some of which included programmes of work sharing different from those involving sharing between generations. The educational- and sabbatical leave schemes already mentioned were, around 1990, set out together with a parental leave-scheme; 'the dustman's arrangement', proposed a few years later by the dustmen in Aarhus but never supported by the powerful unions or the social democrats, were intended to share the amount of work by providing for workers to take each fourth week 'on unemployment benefits'; and there were schemes for further and even earlier exit from working-life, e.g. the transition scheme from the early 1990s which made it possible to leave the labour market from the age of 55.

Already from the outset, the solidaristic discourse had as one of its basic, although often only implicit, assumptions the point that periods with full employment are the exception rather than the rule and that the amount of paid work available, consequently, most often is limited. Under-employment is a widespread and diversified phenomenon which should be partly overcome, so goes the argument, by sharing the work available.

At the same time, although the discourse in its radical forms seems to break away from the work norm, it is still in line with the two other main discourses in its overall assumption that paid work and other types of income-creating work are very crucial means – maybe the most crucial means – for inclusion of individuals, groups and classes.

During the 1980s the solidaristic discourse became related to another most central and topical discourse: about the *importance of the family*. The discourse about the family focuses on inclusion within the family as a place for love, provision and socialisation. For long, it had been observed that the steadily growing divorce rate continued to go hand in hand with a high propensity to co-habitat. As the two-incomes family more and more became the rule, it was also increasingly acknowledged that work pressures dominate life in the nuclear family and drain time resources away from family relations (Carlsen & Larsen 1993). So the family, now in a very different form from that associated with the heyday of the male bread-winner model, is both supported by various legal interventions (e.g. larger family allowances, more day-care centres for children and increased periods of parental leave) and also increasingly conceived as the other most crucial sub-system for the individual to be included into. So with the entrance of the majority of married and co-habitating women into the labour market, there came to be for more and more people two main institutions providing inclusion, paid work and the family. At the end of the period, furthermore, the family was increasingly prioritised both by legal means and ideologically as the place for intimacy and socialisation. The family leave scheme has as one of its intentions that of bridging the distance between the family and work. Part-time employment has for many women already for years constituted such a bridge.

The peak of the solidaristic discourse may, however, very well have passed by now. At the turn of the year 1995/96 more than a quarter of a million people, out of a labour force of 2.8 millions, had chosen some type of work sharing scheme. This was much more than anticipated by the Ministries prior to the outset of the different schemes, which appeared to become very popular among the work force. While the schemes continue to enjoy some social-democratic support, for their evident popularity and their contribution to reducing the unemployment figures, they have come under increasing attack from other sides, notably the liberal oriented and some of the small centre parties, for the growing public costs of financing them. Generally it can be said that none of the work sharing schemes ever got whole hearted support from the political centre and the right (with the exception of the small Christian party, which strongly supported the family scheme). The future of the schemes is uncertain.

Some of the major work sharing schemes were part of the new social democratic dominated government's labour market reform from mid 1993. The general election at the end of the same year was, however, less than favourable to the social democrats, and when the public opinion polls showed a steady decline in the party's popular support, the government 'gave in' in subsequent negotiations with the opposition. The schemes were more and more attenuated, the transition scheme was abolished and the sabbatical leave scheme was severely cut back. It had little influence on the discourse that the then head of the Commission of the European Community, Jacques Delors, officially declared that he saw the leave schemes as an important device to combat European labour market marginality.

The discourse on compulsory inclusion through workfare[8] *and education*

This discourse, which emerged in the early 1990s, links rights to benefits with obligations to participate in various inclusive schemes. It is based on the present social democratic dominated government's and the liberal opposition's thrust towards compulsory activation, education and training schemes. Besides the assumptions made of enhanced social coherence via inclusion of the unemployed and the labour market marginalised into the labour market and via consequent tax reductions, the discourse also rests on the ideology of 'receiving in return for contributing'. This principle is closely akin to the classic liberal social policy notion of 'help to self-help', but it is correspondingly alien to the classic social democratic principle of disconnection between charges (taxes) and benefits, except that entitlement to benefit from unemployment funds has required prior contribution to the funds. The maintenance of this exception is, however, explained by the fact that, via membership payment to the union-steered and overwhelmingly social democratic oriented funds, a high degree of unionisation is achieved.

A key question in the prevailing and sometimes very heated debate is whether the workfare schemes and the compulsory education programmes, at the end of the day, really will bring the labour market marginalised persons within the normal labour market. In other words, how many will end up being normally employed, in a normal job and paid a normal wage? And how many will add activation in one scheme to activation in the next, or walk from one educational/training programme to another, with the not unlikely risk of ending up in a worse situation, e.g. of reduced and steadily declining self-esteem? This is mainly an empirical question, which can be reasonably well answered only after a few years' time.

The compulsory workfare and education discourse includes, as mentioned, emphasis on marginalised groups' inclusion within the sub-system of income-creating employment. As long as it is uncertain, however, which of the workfare schemes do bring otherwise marginalised people into the normal labour market and to what extent, the other debates within the discourse will be much based on emotions. They are, however, further fuelled by the fact that the schemes and the programmes, quite often, are accompanied by reductions in the benefits to those activated, a fact which may well reduce their inclusion via a reduced ability to take part in the consumer regime, in their social networks and in other commonly expected everyday ways of life.

This discourse encompasses a *sub-discourse on greater responsibility on the part of the individual* to provide for him/herself. That discourse was launched by the liberals and included in standard liberal discourse from the beginning of the 1980s (Christoffersen 1981). In the early 1990s it was finally adopted also by the majority of social democrats in connection with the debate on compulsory activation and education. In general one can say that every activation scheme at one and the same time both includes those who succeed in (re-)entering the normal labour market and differentiates by further excluding those who fail. With the introduction of the emphasis on greater individual responsibility, the gap between those who succeed and those who fail may very well be further widened through addition of assumed individual responsibility to existing social processes of differentiation.

The discourse on compulsory inclusion of individuals through workfare and education is furthermore related to, although not necessarily included within, a *discourse on the social responsibility of firms*. This is partly because both discourses turned up at almost the same time, at the beginning of the 1990s, and partly because of growing public concern with the running-down of still larger parts of the work force, one of the explanations for the growing number of people on public support. The idea of recruiting private enterprises for relief of social problems, however, runs counter to a long tradition in Danish social policy according to which it is the state (and to a minor degree the family) which has the overall social responsibility. The classical division of labour between the state and the firm says that it is the task of the firm to produce surplus, while problems about work and natural environments as well as social and human problems are tasks for the state. What is new in relation to this division of labour, however, is increased concern about the state's growing social burdens, the debate about welfare-mix or welfare pluralism (Evers, Novotny and Wintersberger 1987), and an increased awareness of the visible and direct relation between working conditions in the firm and the growing number of worn-out and de-qualified wage-earners. Another part of the background to the discourse was the fact that some (few) firms had started developing a new social profile, particularly on the local level, and this profile corresponded well with the general societal trend towards de-centralisation (Gamst & Bislev 1995).

The third main discourse is the most recent one. It is newer than both the liberal discourse and the discourse on solidarity, and it is remarkable that its proponents include both the political centre, the right wing parties and the employers' federations, as well as major sections of the social democrats, including many unions. There is no doubt that all the most powerful actors in Danish labour market policy stand behind this discourse.

For all the three main discourses it can be asked: how did they come about? What are their ideological roots? In the present paper we shall, however, try to answer these questions only in relation to the discourse on compulsory inclusion through workfare and education. This is partly explained by the limited size of one article, but most importantly by the probability that the workfare discourse not only could turn into a most powerful discourse but also into a hegemonic project, cf. below. So, what did make a well consolidated Scandinavian welfare state, with social democratic dominated governments which were almost free from problems so far as inflation, balance of payments, growth rates, state debts and budget deficits were concerned, follow an ideology which has so clear a liberal origin and so many of its connotations? Why did these governments end up supporting the 'workfare road' and launching a series of compulsory educational, training and activation schemes of the 'food for work'-type for all categories of unemployed people, including drug-addicts and psychiatric patients? How did the social democrats, with a legacy of concern for education, come to neglect the point that success in learning depends on motivation rather than on compulsion?

My answer to these questions builds on the hypothesis that there is a widespread fear among powerful social democratic politicians of declining support for the welfare state, particularly on the part of low paid unskilled workers. The hypothesis rests on a series of more empirical observations. First, it has for long been known that, apart only from the self-employed, support for the welfare state, although predominantly positive, is least among low paid unskilled workers (Goul Andersen 1981; Tonboe 1997). Secondly, their support for the social democratic party has been in remarkable decline over the last decades. Thirdly, the gap between high income wage earners and low income wage earners has been widening in recent years (Hansen 1995). Fourthly, it has – more rightly than wrongly – for long been a growing part of public 'wisdom' that the check-out lady in the supermarket is paid little if at all more than people on unemployment benefits.

Most often the activation schemes and the compulsory education programmes are, as mentioned, officially motivated by the philosophy that activation is inclusive, healthy and builds on the sane and well founded principle of 'receiving in return for contributing'. It must, however, also be noted, although it is seldom publicly said, that social democratic support of the schemes ultimately presupposes the tax payers' continued willingness to pay, which in turn depends on a maintenance of social integration. (For some rare but important examples of explicit attention to the point, see the Minister of Social Affairs, *Berlingske Tidende*, March 29,1996; the Prime Minister in Parliament May, 27,1993; and the Minister of Finance, *Politiken,* April 13,1997). This stimulus to policies of compulsory activation corresponds well with the above mentioned hypothesis about relatively low and declining support for the welfare state from low-wage earners. Indeed, it is otherwise more than difficult to explain – after a period of more than twenty years with high unemployment – why it should have become generally accepted, from almost one year to the next, that compulsory activation is healthy and inclusive. Furthermore, how can it otherwise be explained that the principle of 'receiving only for contributing' should replace the old social democratic principle of 'universal entitlement'- for the deserving as well as (if less) for the non-deserving?

*

In all three main discourses education is, as previously noted, centrally placed. All three also include *two sub-discourses*. The first of these is about *greater involvement of NGOs*, i.e. involvement of voluntary organisations as part of the growing emphasis on and attention to provision from the civil society. The second sub-discourse concerns local/regional development projects. This is part of a still on-going and multi-staged process of *de-centralisation:* from de-centralisation of state activities to the municipal level in the 1970s; via de-centralisation of municipal government to smaller local administrations in the 1980s; to the inclusion of citizens and clients in many types of service provision in the 1990s (Hegland & Hulgård 1998). It is claimed that Denmark has had the most consistent process of de-centralization in Europe (Wilmann 1997).

Conclusion

On the one hand, so far, none of the three main Danish discourses has succeeded in establishing itself as a project of hegemony. On the other hand, the battle about the size, the composition and the quality of the welfare state is far from ended and it might well, at the end of the day, happen that a new hegemonic project will emerge.

The social democrats, the small bourgeois parties at the centre, the left-wing parties and the major and strongest unions have repeatedly declared that they will never follow the *liberal discourse* regarding what they see as 'the cornerstones' of the welfare state: the health system, the educational system, and those parts of the social security and service system which are crucial to the employed population, the pensioners and the family. Most decisive in telling against any future ascendancy of the liberal discourse is the victory of the social democratic government and the defeat of the bourgeois opposition in the general election of March 1998. Furthermore there is in Denmark an almost century long tradition of consensus among the four old political parties (cf. footnote 6) as a precondition for major political changes. So not only will the social democrats and others continue to argue against a more radical version of the liberal discourse, they will also constitute a strongly entrenched barrier to major changes in the 'cornerstones'.

Nonetheless the *solidaristic discourse* has been losing much ground in the latest years. This has been evident from, among other things, the abolition of the transition scheme and the reduction of both benefits and eligibility in respect of the parental- and sabbatical leave schemes. At the moment, the early retirement pension scheme is under heavy attack for its alleged low entitlement age.

What, in contrast to the two other discourses, gives the *discourse of compulsory integration through workfare and education* a fair chance to achieve hegemony is its massive back-up from nearly all political parties, the employers' federations, all major unions, probably the majority of the tax paying population and quite often also the compulsorily activated people and the unemployed themselves. It seems indeed that the unemployed and marginalised groups, at least to some extent, have approved the project of compulsory inclusion into education, training and other activities. It is reported – although how reliably remains unknown – that marginalised people often express satisfaction with 'at last having some necessary work to do'. It seems likely, if so, that they are repressing anxieties that the 'job' is only temporary, that it may not lead to permanent employment in the real labour market, and that in the not so distant future they may be forced into new and once-again temporary activity.

Although new legislation on workfare, to be implemented from the summer of 1998, has been agreed by all major agents, including all political parties with the exception of the small most leftist party, one should be cautious about predicting that the discourse on compulsory inclusion will become the future hegemonic project. The experience from mid 1993 to end 1994 of both a rapid rise and then a rapid decline in the support for the solidaristic discourse suggests the possibility of very fast changes dependent, among other things, on shifts of political configuration and economic climate.

Ostensibly the preconditions seem to be present for the discourse on compulsory inclusion to become a hegemonic project. However, it might well be that a project only about inclusion of marginalised people and the unemployed is too limited to provide a semblance of national unity, or in Gramsci's terms a collective will – a project of hegemony – capable of sustaining and reproducing the social relations of production with endorsement by all the powerful and less powerful actors. It seems then more likely that to achieve hegemony the project, as a minimum, would need to be augmented by some further common denominators regarding economic growth and the welfare state[9]. Equipped with these additional dimensions the project, no matter whether or not it succeeds in being established as hegemonic, would have the following characteristics and thereby differ significantly from the hegemonic project of the 1960s. First, it would not include an expansion of the welfare state but rather a stabilisation around the present level, maybe with moderate reductions. Secondly, class co-operation would not be limited to the issue of what to do with the unemployed and marginalised persons, though the relative weaker position of the unions in the 1990s does not make cooperation beyond the collective agreements on wages and other working conditions a necessity for the employers. Thirdly, inclusion into the subsystem of income-creating employment would be enforced by the state and municipal authorities, not via the market as in the 1960s. Fourthly, unlimited growth is no longer assumed and it is increasingly accepted that full employment is an unrealistic goal for the future. Fifthly, the compulsory inclusion project rests, apart from its moral dimension, on the fears of the most powerful actors about a 'polarisation of the Danish population' and about the threats on that score to 'society's social coherence', i.e. its social integration.

It might be too complicated a task to predict all the likely consequences of a hegemonic project of compulsory inclusion. One issue could, however, sooner or later emerge: a discourse on the relevance of the work ethic. In the longer run a broader debate about the social roles ascribed to all citizens might supersede the centrality of the work norm. This might happen at the time – if not before – when it is generally accepted that full employment is unlikely to return, and that compulsory activation does not create new jobs and successful activation is restricted to the adaptation of labour to match vacant job positions. The relevance of doing income-creating work may then be displaced by a search for new social roles not only for the unemployed and marginalised persons but also for the employed. The hegemonic project from the 1960s concentrated on societal income creation and distribution of wealth. The new hegemonic project may at the end of the day raise a debate about the intrinsic and other meanings of doing work and doing compulsory activities. Issues about 'developmental work' (see Hvid elsewhere in this volume), about new types of societally-, locally- and individually recognised work and activities as well as various forms of Basic Income Systems and other types of inclusion into other sub-systems, could well become the most important themes in the first part of the 21st century.

Notes

1 The main, and only partial, exception is the solidaristic discourse (to be dealt with below) which also builds on the importance of individuals' inclusion within other sub-systems, e.g. the educational, the family, the social network, and thereby to some extent questions the norm that every adult, *in every stage of the life course,* should be doing income-creating work.

2 Social integration is applied in accordance with David Lockwood's classical definition...'as the more or less orderly or conflicting relationships between actors of a social system'. (Lockwood 1992:400). Thus the social integration perspective focuses on actors and their conflictual or co-operative relationships.

3 Hegemony, here applied in Gramsci's conception, consists the ability of a class, classes or sub-classes to represent the 'universal' interests of a whole society and to unite to itself a group of allies (Sassoon 1978). Hegemony is not simply an ideological dimension

unrelated to the sphere of economic relations and 'the political', nor does it imply much of a compromise: 'Undoubtedly the fact of hegemony presupposes that account be taken of the interests and tendencies of the groups over which hegemony is to exercised, and that a certain compromise equilibrium should be formed – in other words, that the leading group should make sacrifices of an economic-corporate kind. But there is also no doubt that such sacrifices and such compromises cannot touch the essential; for though hegemony is ethical-political, it must also be economic, must neccessarily be based on the decisive function exercised by leading groups in the decisive nucleus of economic activity' (Gramsci, *Selections from Political Writings, 1921-1926*, p.161).

Hegemony should not be seen as 'false consciousness' or as indoctrination but rather as arising when one of the ideologies 'or at least a single combination of them, tends to prevail, to gain the upper hand, to propagate itself throughout society – bringing about not only a unison af economic and political aims, but also intellectual and moral unity, posing all the questions around which the struggle rages not on a corporate but on a 'universal' plane, and thus creating the hegemony of a fundamental social group over a series of subordinate groups'(Gramsci ibid, 181-2).

4 As it shall be shown below, education is conceived, particularly by the social democrats, as an important means to further equal opportunities but also for combatting unemployment, labour market marginality and 'structurally generated inflation'.

5 Discourse analysis is here applied in a neo-Gramscian sense as ...'the ensemble of phenomena in and through which social production of meaning takes place'(Laclau 1980). Neither Laclau's nor any other of the main discourse-theoretical approaches will here, however, be considered or adhered to in full. It is also beyond the scope of this article to review and discuss the advantages and disadvantages of the different approaches. Rather, a few central points in my use of the notion will be presented as follows. First, it involves a clear rejection of the economism entailed in capital-theoretical analyses of the state. Secondly, it also involves rejection of an assumption found in some class-theoretical analyses, that classes are the only social forces worth consideration. Thirdly, discourse analysis is focused on ideologies and ideological class struggles rather than the economy, the state and politics as such. Thus, discourse theory is seen as the struggle about which 'meaning' or conception of societal problems shall dominate (who is formulating the agenda?). Fourthly, discourse theory is, however, also conceived as a practice concerned with the complex articulation of extra-discoursive conditions such as the forces of production, the social relations of production and the different forms of SMR. Fifthly, extra-discoursive conditions are effective not only through their prior mediation through discourse but also through their concrete existence. So the focus on discourse as the production of social meaning will not lead to neglect of economic, legal, administrative and other political arenas for class struggles and non-class struggles.

The centrality of extra-discoursive conditions for the constitution of a hegemonic project is underlined by Gramsci (1971). He claims that, however plausible a given hegemonic project may appear in terms of intended articulation of class and non-class subjects and demands, it will only become 'directive' to the extent that strategically significant forces support it and likely sources of resistance are neutralised. It should also be noted how hegemonic projects are typically promoted through a combination of means that include not only persuasion and moral compulsion but also material inducements and physical repression. It should not be ignored that Gramsci viewed state power as 'hegemony armoured by coercion'.

6 Only what is conceived as the three main discourses will here be dealt with at some length. The most important sub-discourses sustaining and shading into the three main discourses will be touched upon only slightly. And the sub-discourses which take place within all four old political parties (the social democrats, the liberals, the conservatives and the smaller

social-liberals) will not be considered at all, partly for lack of space and partly because they are seen as less significant.

7 A survey of the attempts to evaluate the 'crowding out' thesis reveals a much more complex relationsship between welfare state social policies and national competitiveness. Not only does empirical evidence not allow general conclusions to be drawn, it also seems that the effects of social policy on competitiveness is contingent on the institutions of the nation and its place in the global economy (Gough 1995).

8 The conception of workfare varies from one national context to another, and the understandings of workfare in, for example, England and Sweden are not identical with those in Denmark. The Danish understanding of workfare is distinct because it constitutes a sudden and flagrant break with a century old privilege for members of the unemployment funds to receive benefit as of *right* when unemployed. The only condition had been 'to be available in the labour market'; and this has always (by comparison for example with Sweden) previously involved a narrow interpretation of 'labour market' in terms of both geography and trade/skill, so a generous reading of the condition. In England the road to workfare was much more of a process than a sudden break. During twenty years of Conservative rule, entitlements, durations and benefits were frequently reduced. The rights remained but they were steadily cut down and in the end they were of an almost formal character.

9 Gramsci himself also mentions the possibility of combining different ideologies/projcts for the constitution of a hegemonic project (Selections pp 181-2).

References

Amin, A. and Thomas, D. (1996), 'The negotiated economy: state and civic institutions in Denmark', *Economy and Society*, Vol. 25, No. 2.

Andersen Goul, J. (1981), *Vælgernes holdninger til socialpolitikken,* Paper presented to the 6th Nordic Congress of Political Science, Åbo, Finland 17-19 August.

Andersen J. et al. (1993), *Medborgerskab, demokrati og politisk ledelse,* Herning: Systime.

Andersen, J. (1995), 'Solidarity and Social Citizenship in Post-Industrial Welfare Models', in *Proceedings from Symposium in connection with Maastricht II, Copenhagen, September 1995,* The Danish Center for Human Rights, Vol. 25, No. 2.

Evers, A, Nowotny, H. and Winterberger, H. (1987), *Changing Face of Welfare* (Studies in Social Policy and Welfare No.XXVII), Aldershot: Gower Publishers.

Gamst, B. and Bislev, S. (1995), 'Virksomhederne ind i Socialpolitikken?', *Nordisk Tidsskrift for Socialt Arbejde.*

Carlsen, S. and Larsen, J.E. (1993), 'Introduction', in S. Carlsen, and J.E. Larsen, *Den svære balance,* Copenhagen: Ligestillingsrådet.

Christoffersen, H. (1981), 'Ikke alene friheden men også ansvaret og initiativet er smuldret', *Liberal,* No. 1.

Christensen, J. J. et al. (1996), *Tilbage til friheden – den eneste vej frem for Socialdemokratiet,* København: Fremad.

Fonsmark, H. (1990), *Historien om den danske utopi. Et idépolitisk essay om danskernes velfærdsdemokrati,* København: Gyldendal.

Gough, I. (1995), *Social Welfare and Competitiveness,* Copenhagen: CID.

Gramsci, A. (1921-1926), *Selections from Political Writings.*

Gravesen, G. (1992), *Arbejdets betydning, kvalitet og udformning,* København: Akademisk Forlag.

Hansen, F.K. (1995), 'Velfærd og fordeling', *Samfundsøkonomen* No. 6.

Hegland, T.J. and Hulgård, L. (1998), 'Socialpolitik og forsøgsvirksomhed', in J. Elm Larsen and I. Hornemann Møller (eds) *Socialpolitiskgrundbog*, Copenhagen: Munksgård.

Hvid, H. (1997), *Development of work and social (dis)integration*, Paper presented to the conference 'Integration and Differentation', May 4-6, Lund, Sweden.

Jessop, B. (1982), *The Capitalist State*, Oxford: Martin Robertson.

Jessop, B. (1994), 'The Transition to post-Fordism and Schumpeterian workfare state', in R. Borrows, and B. Loader, (eds), *Towards a Post-Fordist Welfare State*, London.

Just, G. (1994), 'Arbejde skal være sjovt', *Velfærd?*, Tillæg til A-Pressen, Nytår 1994.

Knudsen, H. (1990) 'Opbevaring til bedre tider. Kultur & socialt arbejde', *Social Kritik* 7/90.

Kommissionen om fremtidens beskæftigelses- og erhvervsmuligheder (1995), *Velstand og Velfærd – en analysesammenfatning*, København: Erhvervsministeriet, Finansministeriet, Statsministeriet og Økonomiministeriet.

Laclau, E. (1980), 'Populist rupture and discourse', in *Screen Education*, 34.

Lind, J. & Møller, I.H. (1997), *Unemployment or Basic Income – is there a Middle Road?*

Lind, J. (1998), 'Socialpolitikken og arbejdet', in J. Elm Larsen and I. Hornemann Møller (eds), *Socialpolitisk grundbog*, Copenhagen: Munksgård.

Lockwood, D. (1992), *Solidarity and Schism*, Oxford: Clarendon Press.

Lykketoft, M. (1997), 'Truer jobløsheden – eller er der arbejde på vej?', *Politiken*. Debat 13. april.

Mac, B., Møller, F.R., Olsen, L. and Ryom, K. (1989), *Modernisering af den offentlige sektor – en analyse af den politiske debat*. Sociologisk Institut, Københavns Universitet.

Madsen, A. (1992), 'Arbejdets betydning', *Dansk Sociologi* Nr.4.

Møller, I.H. (1978), *Ungdomsarbejdsløshed*, København.

Møller, I.H. (1997), 'Social Integration and Labour Market Marginalisation in Scandinavia', in M. Roche and R. v Berkel, (eds), *European Citizenship and Social Exclusion*, London: Avebury.

Ruysseveldt, J. Van and Visser (1995), 'Revised diversity: from the neo-liberal decade to beyond Maastricht', in *Industial Rela tions in Europe. Traditions and Transitions*, Sage.

Samak (1989), 'Den offentlige sektor som led i den socialdemokratiske velfærdspolitik', in *Fornyelse af den offentlige sektor*, LO-rapport.

Sassoon, A.S. (1978), 'Hegemoni and Political Intervention', in S. Hibbin (ed.), *Politics Ideology and the State*, London: Lawrence and Wishart.

Schjødt, P.J. (1993), *Hvad med de andre?*, Copenhagen: Fremad.

Thorgrimson, F. (1990), 'Efterlyser fælles forslag', *Tillæg til LO-Bladet*, No. 29.

Thorsen, N. (1993), 'Regering bebuder social grundlov', *Politiken*, Indland.

Tonboe, J. (1997), '"Marginalisering" og "integration" som ideologi', in Rasmussen et al., *Egne veje. Festskrift til Per Salomonsen*, Ålborg: Aalborg Universitetsforlag.

Wilmann, Klaus, (1997), 'Nødvendige valg i fagbevægelsen', *Politiken*, Kronik 24 februar.

10. Labour market flexibility and regulation

JENS LIND

Introduction

Labour market flexibility is considered an important factor in offering the best conditions for economic growth and competitiveness in society. This no doubt makes sense in so far as it provides the employers with labour according to their needs and demands. Flexible and cost effective production presupposes a flexible supply of labour. Labour market flexibility, however, does not always correspond to workers' needs for stable employment and sufficient income. The standard employment relationship at one time 'incorporated a degree of regularity and durability in employment relationships, protected workers from socially unacceptable practices and working conditions, established rights and obligations, and provided a core of social stability to underpin economic growth' (Rodgers 1989:1). In this sense some of the costs of the flexible employment of labour are paid by the workers, their families and, in the case of welfare state intervention and compensational schemes, by the tax payers or members of social insurance systems. The price of labour market flexibility is also wastage of productive potential through unemployment and underemployment, as well as a segmented labour market and labour market marginalisation.

During the past almost 25 years of high unemployment, labour market policy in Denmark has been shaped by the shifting influences of and compromises between a liberal and a social democratic political strategy, or in other words between a strategy of competition and a strategy of co-operation (Schmid 1994). The different strategies do not differ in the basic understanding that employers must be supplied with appropriate labour to ensure economic growth, and that this must be provided by means of a more flexible labour market. According to liberal orthodoxy, however, labour market flexibility is to be obtained by strengthening market forces and diminishing of state intervention and collective bargaining regulation, while a social democratic strategy aims to increase flexibility by collectivist regulative measures. These differences imply among other things that social differentiation and integration are interpreted in different ways and have different policy implications. In crude terms, liberals consider social differentiation a means to further or secure social integration, while social democrats intend to reduce social differentiation and thereby improve social integration.

Unemployment has been decreasing in Denmark since 1995 and the present social-liberal government claims that this is due mainly to its sensible economic policy. Every government does so. The conservative-liberal government did the same thing during some years of the mid-1980s in ascribing decreasing unemployment figures to the effects of more liberal policies. This of course raises the question whether any policy matters at all. The cynical judgement would be that unemployment goes up and down no matter what policies are implemented – perhaps because, in the case of Denmark, changing governments have done almost the same thing though with different means, namely increase labour market flexibility.

When labour market flexibility is subordinated to the primary aim of providing employers with appropriate labour it is very difficult to promote a strategy aimed at improved autonomy for workers in working life. A project for workers' autonomy could seek a solidaristic distribution of work and production based upon a notion of a fair contribution to the community, for instance in the shape of a basic income system (Christensen 1993). But the difficulty of implementing such a project comes not only from business cycle related factors (unemployment) but also from structural considerations: it is assumed that autonomy must be kept restricted to secure or improve the competitiveness of the economy. In this way the discourses in society on this matter (Møller 1998) are mainly dominated by concerns to meet employers' needs and demands, which makes it difficult to further wider social interests and so avoid some of the negative social consequences of a flexible labour market.

The analysis on the following pages will outline to what degree flexibilisation and (de)regulation of the labour market has influenced differentiation and marginalisation. The focus will be on unemployment and certain forms of non-standard employments because unemployment and non-standard employment are supposed to be interrelated in the sense that a lot of unemployment is due to non-standard employment, and that non-standard employment increases during periods of high unemployment. Two sorts of labour market regulation are relevant to look into, namely regulation of the employment relationship and unemployment policies; and the thesis is that labour market regulation has gone in mutually contradictory directions. On the one hand flexibilisation has been promoted because it is expected to create more jobs; but on the other hand labour market regulation has also sought to reduce or curb labour market marginalisation.

Flexibility, unemployment and non-standard employment

A relatively diminished importance of the standard employment relationship in society is often termed an increase in labour market flexibility. The standard employment relationship, however, is difficult to define because it varies among different societies, labour markets and segments. In broad terms a standard employment relationship could be defined as paid employment for a non-fixed period and at 'normal' or 'usual' working hours during a day or a week. Deviations from standard employment can focus on the contractual relationship regarding pay, the level of pay and the way labour is actually deployed. It is only the last aspect which will be in focus here. Using the concept of flexibility, the deployment of labour can be described and analysed by distinguishing between functional, numerical, working time, working hours and intensive flexibility;[1] and among these my main concern will be numerical flexibility (temporary employment) and working time (part-time) flexibility because these forms of non-standard employment are directly related to unemployment.

This implies that non-standard employment patterns involving flexible working hours (shift-working, night work, week-end work etc.) will not be considered here. At what time of the day or the week the work takes place does not directly affect the volume of work involved, that is of employment versus unemployment, but it should be mentioned that this sort of non-standard employment has been moderately increasing in Denmark during the past 10-20 years (Schönemann-Paul et al 1992).

Unemployment means that the society loses a potential production of goods and services. In this way unemployment is an indication of an economic malfunction when the society does not make use of the labour available. This again means that the unemployed do not get an income from work and cannot maintain themselves and their families. In a welfare society with state provision for maintenance the unemployed and their families are partly compensated by social benefits. Unemployed people are thus maintained via other people's work either by help from within their own family or by means of some welfare state arrangement. The result is the same: others must do without a proportion of their contribution to production and instead secure the maintenance for them.

In principle, the same takes place when people work less than the usual or normal working hours during a day, a month, a year or an entire life. The work or the production is less than would otherwise have been the case. In quantitative terms non-standard work is just another expression for unemployment, or, the other way round, unemployment is just another way of describing non-standard work. At least this is the case if we assume that all workers want standard time employment.

Part time and temporary work are often the result of a choice or a wish for reduced working time because of personal or family considerations. If so, the reduction of working time takes place because of the worker's preferences and needs. This is an indication of workers' autonomy in the labour market and can be termed a reduction of working time determined by the supply side. In other cases, reduced working time is caused by the fact that the worker cannot find full time work and must be content with less. This can accordingly be termed a reduction of working time determined by the demand side.

Presumably a reduction of working time determined by the supply side is most widespread among groups of workers who are in a labour market position which allows them to set some of their own limits to job conditions. For the labour market in general a reduction of working time determined by the supply side is most likely during a period of very low or no unemployment.

During periods of high unemployment and in segments of the labour market with high unemployment, by contrast, the demand side – that is, the employers' side – has the best opportunities to see its needs fulfilled. Demand side reduction of working time most frequently takes place when the employers can define and enforce a strategy of economizing with the use of labour. At times or in segments of the labour market where the labour supply is not sufficient to meet the demand, management's economizing strategy tends not to include reduction of working time.

In this way, both in terms of definition and in terms of actual occurrence, unemployment and non-standard work are often closely interrelated. According to prevailing economic theory, non-standard employment is presumed to be a remedy for reducing unemployment. The line of reasoning goes that labour market flexibility is necessary for the economy to be competitive to other economies. By flexibilisation of labour the employers can reduce labour costs, be more competitive, make more money and so employ more people.

Labour market regulation

The labour market is regulated by three different institutions and forms of regulation, namely the market (market forces), the state (legislation), and collective bargaining (collective agreement). The basic form of labour market regulation in a capitalist society is the market which consists of the decisions made by the various agents mainly for economic reasons. Market regulation is based on individual contracts. The state upholds the principles of the free market on one hand and establishes rules in the interest of the collectivity, the society on the other. Collective bargaining establishes common frameworks for the individual contracts via collective agreements between the representatives of labour and capital. The main division in labour market regulation is between the individualism of the market on the one hand and the collectivism of legislation or collective agreements on the other.

In principle, all forms of political intervention affect the labour market, but attention here will be restricted to labour market policy although education policy, industrial policy, social policy and also general macroeconomic policy all have significant influence on behaviour in the labour market. It might be maintained that decisions and strategies of major companies have the same sort of regulatory effect in the labour market as collective agreements and policies, but this is not the case in Denmark.[2] What could be termed the 'social mode of regulation' does certainly affect behaviour in the labour market, for instance shifting norms in gender relationships, and changes in attitudes between different generations and age groups together with general patterns of attitudes and behaviour (cf. Hirschmann 1982); but these elements in the social mode of regulation will not be considered here in any detail.

Legislation and collective bargaining

The basic structures of the Danish system of labour market and industrial relations were established in 1899, when the trade unions and the employers signed a basic agreement recognising each other as legitimate parties in the labour market. Since then, industrial relations have developed into a generally consensual relationship between the labour market organisations and the state, where collective bargaining and political regulation support each other in a very pragmatic way although some key areas must be noted as distinctive for each of them. In principle, the regulation of wages is solely a matter for collective bargaining which also regulates most other working conditions – apart from a lot of labour protection matters such as health and safety at work, holidays, mass redundancies, minimum rest periods etc., which together with all matters of social protection, employment and unemployment measures are regulated by legislation (Lind 1991;Due et al. 1994; Knudsen, Lind 1998).

Labour market policies are most frequently decided and implemented with significant influence from trade unions and employers' organisations. This tripartite or corporatist structure constitutes, together with the pragmatic relationship between legislation and collective bargaining, some sort of implicit social contract between the state and the representatives of labour and capital. This social contract is kept alive by common acceptance of, and respect for, some tacit rules about how to achieve goals shared across the society. In this respect, the principle of 'free collective bargaining' is taken as a normal basic rule but may be set aside by the state if the outcome otherwise is seen to threaten the welfare of the society.[3] Collective agreements regulate all public sector employment, but only 50-60 percent of the private sector is covered by collective agreement, so approximately 70 percent of the entire labour market is directly regulated by collective agreements (Scheuer 1996). Indirectly, however, collective agreements influence the rest of the labour market, setting pay and other standards.

An important development in the structures of labour market regulation is the decentralisation of collective bargaining which has taken place since the early 1980s, whereby the main organisations increasingly have lost influence. This process accelerated during the early 1990s mainly for two reasons. Firstly because of radical changes in the organisational structure of the Confederation of Danish Employers, the DA, where collective bargaining has now become a matter for the member organisations organised in 5 groups (manufacturing, printing, construction, retail etc., wholesale etc.), of which manufacturing, the DI (Dansk Industri), is by far the most powerful. Secondly, decentralisation has accelerated because the collective agreements at industry level have increasingly developed into so-called 'framework agreements' only, the details of which are then negotiated at company level.

Decentralisation of collective bargaining has also taken place in the public sector, but almost entirely concerning pay. Other issues are still bargained at national level.

Two strategies on political regulation

As mentioned in the introduction, two strategies on the role of the state in the labour market can also be distinguished in Denmark. The liberal strategy became fashionable when the conservative liberal government took office in 1982, and since the mid 1980s the political debate on labour market issues in Denmark has been strongly dominated by analyses which claim the presence of structural unemployment. The assumption – derived from the monetarist thesis of the existence of 'natural unemployment' – is that the labour market has structural rigidities which restrain optimal functioning of market mechanisms, so causing a certain minimum level of unemployment when some main economic indicators (mainly inflation) remain stable. If the structural rigidities could be removed and wages could be reduced for the groups with the highest unemployment rates, more unemployed would find employment and marginalisation would be restrained. The rigid (and relatively centralised) bargaining system and wage structure have the effect that the 'insiders' price the 'outsiders' out of jobs. The 'outsiders' are not in a position where they can choose to accept wages at a sufficiently low level to be offered a job (Det økonomiske råds formandsskab 1988).

A further statement is that the 'outsiders', who normally are the lowest paid workers, often do not have an incentive to accept a job when unemployment benefits are 90 percent of previous earnings (Arbejdsministeriet et al 1989). The solution to the problem of structural unemployment is accordingly said to be a decentralised wage bargaining system, where the market determines the level of pay which would secure the 'outsiders' a job, combined with reduced unemployment benefits and/or a financing of unemployment insurance whereby the groups with high unemployment risk and so the 'overpaid' groups (typically the lowest paid) pay the marginal costs themselves. According to this line of reasoning, the unemployed will be able to choose either the combination of lower wages, lower risk of unemployment and lower contributions to unemployment insurance, or the combination of higher wages, higher risk of unemployment and (consequently) a higher contribution to unemployment insurance.

This way of reasoning has sole focus on the motivation of the unemployed to accept a job for economic reasons alone. Emphasising this sort of economic rationality, a recent study concludes that around one fourth (25 percent of men and 28 percent of women) of the unemployed have no economic incentive to accept a job (Smith 1998:200). Accordingly the study recommends increasing the economic incentives of low paid workers by tax reductions and lower unemployment benefits; but the study also reveals the fact that 20 percent of the already employed have no or very little economic incentive to work (Smith 1998:191). Obviously, this result indicates that people do not work for economic reasons alone.

The liberal assumptions of structural unemployment are usually presented as derived from an 'objective economic analysis', but have in reality very strong political colouration in liberalist direction. Although adherents flourished most notably during the period of conservative/liberal governments till 1993, when they were active as advisers and members of various commissions (Udredningsudvalget 1992, Socialkommissionen 1992), they are still influential especially in the Ministry of Finance and among so-called 'experts', but traditional strongholds of social democratic orientation, for instance the Danish Federation of Trade Unions (the LO), are increasingly influenced by liberal thinking.

According to social democratic interpretations, structural problems in the labour market are synonymous with a mis-match between the demand for and the supply of qualifications and/or their geographical locations. In principle this way of reasoning is the basic idea behind 'the active labour market policy' which was developed during the 1950s under the inspiration of Swedish policies (the Rehn-Meidner model), and implemented in Denmark during the 1960s by the establishment of labour market training institutions and by reform of the employment exchange system (Lind 1985). The aim of the 'active labour market policy' is to support general economic policies to strengthen economic growth, combat unemployment and inflation, and secure an acceptable level of social fairness (redistributive policies). In theory, qualificational and geographical imbalances between various segments in the labour market should be reduced by education and training of the unemployed in one segment to qualify them for another segment where labour demand exceeds supply and in this way reduce inflation, or, in the case of unemployment in one geographical segment of the labour market, induce workers to move to a segment with excess demand.

As the active labour market policy is intended to smooth the allocation process by adjusting qualifications and the geographical distribution of the labour force to the structure of demand, the policy enhances flexibility of labour and encourages the establishment of temporary employment relationships. If the employers' opportunities for getting easy access to labour are improved, their transaction costs are reduced and they might take advantage of this to develop a pattern of temporary employment relationships. In fact, this is a visible and documented effect of how the public employment service has worked in certain segments of the labour market (Jørgensen et al. 1990).

According to the social democratic strategy labour market marginalisation can be avoided by a number of regulative initiatives among which training and education of the labour force is the most important. To improve employment chances for people who are potentially or actually marginalised all sorts of incentives may be used, for instance stricter obligations for the unemployed to accept any vacant jobs and subsidies for employers who take on long-term unemployed, disabled or other sorts of relatively less attractive labour.

In a sense, the difference between the liberal and the social democratic strategy is that liberals maintain that the productivity of the unemployed is not high enough relative to the expected wage level. The solution is to lower wages. The social democrats have the same starting point, but instead of lowering wages they seek to increase the potential productivity of the unemployed by raising their level of qualifications. The result is the same: the unemployed are employed if the level of wages comes into level with productivity.

In a wider perspective the two strategies represent different strategies for economic growth. The liberal strategy represents what could be termed a 'quantitative' strategy for economic growth based upon wage differentiation and competition. The social democratic strategy has common traits with a 'qualitative' strategy based upon improving the quality of labour (and working life) and the implementation of new technology.

Unemployment policy

The main functions of labour market policy with specific reference to unemployment are the maintenance and the employment (or activation) functions. The maintenance of the unemployed takes place by way of unemployment benefits, social benefits, leave schemes and early retirement; and activation of the unemployed consists of subsidised or special jobs for the unemployed and training and education schemes. During the past 25 years or so, the overall trends in use of such measures can be categorised into six phases.

Until 1979 (phase 1) unemployment was considered a temporary phenomenon and legislation concentrated on ensuring that unemployment benefits kept pace with inflation, and that unemployment benefits were made accessible for the widened group of people who became unemployed, including the increasing numbers of long term unemployed. From 1977-79 a youth employment scheme, an early retirement scheme and a job offer scheme for the long term unemployed were introduced. Between 1979 and 1982 (phase 2) unemployment benefits fell by approximately 4 percent relative to wages. Apart from strengthening of the obligation to be available for work, the limitations in benefit access hit almost the same groups which during the 1970s had benefited from the widening of access (young people, part-time workers, the long term unemployed). Apart from a reduction in pay for participants in youth employment schemes below the level of collective agreements (1981), these schemes and the long term unemployment scheme were slightly improved till 1982.

The change to a liberal-conservative government in 1982 and a period of economic growth mark phase 3, from 1982 to 1988. The new government further reduced the level of benefits relative to wages, shortened the period of a public (but not a private) job offer for the long term unemployed from 9 to 7 months, and gradually widened the access of the long term unemployed to education instead of a job offer. In 1985 a scheme of 'enterprise grants' was intended to stimulate the unemployed to start their own businesses. Subsequent changes in unemployment policy strengthened the element of educational opportunities and offers for the unemployed – alongside cuts in the budgets for labour market education.

During the period from 1988 to 1993 (phase 4) access to unemployment benefits was reduced for young people, part-time workers and the long term unemployed; the age for entitlement to early retirement was lowered to 55 years; a maximum limit of pay was set for all persons employed with a subsidy in the public sector; and temporary leave for education and child care was introduced at 80 percent of the unemployment benefit maximum.

The liberal-conservative government resigned in 1993 and the new government, headed by the social democrats, introduced an ambitious labour market reform. Some of the ideas of this reform could be labelled as a new phase (5) in unemployment policy. The main elements in the reform have been to bring together existing activating measures into a coherent scheme, to improve temporary leave schemes and to remove the right to qualify for unemployment benefits by participation in subsidised employment and training. The 1993 legislation curtailed access to unemployment benefits by imposing a 7 or 9 years limit to the period of entitlement and stricter regulations about the obligation to be available for the labour market. But it also opened the way to minimising that obligation for persons on leave; and in particular it introduced new provision for sabbatical leave, which makes it possible for the leave taker to do whatever he/she wants to do during one year, on 70 percent of normal benefit maximum (60 percent from 1997).

The sabbatical leave scheme was, and still is, by far the most controversial element, and since 1994 subsequent adjustments of the scheme restricted access to it. This has reduced the number of persons on the scheme. The provision for temporary child care leave has been the most popular, mainly among women in public sector jobs, but access to this scheme has subsequently been restricted in order instead to promote the educational leave scheme. Because of its potential to increase the functional and numerical flexibility of the labour market, educational leave is the scheme most favoured by the Government. It can easily be conceived of as part of a more conventional active labour market policy. Consequently, educational leave has the highest remuneration level (100 percent benefit) and the fewest restrictions on access (Lind 1995).

During the second half of the period 1994 to 1998 unemployment fell to a level just above 200,000 persons, and together with a weakening of the social democratic government this reignited the debate on structural unemployment with emphasis on devastating 'bottlenecks' in the labour market. The resulting policies from 1995 on (phase 6) contained further restrictions on unemployed persons' access to benefits. Among other things, the age of entitlement to membership of an unemployment fund was raised from 16 to 18 years, the qualifying period for entitlement was changed from 6 to 12 months, the maximum period on benefits was reduced to 5 years, and a number of strict obligations to accept a so-called 'pool job' were imposed on the unemployed if they stayed unemployed for more than 2 years.

In order to strengthen the 'activation' profile of unemployment policy the government strongly recommended the trade unions and the employers' organisations to include so-called 'social chapters' in the new collective agreements of 1995. With some hesitation especially among trade unions, such social chapters were included in most collective agreements. They are typically not very detailed but rather general statements of willingness 'to create understanding among management and employees to ensure that persons who cannot follow the normal standards of the collective agreements can find a place in the labour market.' So, the parties to an agreement are bound 'to consider appropriate suggestions to further the employment of persons who due to health problems, reduced working ability or long term absence from the labour market cannot be employed in a full time and normal job. The intention must be to make local agreements in this matter which must be approved by the parties to the collective agreement and which may include deviations from the normal regulations on wages, working time etc. set in the collective agreement' (quotation from the adopted proposal of the Official Conciliator 1995). Although some social chapters are more detailed, the main idea is that they are to be locally bargained and subsequently approved by the parties to the collective agreement.

This strategy for privatisation of the responsibility for labour market re-integration of some marginalised groups clearly changes the borderline between the state and the organisations of the labour market, between legislative and collective bargaining regulation. A consequence may also be that workers increasingly are employed under conditions that do not apply to normal pay and other working conditions. In fact, this is the general idea: flexible pay and working conditions are introduced by means of regulation and not by the competitive forces of the labour market. From the trade union point of view this has the advantage of giving them some control over the creation of such jobs, but on the other hand the unions had not originally wanted thus to contribute to the legitimation and the creation of non-standard pay and employment patterns.

The campaign for 'protected employment' (*skånejob* or *flexible jobs*), which was launched at about the same time as the implementation of the labour market reform, has almost the same target group as the social chapters, namely those people who are potentially and actually marginalised. This campaign, originally called 'It concerns all of us', aims at furthering (mainly) private sector companies' employment of this group of persons by imposing a 'social responsibility' on the companies. The target group is both the people still employed but for some reason losing part of their productive capacity and people maintained by public provision. The scheme offers the employers a subsidy from 1/3 to 2/3 of the minimum wage dependent on the level of reduced work ability.

Like the social chapters in collective agreements this provision for protected employment is not new, but the campaign rightly points out that if labour market marginalisation is to be curbed, and the increasing number of marginalised people are to be withdrawn from permanent public provision, then private sector companies especially will have to include some of these people in the labour force (Arbejdsministeriet, Socialministeriet 1995 and 1996).

The employers do not reject this, but warn that expectations should not be too high. It might be so that private sector employers could take on some sort of social responsibility for their own employees with decreasing productive capacity, and in this way reduce the externalisation of costs towards maintenance of these people, but according to the director of the Confederation of Danish Manufacturers (the DI) an estimate of a 'realistic potential (...) comes to some 20-30,000' persons (Christensen 1996:33). A recent survey confirms the point that expectations of acceptance of this sort of a social responsibility among private sector employers must be modest. Very few companies are ready to contribute to reduce labour market marginalisation (Holt 1998).

In sum, the features of the Danish unemployment policy mentioned here are concerned to limit labour market marginalisation but are simultaneously very conducive to employment patterns flavoured by numerical flexibility. A fairly high compensation level of unemployment benefits relative to wages favours numerical flexibility. Workers' resistance to redundancies is presumably lower if their economic loss is relatively small. This is the case with the low paid segments of the labour market. On the other hand the relatively high compensation rates have fostered assumptions that the unemployed do not have sufficient incentives to accept a job.

Table 10.1 The level of unemployment benefit compared to wages

	1982	1984	1986	1988	1990	1992
Male, skilled workers	0.61	0.58	0.53	0.51	0.53	0.53
Male unskilled workers	0.69	0.64	0.6	0.58	0.6	0.58
Female unskilled workers	0.77	0.72	0.68	0.66	0.67	0.66
Male salaried employees			0.48	0.45	0.46	0.45
Female salaried employees			0.66	0.63	0.63	0.61

Notes: Maximum UB-rate compared to wages. Working hours a week: 1982, 1984, 1986: 40 hours, 1988: 38.5, 1990: 37.5, 1992: 37. Average no. of weeks per month: 4.33. Due to a change in pay statistics it has not been possible to calculate comparable figures after 1992.

Source: Own calculations from Danmarks Statistik and table 11 in Arbejdsministeriet: Arbejdsmarkedspolitisk årbog 1993.

Flexibility has also been furthered by gradual tightening of the obligations of the unemployed to be available for vacant jobs, intensification of control and punitive measures, together with shortening of the time period of access to benefits and increasing emphasis on activation programmes. These measures can all be seen as disciplining factors which increase the incentive of the unemployed to take paid labour and lower their resistance to the acceptance of a poorly paid or temporary job. But again, on the other hand, they might also increase opposition on the part of the already employed to being made redundant, and in this way reduce employees' readiness to accept a high level of numerical flexibility and the creation of temporary employment relationships.

Unemployment and labour market marginalisation

Perhaps the most general observation on labour market developments is that the proportion of the population in employment has remained almost constant during the past many years. In quantitative terms, unemployment is, apart from small fluctuations, due mainly to the fact that the labour market participation rate has been increasing, especially because of the great influx of women into the labour market, while the demand side has not been able to provide a correspondingly additional number of jobs. At the beginning of this influx, expansion of the public sector secured employment for the increasing number of women seeking paid work; but since the early 1970s, after the growth rate of the public sector had begun to fall, the increase in labour market participation among women has been followed by unemployment because private sector jobs have not increased sufficiently.

Unemployment is unevenly distributed among the work force. During the last ten years some 700-850.000 people have been affected by unemployment in shorter or longer spells during a year, which gives an annual calculated average of 220-350,000 full time unemployed. Short periods of unemployment for many people contribute to this average number of unemployed which indicates how much available labour is wasted in society, but a lot of this unemployment does not necessarily cause social problems for the unemployed. It can instead indicate a high level of numerical flexibility and temporary employment, which does not always entail serious social problems. That may, however, be the case for the long term unemployed, or people who during a long period can only find employment for short periods of time.

Table 10.2 Population, labour force, employment (000s), and participation rates (percent)

	1960	1965	1970	1975	1980	1985	1990	1994
Population 15-64	2923	3077	3159	3238	3306	3394	3454	3506
Labour force	2176	2313	2371	2468	2626	2783	2836	2837
Employment	2137	2293	2341	2338	2442	2532	2564	2493
Employment rate (%)	73	75	74	72	74	75	74	71
Labour force participation rates (%)								
All	70	70	70	71	74	77	77	76
Men	98	94	86	84	82	83	82	80
Women	43	47	54	58	65	70	71	71

Note: The participation rates are calculated from a modified database which causes slightly lower figures.

Source: Danmarks Statistik: 50 års oversigten.

This group of people actually or potentially marginalised from the labour market is difficult to define in any agreed sense and with no ambiguities, because in some industries some periods of unemployment are part of a 'normal' pattern of working life for certain parts of the work force, and because some unemployed are in a more hopeless position than others because of personal capacities or prospects specific to their particular qualificational or geographical segment of the labour market.

People actually or potentially marginalised from the labour market within normal working age are most frequently defined as those on some sort of scheme for permanent withdrawal from the labour market and persons who are on short term schemes for a fairly long period. Definition of the latter group especially is disputed: how long a time on some sort of short term scheme (unemployment, social, sickness benefits and activation schemes for the unemployed) is an indication of prospective difficulties in returning to a normal pattern of employment and of not being able to find a job in the future? Apart from personal characteristics of the unemployed individual this is determined by a lot of other factors, among which future labour market developments and labour market policies are the most important.

Table 10.3 Total number of unemployed during a year, degree of unemployment and calculated full time unemployment (000s)

	1985	1986	1987	1988	1989	1990	1991	1992	1993	1994	1995	1996
Unemployed	741	699	716	705	720	737	761	796	842	818	783	756
Degree												
0.001-0.100	213	223	241	199	184	187	179	177	180	191	220	251
0.101-0.200	99	98	97	97	96	98	89	95	102	99	102	100
0.201-0.300	83	78	79	79	80	83	92	92	93	84	86	86
0.301-0.400	76	71	68	71	71	72	72	79	79	68	67	65
0.401-0.500	72	60	61	66	70	73	80	80	85	69	63	59
0.501-0.600	47	41	40	44	47	48	52	56	58	53	48	42
0.601-0.700	39	35	34	37	42	45	48	55	55	51	45	37
0.701-0.800	32	26	27	30	36	36	41	42	45	43	37	29
0.801-0.900	28	23	23	27	31	31	35	37	42	41	31	25
0.901-1.000	52	43	46	55	62	64	75	84	103	119	82	61
Full time unemployment	252	220	222	244	265	272	296	318	349	343	288	246

Source: Danmarks Statistik: Tiårs oversigt 1996, 1997.

That debate is as old as mass unemployment itself. When a main question posed from the 1970s and the early 1980s on was mainly 'who are the genuinely unemployed', the point was often to emphasise that unemployment to a high degree was voluntary because of the economically attractive unemployment benefit scheme (Pedersen 1981). During the late 1980s the intention became rather to show the vast number of marginalised people and so to prove that society still had a serious problem (Møller 1989); and during the 1990s the main issue became the heavy burden on public finances and the overall passive profile of unemployment policies. A number of commissions and official estimates dealt with this topic (Socialkommissionen 1992, Velfærdskommissionen 1995, Finansministeriet 1995) using different definitions of core and periphery in the labour market.

The most recent analysis from this generation of estimates based upon social registers (Ingerslev & Pedersen 1996) operates with five groups of labour market attached people among the 18-66 years old, namely the core, the loosely attached, the marginalised, those permanently on public provision, and the alternatively maintained.[4]

Table 10.4 18-66 year olds according to labour market status (000s)

	1990	1991	1992	1993	1994
Core	2255	2241	2225	2189	2201
Loosely attached	381	402	411	431	429
Marginalised	178	198	219	250	255
Perm. on public prov.	331	339	344	357	370
Alternatively maintained	186	171	168	158	150
All	3331	3351	3367	3385	3405

Source: Ingerslev & Pedersen 1996.

From 1990 to 1994, which was a period of increasing unemployment, the core group and the group of alternatively maintained were decreasing. In both 1990 and 1994 women were underrepresented in the core group and overrepresented in all the other categories. Persons aged 18-40 comprise the highest proportion among the loosely attached and the marginalised, 41-50 years old the highest proportion in the core group, and people between 51-66 years the highest proportion in the group permanently on public provision. Persons with no formal education comprise the highest proportion in the groups of people who are loosely attached, marginalised and permanently dependent on public provision, while persons with formal education have a relatively higher representation in the core group.

This is well known stuff. It fits with common knowledge about the groups who have some sort of disadvantage in the labour market. Similar results would be found for foreigners (immigrants), disabled people etc. showing that these groups have a low propensity to join the core and a high propensity to be marginalised or expelled from the labour market. It is also a well known fact that the labour market is segmented in the sense that the propensity to stay in one of the groups is very high. For some people the labour market provides stable employment while other people never or only occasionally are able to find a stable job.

Mobility between the core and periphery is limited. Among those who were in the core group in 1994, 75 percent had also belonged to that group in 1990, 7 percent were previously in the group of loosely attached while 13 percent were under 18 years in 1990. At the other end of the scale, 57 percent of the group permanently on public provision in 1994 had also been in this group in 1990; and 33 percent of the group of marginalised people in 1994 had belonged already to that group in 1990. There was some exchange between the core group and the group of loosely attached people and also some between the loosely attached and the marginalised group.

This analysis does not tell the whole story about unemployment and marginalisation. The average number of unemployed during a year indicates the number of full time persons who on average do not work. Adding in the number of persons on permanent public provision we can then estimate the number of persons who could contribute to production in society if there were sufficient demand for labour. Some of these people would not be able to work properly because they have lost their skills or have otherwise been out of touch with the labour market for too long or have physical or mental disabilities. An estimate of the size of this group is difficult because at the end of the day it also depends on the demand side: at times of excess labour on the market, the employers tend to increase their standards for the quality of labour they are willing to employ.

The difficulty in estimating this 'wastage of labour' and the numbers of people actually and potentially marginalised from the labour market is compounded by the question about persons on various forms of labour market schemes. Is a job training scheme a path into or out of the labour market, are temporary leave schemes just a phase intervening between active periods or a path to dead end jobs? The same sort of questions can indeed be asked about non-standard employment. Is it determined by the supply or the demand side, is it a permanent status for the persons affected or is it a path towards labour market integration or towards marginalisation, into the core or out to the periphery?

The effects of the various job training schemes have been highly disputed during the past 20 years or so. In general terms, subsidised job training in private sector companies has had the highest success rate in leading to ordinary employment (without a public subsidy). This is mainly due to the fact that private sector job training has been offered to the best qualified persons among the unemployed, and because public sector job training most frequently has been of fixed duration in order to make room for the next in the queue. Despite the public subsidy for private sector job training only a minority of the unemployed have received job offers in the private sector, so the direct effect in terms of ordinary employment has always been very limited. Until 1994 the major consequence of job training for the young unemployed was to qualify them for membership of unemployment funds, and for the long term unemployed to re-qualify them for entitlement to unemployment benefits. The removal of this consequence has strengthened the economic incentives for the unemployed to accept a job; and, if they should not succeed, it has furthered labour market marginalisation.

Educational leave may in some cases have an integrative effect by providing the leave takers with better skills for a job, but both sabbatical and child care leave may lead to a more insecure job situation because the employers in most cases presumably do not see any advantage in these schemes. The high proportion of women on child care leave is especially a problem in this respect because it underlines the impression that women are an unstable labour force. At least this line of reasoning tends to be applied to those on leave from employment. For unemployed women on child care leave the effect is mainly an opportunity to concentrate on family matters without having to be available for the labour market.

Table 10.5 Job training and leave schemes (000 persons)

Job training	1990	1991	1994	1995	1996
Private sector	9	13	15	9	8
Public sector	41	49	24	21	22
Unknown sector	-	-	5	7	7
Start of own firm	8	13	16	14	12
Total job training	58	75	60	51	49
Sabbatical leave			3	7	1
Child care leave			36	42	31
Educational leave			12	33	31
All leave schemes			51	82	63

Source: Arbejdsministeriet: Arbejdsmarkedspolitisk Årbog 1993, Danmarks Statistik: Statistiske Efterretninger 1996:33, 1997:14.

Regulation of the employment relationship and non-standard employment

Regulation of the establishment of an employment relationship is based upon the principle of contractual freedom, and legislation is very sparse except in respect of such special matters as discrimination. Legislation does not prevent anybody from making a contract for part-time or temporary work, but if a person is employed in several subsequent employment relationships by the same employer, the relationship will be considered as permanent with the consequence that the employee is given the same protection as in a standard employment relationship.

Many collective agreements contain rules for part-time employment.[5] Most frequently they specify that part-time employment must be for a minimum of 15 hours and a maximum of 30 hours a week in order to secure the employee some rights under labour market and social legislation (the act on white collar workers, unemployment and sickness benefits). In some cases the rules also restrict the employers' opportunities to establish part-time jobs for instance by prohibiting the transformation of full time into part time jobs (Jensen 1987:343, Nielsen 1996:223).

Such regulation of the establishment of non-standard employment relationships may have been eased slightly during the past 10-20 years because trade unions' opposition, at least vis à vis part-time jobs, has been decreasing.

Table 10.6 Weekly working hours (000 persons)

	1984	1986		1988	1990	1992	1993
Hours			*Hours*				
Under 15	169	160	Under 15	179	200	212	216
15-19	80	78	15-19	73	71	62	56
20-24	173	176	20-24	145	126	117	113
25-29	93	92	25-30	201	180	187	183
30-34	115	117	31-36	119	132	141	131
35-39	114	133	37	43	238	1299	1274
40	1359	1410	38-39	1431	1170	51	52
41 and more	331	322	40 and more	485	489	560	530
Unknown	55	65	Unknown	20	65	23	28
Total	2488	2553	Total	2695	2670	2652	2584

Source: Danmarks Statistik: Arbejdsstyrkeundersøgelsen, various years.

On the other hand, it seems from collective agreements that the period of notice which employers have to give when terminating an employment relationship may have grown slightly longer during the past 10-20 years.[6] Likewise, the legislation on mass redundancies has had the consequence of lengthening periods of notice for some employees. However, it is difficult to say if this development has promoted or inhibited temporary employment patterns, but because the changes are minor it may be assumed that the effect either way has been very limited.

In sum, regulation of employment relationships in non-standard employ - ment by way of legislation and collective agreements has not changed significantly during the past 10-20 years. There is no evidence of a deregulative tendency but the minor changes introduced may have made it easier to establish part-time jobs while perhaps more difficult to establish temporary jobs.

Table 10.7 Part time employment

	1976*	1978*	1980*	1982	1984	1986	1988	1990	1992	1994	1996
Employed											
All	2337	2365	2552	2521	2540	2675	2741	2674	2626	2585	2648
Men	1394	1398	1430	1399	1410	1482	1500	1454	1426	1396	1444
Women	943	967	1121	1122	1130	1192	1241	1219	1200	1189	1205
Part time											
All	501	537	520	512	498	502	502	488	471	409	387
Men	76	76	115	111	113	125	139	148	157	144	151
Women	425	461	405	401	385	377	363	340	314	266	236
Part time as % of total											
All	21	23	20	20	20	20	18	18	18	16	15
Men	5	5	8	8	8	8	9	10	11	10	10
Women	45	48	36	36	34	32	29	28	26	23	20

* Not the same method as following years. Numbers are a bit overestimated compared to following years.

Source: Danmarks Statistik: Tiårs oversigt, various years.

As mentioned above, working time is regulated by collective agreements which cover all public sector employees and 50-60 percent of employees in the private sector. Standard working time was 40 hours a week from 1974 to 1986 whereafter it was gradually reduced to 37 hours in 1990; and the average number of hours actually worked per employed person has been reduced from about 2,000 per year in 1960 to about 1,500 in 1994. Most employees work standard hours, but there is and has always been a significant range of variation in weekly working hours. The reduction in standard working time since 1986 can clearly be observed in actual working time patterns as the majority of people have had their number of hours worked gradually reduced, but it seems that the extremes have been slightly increasing during the past ten years or so: an increasing number of people work either less than 15 hours or more than standard working time.

Part-time employment usually refers to those working less than standard working time as set in collective agreements. There is no official definition of part time employment apart from definitions in various sorts of legislation, where for instance eligibility for unemployment insurance in part-time work requires a weekly working time between 15 and 30 hours. Other legislation includes some minimum working time as a condition for being covered by the legislation. For instance the law on white collar workers (*Funktionærloven*) requires a minimum of 15 hours a week and the law on sickness benefits (*Lov om dagpenge ved sygdom eller fødsel*) 120 hours of work within the last 13 weeks.

The frequency of part time work has been decreasing since 1978. The decline is first and foremost due to changes in the unemployment insurance system which reduced access to unemployment benefits for part time employees, cf. the description of the unemployment policy earlier. This is a very clear indication that both employers and employees adjust their behaviour according to welfare state provisions. Part time employment is not solely the result of employer demand for flexible labour but is a result of many factors. The significant reduction in part time work among women and the simultaneous increase among men is first and foremost the result of the change in legislation but might also be interpreted as showing more gender equality in the labour market since a lot of men, especially young and elderly, now want part-time jobs. It may be assumed that most of the people who are employed part time actually want that kind of employment: among persons who looked for a job at the beginning of the 1990s about 10.5 percent of the men and 21.5 percent of the women wanted a part time job. These figures correspond almost exactly to the actual part time rates.[7] Although women's part time rate is still twice that of men, the increase in the rate for men may be seen as a sign of narrowing differences in the still gender segmented labour market.

As mentioned above, the large number of people who have been unemployed for short periods during a year indicates the existence of a high degree of numerical flexibility in the labour market. The relatively high compensation rate in case of unemployment (unemployment benefits relative to wages) favours employees' acceptance of being laid off for fairly short periods and their acceptance of temporary jobs. During periods of economic growth companies can offer more 'permanent' employment than in periods of economic crisis, so temporary employment may not be just a management strategy for more numerical flexibility independent of the business cycle. In fact, the number of temporary jobs decreased during the economic growth of the mid 1980s when unemployment rates were also reduced; and it increased again later when unemployment also increased. During the 1990s the same pattern seems to occur: temporary employment co-varies with unemployment (compare table 8 with table 3). So, if we accept the relatively small fluctuations in the rate of temporary employment as a useful indication, the variations in temporary employment cannot be seen solely as the result of management's strategy for more labour market flexibility, a structural tendency, but certainly also as the result of the economic cycle and the growing number of people on temporary activation schemes during periods of high unemployment.[8] At any rate, temporary jobs are not in any sense expanding to major parts of the labour market. At least not yet.

Table 10.8 Temporary employment

	1984	1986	1988	1990	1992	1993	1995	1996
Persons in 000s:								
Total employment	2488	2662	2695	2670	2652	2584	2601	2623
'Not possible to get a permanent job'	117	88	75	91	111	121	125	107
'Do not want a permanent job'	65	75	77	64	61	46	71	63
Persons in temporary jobs	182	163	152	155	172	167	196	170
Percent:								
'Not possible to get a permanent job'	4.7	3.3	2.8	3.4	4.2	4.7	4.8	4.1
'Do not want a permanent job'	2.6	2.8	2.9	2.4	2.3	1.8	2.7	2.4
All persons in temporary jobs	7.3	6.1	5.6	5.8	6.5	6.5	7.5	6.5

Source: Danmarks Statistik: Arbejdsstyrkeundersøgelsen, various years. Eurostat: Labour Force Survey, Results 1995 and 1996, 3c.

During the 1990s approximately one third of the persons in temporary jobs have been working less than 37 hours a week, so, given an overall part time rate of about 18 percent, temporary employment is more widespread among part timers than among persons working full time.

Underemployment, marginalisation and flexibility

To sum up some of the findings of this overview of unemployment and non-standard work, the amount of underemployment, the amount of labour which is available in society but not used actually or potentially (persons on training and education) for productive purposes, is suggested as comprising the estimated number of full time unemployment and the number of persons under pension age on permanent public provision. To this must be added the number of people on temporary leave. Although temporary leave is voluntary, sabbatical and child care leave takers (or their substitutes in case of jobrotation) are in essence unemployed. On the other hand people in part time employment are assumed to have such a job voluntarily, and only very few persons in temporary jobs can be assumed to be underemployed. Adding these groups together, the amount of underemployment has varied between 600,000 and 750,000, or between one quarter and one third of the employed labour force, during the first half of the 1990s.

Table 10.9 Underemployment

	1990	1994	1996
Full time unemployment	272000	343000	246000
Persons on permanent public provision	331000	370000	420,000*
Persons on sabbatical and child care leave	12000	39000	32000
All	615000	752000	698000

* Estimated.

Source: see above, plus Regeringen 1997.

The number of those marginalised in the labour market includes persons on permanent public provision and the group termed 'marginalised' in the above analysis. Persons in public sector job training and schemes on start of own firm must also be included in this group because they cannot in general expect significant improvement of their employment chances. It is not easy to define how many of the temporary leave takers should be termed marginalised, but it might be sensible to include at least some of those who are on leave from unemployment, especially those unemployed who are on child care leave, because they are not improving their attractiveness in employers' eyes. Among the persons in temporary jobs some must be potentially marginalised, but apart from those on job training schemes it is perhaps most sensible to label them as a group of people loosely attached to the labour market while not really marginalised. During the 1990s, the number of those marginalised from the labour market have amounted to around one fifth and one fourth of the number of employed persons in the labour force, and, as is the case for the figures on underemployment, marginalisation is closely related to the development of unemployment.

Table 10.10 Labour market marginalised

	1990	1994	1996
Persons on permanent public provision	331000	370000	420,000*
Marginalised (Ingerslev & Pedersen)	178000	255000	130,000*
Job training	49000	45000	37000
Temporary leave	0	16000	15000
All	558000	686000	602000

*Estimated

Source: see above, plus Regeringen 1997.

This brief summing up of recent developments in underemployment and marginalisation can of course be disputed if other definitions are chosen, but they show that the official unemployment figures do not represent the entire wastage of human resources involved and the number of people facing labour market marginalisation. Unemployment figures are only the top of the iceberg.

The assumption that high unemployment rates are followed by an increase in non-standard employment can only partly be confirmed. In respect of part-time employment there is no evidence that employers take advantage of their favourable market situation and their thus improved possibilities of designing part-time jobs during periods of relatively high unemployment. Rather it seems that employers and employees adjust to changes in regulation, such as in the unemployment insurance system, and reduce the number of part-time jobs when part-time employees experience restrictions of their access to unemployment benefits. This must be the main explanation for the decrease in rates of part-time work since no other regulation on this matter has become more restrictive.

Another reason for the decline in part-time employment might be that people have changed their priorities as between work and freedom from work. More women wanting full time jobs could indicate a higher interest among women in achieving economic independence, for various reasons. On the other hand, as part-time employment is still dominated by women, it is obvious that people make priorities as between work and family, and that women do still bear the prime responsibility for work within the family. At least, part-time employment is not in general closely related to labour market marginalisation, though of course some part-time employees do want a full time job and perhaps more stable employment.

Temporary employment of involuntary character co-varies with the rate of unemployment, though when of voluntary character it varies inversely with unemployment. There is no evidence that deregulation has improved the scope for employers to create temporary jobs. Regulations of the employment relationship have remained almost unchanged (very liberal) during the past many years apart from stipulating longer terms of dismissal notice. Some of the people in temporary jobs are on job training schemes, and as the number of these persons tends to co-vary with the number of unemployed, this may be an important explanation for the variations of involuntary temporary employment. In any case it reduces the weight of the argument that employers tend to create more temporary jobs at times when they are in a better market situation vis-á-vis the workers.

In sum, the Danish labour market has not become more deregulated, and high unemployment rates have not caused significantly higher levels of non-standard employment with a minor exception in the case of temporary employment.[9] At least there is no structural tendency to a more flexible labour market as conceived in liberal terms. But labour market regulation in Denmark is nonetheless now deeply set within a strategy to secure the flexibility in the labour market necessary to provide employers with appropriate labour.

The welfare provisions for the unemployed basically ensure a high level of numerical flexibility. This is still the case for the core group of the labour market. People with relatively stable employment patterns and relative low wages do not object fiercely to being made redundant because they are relatively well compensated by unemployment benefits. They are 'made flexible' by means of the carrot. The marginalised who are not on permanent public provision, however, are increasingly 'made flexible' by means of the stick. They have to accept less attractive jobs either because they are not entitled to unemployment benefits or because they have no other options than to be 'activated' in some sort of scheme. Welfare for the core and workfare for the marginalised.

Notes

1 I shall not go further into the debate on these concepts here. My definitions are inspired by Atkinson (1984) and Jørgensen et al. (1990). The distinction between working time and working hours flexibility is that working time flexibility is the number of hours worked and working hours flexibility is about when during the day or week the work is done.

2 The behaviour of some major companies might have a norm-setting effect on other companies. However, in a relatively highly regulated labour market such as the Danish and given an industrial structure with only few big companies and many small and medium sized ones, it may be assumed that collective agreements and policies are of a relatively higher importance.

3 Direct state intervention in collective bargaining has taken place in 1975, 1977, 1979, 1985 and 1998, and various governments have been active in setting a level for wage increases or direct law regulating single elements in the agreements in 1981, 1983 and 1991. Indirectly, governments have influenced most agreements by dictating or 'recommending' a general level of wage increases.

4 *The core*, persons with no more unemployment than 8 weeks per year during the last 3 years, *the loosely attached*, persons with 8 to 36 weeks of unemployment per year during the last 3 years, *the marginalised*, persons with more than 36 weeks of unemployment per year during the last 3 years, *those permanently on public provision*, persons on early retirement schemes (førtidspension, efterløn, overgangsydelse), *alternatively maintained*, mainly students and people provided for within the family. For a more detailed definition of the five categories, see Ingerslev & Pedersen 1996 and 1997.

5 Specific and up to date knowledge about this is absent, but Jensen (1987) estimates that about 50 percent of collective agreements within the LO contain rules on part-time agreements.

6 There is no firm evidence on this, but comparing the collective agreements for manufacturing for 1981 and 1995 the period of notice have been prolonged for employees with relatively short time employment (*Løn og arbejdsforhold inden for jern- og metalindustrien 1981* and *Industriens overenskomst 1995*).

7 A survey among members of trade unions affiliated to the LO (1,500,000 workers) supports the assumption that most part time employment is voluntary and that a lot of full time employed people would actually like to have a part time job: 72 percent of the workers were working full time(11 percent part time and 17 percent unemployed) but only 66 percent would have preferred a full time job if they could decide for themselves and 23 percent would have preferred a part time job (Jørgensen et al 1992). This could indicate that more people want to work part-time if regulation (provision for unemployment insurance) were more favourable and employers allowed them to.

8 I am aware that temporary employment differs widely between different industries. In some cases temporary employment cannot be considered as non-standard: if it is part of a normal pattern of behaviour this pattern must be the standard. For various industries etc., see Anker (1990).

9 As mentioned earlier in this article, I have not dealt with all forms of non-standard employment. In particular, working hours flexibility has presumably increased during the past ten years or so. This might, however, not be the result solely of employers' interest, but also because workers prefer increasingly flexible working time for family reasons or whatever.

References

Anker, N. (1990), *Fleksibilitet på arbejdsmarkedet*, København: Socialforskningsinstituttet.

Arbejdsministeriet et al. (1989), *Hvidbog om arbejdsmarkedets strukturproblemer*, København: Arbejdsministeriet.

Arbejdsministeriet, Socialministeriet (1995), *Rapport fra udvalget om skånejobs*, København: Arbejdsministeriet, Socialministeriet.

Arbejdsministeriet, Socialministeriet (1996), *Redegørelse til regeringen om etablering af skånejob på arbejdsmarkedet*, København: Arbejdsministeriet, Socialministeriet.

Atkinson, J. (1984), *Flexibility, uncertainty and manpower management*, Brighton: IMS.

Christensen, E. (1993), *Borgerløn – på vej mod et paradigmeskift i arbejdsmarkeds- og socialpolitikken?*, Aalborg: Institut for Politik, økonomi og forvaltning.

Christensen, H.S. (1996), 'Virksomhedernes sociale ansvar', *Social Forskning*, September 1996, København: SFI, pp. 31-35.

Det Økonomiske Råds Formandsskab (1988), *Dansk Økonomi*, København: DØR. Maj.

Due, J., Madsen, J.S., Jensen, C.S. and Petersen, L.K. (1994), *The survival of the Danish model*, København: DJØF Forlag.

Finansministeriet (1995), *Finansredegørelse 95*, København: Finansministeriet.

Hirschmann, A.O. (1982) *Shifting Involvements*, Oxford: Martin Robertson.

Holt, H. (1998), *En kortlægning af danske virksomheders sociale ansvar*, København: SFI.

Ingerslev, O. and Pedersen, L. (1996), *Marginalisering 1990-1994*, København: SFI.

Jensen, P.H. (1987), 'Decentrale tryghedsbestemmelser', in Landsorganisationen, *Tryghedsreform – tryghed i jobbet, bilag*, København: LO.

Jørgensen, H., Lind, J. and Nielsen, P. (1990), *Personale, planlægning og politik*, Aalborg: ATA-Projektet.

Jørgensen, H., Lassen, M., Lind, J. and Madsen, M. (1993) *Medlemmer og meninger*, København: LO.

Knudsen, H. and Lind, J. (1998), 'Trade Unions in Denmark', in ETUI, *Handbook of the European Trade Unions*. Brussels: ETUI.

Lind, J. (1985), *Arbejdsløshed og velfærdsstat*, Aalborg: Aalborg Universitetsforlag.

Lind, J. (1991), 'Industrial relations and labour market regulation in Denmark', in Hans-Jeppe Jeppesen & Jens Lind (eds), *Changes in labour market and industrial relations in Europe*, Aalborg: CARMA, pp. 37-54.

Lind, J. (1995), 'Unemployment policy and social Integration', in N. Mortensen (ed.), *Social Integration and Marginalisation*, København: Samfundslitteratur, pp. 183-205.

Lind, J. (1996), 'Trade unions: Social movement or welfare apparatus?', in P. Leisink, J. Van Leemput and J. Vilrokx (eds), *Innovation or adaptation: Trade unions and industrial relations in a changing Europe*, Cheltenham: Edward Elgar, pp. 105-120.

Møller, I.H. (1989), *Samfundet polariseres*, Aalborg: ATA-Projektet.

Møller, I.H. (1998), *Trends in the Danish social mode of economic regulation*, in this book.

Nielsen, R. (1996), *Lærebog i arbejdsret*, København: DJØF-Forlag.

Pedersen, P.J. (1981), *Økonomiske effekter af arbejdsløshedsforsikring*, København: SFI.

Regeringen (1997), *Danmark som foregangsland*, København: Regeringen.

Rodgers, G. (1989), 'Precarious work in Western Europe: The state of the debate', in G. Rodgers and J. Rodgers (eds), *Precarious jobs in labour market regulation*, Geneva: ILO, pp. 1-16.

Scheuer S. (1996), *Fælles aftale eller egen kontrakt i arbejdslivet*, København: Nyt fra Samfundsvidenskaberne.

Schmid, G. (1994), *Reorganisation der Arbeitsmarktpolitik*, Berlin: WZB.

Smith, N. (1998), 'Økonomiske incitamenter til at arbejde', in N. Smith (ed.), *Arbejde, incitamenter og ledighed,* Aarhus: Aarhus Universitetsforlag, pp. 179-209.

Schönemann-Paul, H., Körmendi, E. and Gelting, T. (1992), *Den faste arbejdstid er fortid,* København: Spektrum

Socialkommissionen (1992), *Uden arbejde*, København: Socialkommissionen.

Udredningsudvalget (1992), *Rapport fra udredningsudvalget om arbejdsmarkedets strukturproblemer*, København: Udredningsudvalget.

Velfærdskommissionen (1995) *Marginalisering på arbejdsmarkedet*, København: Velfærdskommissionen.

Part III

The European experience

11. European convergence or national specificities?

JENS LIND AND IVER HORNEMANN MØLLER

The first major theme addressed in this book is the issue of freedom *from* work or freedom *through* work. Two recurrent and factual themes are analysed, namely citizen's income and the development of work (Part I). In a sense these two themes combined can draw up an attractive scenario where people on the one hand are guaranteed an income at a level which enables them to maintain a decent standard of living independent of their participation in working life, and on the other hand secure a working life which is designed to satisfy human needs. At a time when unemployment comprises a major obstacle for social inclusion in Europe, citizen's income is an obvious choice to pave the way towards social inclusion via forms of participation other than paid work. If paid work for those who are needed in production could be rearranged to avoid abuse of human resources and instead be reshaped into a democratic, participative and developmental work relationship the future would suddenly look promising.

The idea of citizen's income is not new and, as is shown in Christensen's article, it has cropped up in various societies under different circumstances. The recent Danish discourses, analysed here, range across numerous aspects of citizen's income, but the basic idea is a further development of democratic and social citizenship. Furthermore, it challenges commodification in society and it also aims to achieve some autonomy for the citizen vis-a-vis the state. Such fundamental changes in social relationships are not on the every day political agenda in Europe! But, as argued in the article, there is scope for an important political discourse to built up around citizen's income to help shape future policies.

The prospect of some such, if still uncertain, impact on actual policy making may be less when we look at steps towards widening the nature of work. As we mentioned in the introduction to this book we can see the outline of a strategy on economic growth in Europe which, at least compared to the USA, would pay closer attention to the qualitative aspects of working life. This resembles what in Denmark is called the development of work. In a sense it has the same features of discourse as does the debate about citizen's income: it is possible to identify almost similar ingredients in fashionable management strategies, trade union strategies and government programmes. But when it comes to reality differences among the three social actors appear. The has not prevented the development of work from so far being implemented in one form or another on a small scale. It is not in any sense, however, a dominant feature of the ongoing restructuring of working life, either in Denmark or in the rest of Europe.

Combinations of citizen's income programmes and 'work developmental' strategies may well be important parts of a future European strategy for combatting and preventing social exclusion. But actual policy making has up till now been far more modest in scope and in general terms rather country-specific. Some trends in labour market policies, however, could indicate converging processes.

A common feature in the regulation of labour markets in Europe is evidently the growing importance in all West European countries of labour market policies for greater flexibility of the labour force. The establishment in almost all West European countries, from the beginning of the eighties, of training programmes and job-creation schemes for poorly-qualified people is just one example of these policies of flexibility.

In the nineties most West European countries have linked these schemes not to citizen's income but on the contrary to policies of workfare. Workfare stems from the view that the unemployed and the groups marginalised in the labour market need guidance away from 'state dependency'. Consequently entitlements to social benefits are made conditional on clients' participation taking in various types of 'activities', including compulsory and labour market oriented education and training schemes as well as other 'socially responsible' activities. Workfare inexorably leads in the direction of coercion: benefits are given in return for activities and those claimants who refuse to take part in the required activities will then receive only what 'they deserve'.

To identify the general trends in Western European countries which point to either convergence or national specificities we shall now make a short comparative analysis of the four countries chosen for the study while also paying some attention to the extent to which each of the countries can be seen as representing one of the four types of welfare state regime schematically set out earlier: a Scandinavian, social-democratic model; a liberal, Anglo-Saxon model; a corporate, 'Bismarckian' model; and a southern 'variant'.

Portugal and the southern 'variant'

In the southern 'variant' part-time employment is low and stable. With the exception of Spain which has the highest rate of temporary employment in Europe (1/3), this type of non-standard employment is moderate and shows in some countries declining tendencies. Self-employment is high and increasing.

Portugal is unique in the sense that it is the only non-core society in our sample and therefore, according to most commentators, more exposed to detrimental effects from the 'hyper-mobility of global capital'. These effects are, among others, under-employment, unemployment and community decay.

The semiperipheral position of Portugal in the hierarchical world context is in part associated with a relative weak position of the state. This is further exacerbated as a result of the rather short experience of democracy (since 1974). Not only had the state in the late seventies and early eighties to submit to the neo-liberal demands of the IMF, with increasing unemployment and reduced GNP among its consequences. Responsibility for policy in the new democratic state is also somewhat ineffectively divided among governmental departments, which contributes to the pursuit of ambiguous and mutually incompatible modes of regulation as far as unemployment and social security are concerned. The weak position of the state is also illustrated by its inability to implement some of its labour laws and by the fact that, after the social cuts in the 1980s, around 70 percent of the nation's social expenditures is now paid out by NGOs.

At the other end of a North-South dimension we find a strong Danish state which is well integrated into 'the core of economic globalization': a strong balance of payments, low inflation and low rates of interest, balanced state finances and rather high economic growth rates.

In recent years the Danish way of combatting unemployment and labour market marginality has moved surprisingly fast towards various forms of workfare, including compulsory education and training schemes, partly following the example of the Netherlands. The Portuguese modes of social regulation have taken several and rather different directions. First, Portugal, along with the other countries in the southern 'variant', has experienced only very moderate doses of workfare programmes. Secondly, another track has been set by a competitive logic prioritising low wages and institutionalising more flexible work contracts: short term, temporary, sub-contracting, domiciliary work. The third track has encouraged two very different types of self-employment. On the one hand the threat of long-term unemployment following from economic re-structuring and de-industrialisation processes has led many wage-earners to 'fall back' into rural production. This has had the consequence that, contrary to most of the rest of West Europe, agricultural production is as widespread a phenomenon in Portugal today as it was decades before (20-25 percent of the population is 'attached' to the sector). On the other hand, a new cultural attitude encouraging the search for personal success, fuelled by neo-liberal ideology – and in this respect parallel to the policy pursued by the UK conservative governments – has created a climate favourable to the development of self-employment. Such self-employment is characterised by rather few but highly paid jobs (e.g. auditing, accounting, soliciting and finance).

The two tracks of self-employment have – directly and indirectly – been furthered by the entry of EU funds (from 1986) which have favoured modern competitive activities but not a re-structuring of traditional activities, particularly rural, to which many of the unemployed, as mentioned, turn when the sectors in which they work undergo a crisis.

Policies aiming at the inclusion of unemployed persons within the labour market have in Portugal somewhat followed the same main lines as in the UK: increasing employment through lowering wages and stimulating self-employment. The specific semiperipheral types of non-standard employment in Portugal – home working, multiple job holding and use of unpaid family workers – are, however, not only rare in the UK but also (in respect of some of the forms) less frequent in other Southern European countries.

These types of jobs are often associated with low pay, high insecurity, no or low social protection and no or few other rights. They involve also often unskilled work and have long working weeks. At the same time, however, these types of non-standard employment strongly contribute to holding down the Portuguese level of unemployment – to far below the levels in all other South European countries and most other West European countries as well. Another question is whether they constitute a lesser evil for the worker than a situation of unemployment? If inclusion into the sub-system of income creating activities – regular or not – implies the recognition by one's surroundings and by oneself of contributing to one's own and the society's reproduction, the question should be answered affirmatively.

As far as characteristics of the four regimes are concerned, figures about home working and work in the informal economy are too sparse to allow any general conclusions. An exception is home working in Portugal where work so recorded because carried out under contract accounted for about 4 percent of all employed in 1995. Another exception is the prevalence of informal work in Southern Europe, which is estimated to comprise around 20 percent of the labour force in 1985 in the case of Spain and 19 percent in 1991 in Portugal.

It should be noted that almost all West European countries since the beginning of the 1980 have introduced alternative training programmes and job creation schemes. The intensity and comprehensiveness of these programmes, however, varies a lot from country to country, with the Netherlands at in the high end and Portugal at the lower end.

Last but not least it should be kept in mind that, in Portugal and in the other countries of the southern 'variant', the family, the local community, the church and charity organisations still play the most important role as welfare providers.

Denmark and the Scandinavian social democratic model

In the other end of the North-South divide the strong Danish state actively supports class collaboration, provides the unions and the employers' federations with institutional frames for their own agreed system of effective conflict resolution, and make, comprehensive interventions in the labour market characterised by corporatist decision making processes and implementation structures.

The Scandinavian countries are characterised by high but significantly declining rates of part-time employment. Temporary employment is rather high and stable, while self-employment is low and shows different tendencies in the three countries.

Apart from flexible working hours (shift work, night work, week-end work, etc.) which have been moderately increasing during the last 10-20 years, non-standard employment in Denmark has, remarkably, been declining over the last more than 10 years. Within the same period the labour market has been very little deregulated.

Rates of part-time employment have long been high. But with reduced access to unemployment benefits for part-time employees from around 1980, women's part-time employment commenced to decline and there is no doubt that this was in part because both employers and employees were adjusting to the reduced access to benefits. But this might not be the whole explanation for the following fifteen years' decline in Danish women's part-time jobs. Part-time jobs in Denmark – unlike part-time jobs in the UK, in Portugal, and in the Netherlands – are as secure and stable and associated with almost the same rights and protections as full-time jobs. The last decades' strong expansion of public child-minding facilities (where Denmark now together with Sweden has the highest level of state-provided child care in Europe) may justify a hypothesis that the decline in women's part-time employment was also a result of many women's deliberate decision to go for full-time employment instead.

While there has been very little deregulation of the Danish labour market, workfare discourse has increasingly dominated unemployment policy since the early 1990s. This recent change in the social mode of regulation is also to be seen in the two other Scandinavian countries, Norway and Sweden.

Besides the assumptions made of enhanced social integration via inclusion of the unemployed and the marginalised into the ordinary labour market and into activation projects of various character in non-standard labour markets, the discourse on workfare looks also to a need to satisfy the tax payers. For long the tax burden has been growing, particularly for the low paid wage-earners among whom support for the welfare state has proved weakest. By introducing activation the dominant political parties supported by the employers and most unions, hope that the tax payers will acknowledge that they now get value for their money.

The discourse on workfare is based on the principle of receiving only in return for contributing. While this principle is closely akin to a classical liberal social policy of 'help to self-help', its support now also by the traditionally welfare state sustaining Scandinavian social democratic parties has to be seen against the background of the demise of their Keynesian policies and of their wish to maintain the tax payers' continued willingness to pay as an essential component of social integration.

Around the turn of the next century it should be clear whether 'the accumulated evidence of workfare induces enough of its adherents to consider options for a better route', as Standing has prophesied (Standing 1997). Some years later it may also become clear whether the relevance of the work ethic and with it the priority for doing income creating work will be displaced by a search for new roles not only for the unemployed and the marginalised but also for those employed in the ordinary labour market.

While liberals and conservatives traditionally have emphasised the responsibility of the individual, it was only from the early 1990s that they were followed in this matter by the Scandinavian social democrats. This happened precisely by way of growing social democratic support for the notion of workfare. Prior welfare policy had accorded society a key responsibility ; now it was emphasised 'that first and foremost the individual is responsible for her/his life' (Nordic Ministers' Council 1996). The Scandinavian social mode of economic regulation has in this respect lined up with the policies in most other Western European countries – with the southern 'variant' as the only exception.

The UK and the liberal Anglo-Saxon model

The development in the UK in respect of non-standard employment and its regulation represent in nearly every aspect the opposite of trend in Denmark: while Denmark has had almost no experience of growth in non-standard employment, rather the contrary, in Britain both part-time work, self-employment and temporary employment have been increasing in the last decade or more. In Britain, over the last four years (to 1996) only 38 percent of new jobs created have been for permanent full-time employees. And while Danish labour market policies and labour rights have been very little deregulated, the British population have experienced such great changes in their social mode of regulation that some commentators talk about a 'drawbridge mentality', where concern is directed at making sure yourself are inside the castle rather than caring about what happens to those who are not.

More specifically, deregulation has not only facilitated the process of labour flexibilisation but has also extended much beyond the labour market to affect provision for housing, transport, etc. Alongside deregulation has gone privatisation. Private provision has been encouraged, and subsidised, in education, health and social services. A third feature of the drawbridge mentality has been a residualisation of those services which have remained in public control – i.e. a gradual process of qualitative decline in public services which are now offered to those who cannot afford to protect or insure themselves through the market.

Even with regard to the issue of workfare the British experiences are very different from the Danish. Although widely debated in some British policy circles, no direct commitment to introduce workfare was made until very recently. The big change then came with the new Labour government whose assumption seems to be that any employment is better than unemployment. Consequently comprehensive workfare schemes have been launched, some of which contain strong elements of compulsion, such as the New Deal for the young and the unemployed, while others have been based around voluntarism, such as the new deal for lone parents and people with disabilities. How effective these schemes will be in (re)including people into employment of a kind which provides participation/activation of quality has yet to be seen. One key worry arising from the British discourse on this work-centered approach to individuals' inclusion concerns the risk of driving a wedge between those on in-work benefits and those on unemployment benefits. What happens to those who cannot work?

It is true for West European countries that where an increase in non-standard forms of employment is observed it is a consequence not only of deliberate policy initiatives but also of structural changes in productive activity associated with decline in manufacturing industry and growth in services. What is rather specific, however, to the growth of non-standard employment in Britain is the importance of changes in the social and economic status of women.

As in most other European countries, the British female labour market participation rate is still growing. Britain, however, has the lowest level of state-provided child care in Europe, and many women work in non-standard employment in order to fit in care of their children. This applies especially to part-time employment for which Britain has one of the highest rates in Europe – next to The Netherlands, Norway and Sweden – and which despite the lack of legislative protection does not seem to be much more insecure than full time employment. The rates of pay, however, are considerably lower.

Another way in which women combine paid work with childcare is to work from home. We do not know exactly the extent of home working but both British and Portuguese data indicate that the amount is limited, probably below 5 percent of the work force.

Consequently, huge barriers remain in place which hinder women's full inclusion into paid work. The need to reconcile work and family life remains central to inclusion of women into the labour market, and forms a central focus of the current debate around British labour market regulation with respect especially to working time and flexible employment.

The Netherlands and the corporate 'Bismarckian' model

With the exception of the Netherlands which has the highest rate of part-time employment in Western Europe, the countries of the corporate

'Bismarckian' model show moderate but growing rates of part-time employment. The rates of temporary employment are moderate to high, with different directions of development from country to country over the last decade. Self-employment is in general declining from a rather low level.

In the Netherlands non-standard employment is not only a widespread phenomenon – almost 40 percent of all jobs are part-time and flexible jobs – it also seems steadily to be taking new forms. Furthermore, non-standard employment is more gender biased than in other West European countries, with the UK as the only possible exception: two in three working women work part-time, and women make up 85 percent of all part-time workers in the Netherlands. At the other extreme, the corresponding Danish figures are one in five and 60 percent, respectively, and while part-time work is declining in Denmark it is growing in the Netherlands.

Non-standard employment in the Netherlands has recently taken new forms: not only are stand-by contracts and destandardisation of working time increasing. But systems have also been introduced for employees to 'buy' and 'sell' extra free time, as well as schemes by which employees, while having a contract with an agency, rotate between a number of other companies where they perform comparable tasks. Another kind of pool is where employees no longer find employment in their present job. They are taken on instead by an agency for some years, and the agency tries to get them employed in other companies.

The growth of non-standard employment has in the Netherlands been significantly furthered by a gradual change in the social mode of economic regulation. The state-subsidized, low paid, low skilled and often non-standardized types of employment provided for the long-term unemployed which have brought, among other problems, the issue of poverty into focus, are only a first and rather superficial sign of this change. Digging somewhat deeper one discovers a dramatic shift of paradigm from protection to participation. Until the late 1980s, Dutch labour market policy, social policy and societal norms were founded on the protection paradigm. Rather than encouraging the growing number of labour market marginalised people to (re-)include within employment, policies aimed at providing relative generous levels of income protection and contributed to decreasing levels of labour market participation. This system became more and more expensive and, gradually, a paradigm shift from protection to participation took place.

Since then any type of participation in paid work (and sometimes unpaid work as well) has been regarded by policy-makers, organisations and social movements as preferable to public provision. Together with restrictions of social policy, restraints on wage increases and deregulation of labour market policies – all ingredients of the new social mode of regulation-governmental institutions and local authorities have during the last decade set up so many participation schemes that, today, it is difficult to find a person who has a complete overview.

The shift from protection to participation has created new patterns of inclusion and exclusion. First, workers on non-standard employment contracts have, in general, less legal protection than 'regular' workers have. Secondly, entitlements to benefits have been tightened but still depend on contributions, which means that they protect best those with strong labour market positions. Thirdly, in respect of state subsidized jobs and activities, some people participating in governmental schemes may find themselves trapped in dead-end jobs, while others in unpaid work may experience enhanced inclusion; but the same scheme may also imply more definite forms of labour market exclusion. Those unemployed and disabled who do not manage to benefit from the new participation opportunities have less money and are therefore more excluded from the consumer regime and the associated social contacts than they used to be. At the same time, however, experiences from target-group oriented projects to help people to find employment as well as to keep their jobs, provide evidence that given the right mix of participation and protection, participation opportunities for vulnerable groups can be increased dramatically.

Lessons for the future

The experiences of labour market issues and regulation from European countries obviously differ a lot. Apart from some common traits among West European countries in the development of non-standard employment and its regulation, the variety of national differences is both so striking and so persistent that one is tempted to conclude that national diversities are more evident than 'Europeanization'. At least this is the lesson if we focus on the development of non-standard work and the varying configurations of national regulations and institutions. They seem each to live their own life generating new national specificities regardless of either the application of common European regulatory principles or the influence from some general trends or fashions in labour market regulation.

Another lesson is that no single model or strategy for labour market regulation has so far been implemented thoroughly, and that models and regulative ideals have been ever shifting. In a sense everything tried has failed after some years. The social democratic models in Scandinavia based upon elaborated Keynesian strategies were abandoned during the 1980s; and during the 1990s the neo-liberal strategy, most thoroughly implemented in the UK, has lost a lot of support because the social costs have proved to be too high. If we are facing any common tendency now in Europe, it can be termed either left-wing liberalism by itself or right-wing social democracy by itself. A compromise between left and right may be an important step in the direction of a more unified strategy on labour market regulation among the various nations in the European Union, and may be a stepping stone towards further convergence in Europe. The basic regulatory principle in this strategy is the market, but significantly supplemented by comprehensive political intervention.

The revitalisation of the campaign for a single European market during the 1980s, the social regulations (the Maastricht and the Amsterdam Treaties) and the project on the EMU during the 1990s may certainly give new incentives, both at national and European level, for the development of more convergent patterns of labour market regulation. It is, however, still an open question whether national specificities will become less significant than is the case now. A repeatedly heard argument is that continuing economic co-ordination (the EMU and onwards) requires the preconditions of further political co-ordination and social integration. If we apply a general perspective to what is going on in Europe, this process is already taking place. In a more detailed perspective co-ordination of labour market policies has already been attempted to a fairly high degree, cf. the 1998 Employment Guidelines (Luxembourg European Council 1997); but when it comes to harmonisation of social security systems and core areas of social policy, the commonly agreed view is still that this is not desirable. If this continues to prevail, then national specificities will be enhanced, because national regulations of the labour market have to be coordinated with national social policy.

This does not completely rule out inspiration from a common European ideal or model. Whether the outcome is a European model of labour market regulation based upon the middle of the road compromise we can identify now, or the next century will provide us with a more coherent and new configuration of labour market regulation constituting a new paradigm, is difficult to say. It is, however, already evident that the economic and social capacity of Europe allows us to question and discuss the future status and role of work. This is perhaps the most important discourse for the future.

References

Luxembourg European Council (1997), *The 1998 Employment Guidelines,* Council Resolution of December 1997.

Standing, G. (1997), 'Globalisation, Labour Flexibility and Insecurity: the Era of Market Regulation', *European Journal of Industrial Relation,* Vol. 3, No. 1, March.

For Product Safety Concerns and Information please contact our EU representative GPSR@taylorandfrancis.com
Taylor & Francis Verlag GmbH, Kaufingerstraße 24, 80331 München, Germany

www.ingramcontent.com/pod-product-compliance
Lightning Source LLC
LaVergne TN
LVHW010621300926
849162LV00001B/25
* 9 7 8 1 1 3 8 3 2 0 5 4 3 *